PIGSKIN

PIGSKIN

The Early Years of Pro Football

ROBERT W. PETERSON

OXFORD UNIVERSITY PRESS
New York   Oxford

Oxford University Press

Oxford   New York
Athens   Auckland   Bangkok   Bogotá   Bombay   Buenos Aires
Calcutta   Cape Town   Dar es Salaam   Delhi   Florence
Hong Kong   Istanbul   Karachi   Kuala Lumpur   Madras   Madrid
Melbourne   Mexico City   Nairobi   Paris   Singaore   Taipei
Tokyo   Toronto

and associated companies in
Berlin   Ibadan

Copyright © 1997 Oxford University Press, Inc.

First published by Oxford University Press, Inc., 1997

First issued as an Oxford University Press paperback, 1997

Oxford is a registered trademark of Oxford University Press

Library of Congress Cataloging-in-Publication Data
Peterson, Robert, 1925–
Pigskin: the early years of pro football
/ Robert W. Peterson.
p.   cm.
Includes bibliographical references and index.
ISBN 0-19-507607-9
ISBN 0-19-511913-4 (Pbk.)
1. Football—United States—History.
I. Title.
GV954.P48   1996   796.332'64'0973—dc20   96-22810

10 9 8 7 6 5 4 3 2 1

For Margie and Rick,
and for Tommy,
a great linebacker prospect

PREFACE

This book is about professional football long before Super Bowls, *Monday Night Football*, and megabuck contracts for players. It tells what the game was like and what players and fans thought about it, beginning more than 100 years ago, when the first pros appeared, and continuing up to the time when televised football was becoming a national passion. The tipping point was the National Football League's 1958 championship game, when a crewcut quarterback named Johnny Unitas engineered a thrilling victory for the Baltimore Colts over the New York Giants in the first sudden-death overtime in a title game. An estimated 30 million television viewers saw that game, a harbinger of the immense television audiences for the Super Bowls of the past decade.

Sheldon Meyer, senior vice president at Oxford University Press and an editor of rare talent and even rarer patience, suggested that I write this book. But I think the book's real genesis was a game played on an autumn Sunday afternoon in 1938 in Warren, Pennsylvania, a town of 14,000 in the skirttails of the Allegheny Mountains. The game matched the Warren Red Jackets—semipros who were factory hands, schoolteachers, and laborers in the workaday world—against the Pittsburgh Pirates of the NFL. The Pirates, renamed the Steelers two years later, were coached by Johnny Blood, a legendary flake in pro football annals, and starred Byron R. (Whizzer) White, a University of Colorado All-American and prospective Rhodes scholar. White was being paid $15,800 for the year, a salary roughly twice that of anyone else in the NFL. (Whizzer White led the league in rushing yardage that year and later played for two years with the Detroit Lions. Later still, he served for thirty-one years as an associate justice of the Supreme Court, retiring in 1993 at the age of seventy-five.)

The Pirates–Red Jackets game is a measure of pro football's place on the sports spectrum before World War II. To meet the payroll, an NFL team with the league's best-paid player had to fill an open date on its schedule by riding a bus for 120 miles, changing into football uniforms at the Warren Moose Club, playing a semipro team before 4,000 spectators, and then riding the bus back to Pittsburgh.

The Pirates beat the Red Jackets, 23 to 0, with Whizzer White rushing for 150 yards on eighteen carries, scoring one touchdown, and kicking an extra point. At half-time, because Warren's Russell Field had no locker rooms or fieldhouse, Whizzer White and the other Pirates—big leaguers all—had to sit on the ground at one weedy end of the field while gaping kids ringed their circle like Indians surrounding a wagon train.

Among those kids was a thirteen-year-old hero worshipper—none other than your author. What, I wondered, were these demigods like? This book is a belated attempt to answer that question.

As with my earlier books of sports history (*Only the Ball Was White*, a history of Negro baseball before Jackie Robinson, and *Cages to Jump Shots: Pro Basketball's Early Years*), my method is to weave oral history into the narrative. My purpose is to flavor the story with first-person recollections of professional football long ago.

For the skeleton of the story, I have relied primarily on several encyclopedias on pro football and the research of some dedicated people in the Professional Football Researchers Association (PFRA). This organization has some 250 members, perhaps two or three dozen of whom are serious researchers and contribute regularly to PFRA's *Coffin Corner*, a twenty-four-page magazine that appears six times a year. First among equals in PFRA is Bob Carroll, its executive director and chief editor. Other PFRA stalwarts whose work I have consulted are Bob Barnett, Bob Braunwart, Jim Campbell, Bob Gill, Stan Grosshandler, John Hogrogian, Joe Horrigan, Emil Klosinski, Milt Roberts, David Shapiro, Robert B. Van Atta, and Joe Zagorski. In addition to being an active PFRA researcher and writer, Joe Horrigan is the curator at the research center of the Pro Football Hall of Fame in Canton, Ohio. He and his staff were very helpful during my visit there.

I am indebted to the old players and coaches who sat with me for hours and patiently answered my questions about pro football before it was of much consequence on the nation's television screens or sports pages. Three of them have been elected to the Pro Football Hall of Fame, and perhaps others should be, but I did not seek out only former stars. Rather, I tried to talk with men who played for various teams from the late 1920s to the mid-1950s. All of them contributed much to this book.

They are Vincent J. Banonis, George Buksar, Louis P. DeFilippo,

Don Doll, Robert L. Dove, Daniel M. Edwards, Robert Emerick, Richard J. Evans, Edward C. Frutig, Mario Gianelli, Louis R. Groza, Lindell L. Houston, Chester (Swede) Johnston, Kenneth W. Kavanaugh, Harold W. Lahar, Dante Lavelli, Raymond L. Mallouf, Joel G. Mason, Frank Maznicki, Chester A. Mutryn, Charles C. O'Rourke, John R. Panelli, Stephen Romanik, Edmund J. Skoronski, Robert A. Snyder, Albert Henry (Hank) Soar, Flavio J. Tosi, Wallace Triplett, and Clyde D. (Bulldog) Turner.

I also interviewed Marion Evans, widow of Lon Evans, an all-pro guard for the Green Bay Packers during the 1930s, and Clementine Halicki, whose late husband, Eddie, was a star halfback for the Frankford Yellow Jackets of Pennsylvania and the Minneapolis Redjackets in 1929 and 1930.

I am grateful to several people who assisted me in the research: William F. Himmelman, president of Sports Nostalgia Research; J. Thomas Jable, who shared his research materials for his study of the first known professionals; Pearce Johnson, the oldest member of PFRA, who was in the front office of the Providence Steam Roller team before the NFL was founded; Mike Murray, director of media relations for the Detroit Lions; and James Reeser of the staff of the *Daily Collegian* at Pennsylvania State University.

Finally, I must thank my wife, Peg, who transcribed the tapes of many of my interviews and typed much of the manuscript, as well as making my world a better place. She is like an offensive lineman (although, I hasten to add, she doesn't look like one) in that she is underappreciated and vital to success.

Ramsey, N.J.   R.W.P.
April 1995

CONTENTS

PIGSKIN

1

BEFORE THE TELEVISION BONANZA

Professional football is more than 100 years old, but for its first 50-odd years the sport was the sad-sack cousin of college football. When the National Football League (NFL) was born in 1920, crowds as small as 800 turned out for some games. Average attendance was probably on the order of 3,000, one-tenth to one-twentieth of the number at major college games that year.

By the late 1940s, when the NFL was well established and beginning to enjoy the first stirrings of prosperity, attendance averaged more than 25,000. Still, pro football played second fiddle to the top college teams on the nation's sports pages and was far behind major league baseball in the devotion of sports fans.

Today pro football is far and away the most popular spectator sport. Roughly half of all males twelve years of age and older name it as their favorite, according to a 1993 survey by the Sports Marketing Group. The pro game has long since surpassed college football in fan interest. Baseball, once the unchallenged national pastime, has lost favor. In 1994 a CBS News telephone survey found that 40 percent of Americans considered themselves baseball fans, a drop of 20 percent from a similar survey four years earlier.

Many learned treatises have expounded on the reasons for pro football's ascendancy. Its controlled violence is said to match the psychological pulse of today's American male. Baseball, it is said, is too slow-paced, cerebral, and open-ended—a relic of the nation's bucolic past.

In my view, no deep thinking is required to account for the popularity of pro football. It is the quintessential television sport, and we are addicted to television. Although the playing field is 120 yards long (including end zones) and 53⅓ yards wide, the action is generally confined to less than one-third of that space. All twenty-two players on the field are clearly visible nearly all the time, and instant replays can bring any one of them into intimate closeup. Expert commentators can stop the action on replays and show us, with diagrams and reruns, who threw the decisive block or how a receiver faked free of a cornerback on the game-winning touchdown.

The same techniques can, of course, be used to stop and repeat baseball action, but we do not see the full playing field or the reactions of all nine defenders to every pitch. In short, we do not see the game that fans at the ball park do. By contrast, football fans at home not only see the same game as those at the stadium, but see it more clearly and with the guidance of experts who can clear up the mysteries of pass receivers' routes, counter plays, and strategy decisions as a tight game winds down to its final seconds.

Television has made pro football fans of hundreds of thousands of people who have never been near an NFL stadium. On Friday night, they watch the local high-school team, and on Sunday afternoon and Monday night they cheer or hiss the behemoths of the NFL on the tube.

It might be argued that if my theory is true, basketball and hockey should be much higher on the attention scale than in fact they are. Both of those games are played in confined spaces, with all players visible nearly all the time, just as football is. I think, though, that those sports are inherently less interesting to spectators than either football or baseball. Like many other fans, I find my attention straying from the screen during televised basketball until the last two or three minutes of a close game, despite the fact that National Basketball Association (NBA) players often perform breathtaking feats of athleticism and are often said to be the best athletes in all of sports. That may be true, though their basketball skills do not necessarily carry over to other sports, as demonstrated by Michael Jordan's shortcomings as a hitter in minor league baseball during his sabbatical from the Chicago Bulls. On the basketball court, Jordan defies gravity and most of the principles of kinesiology, but he had a lot of trouble with a curve ball.

Like other major sports, pro football has changed a great deal since its beginning in the nineteenth century—much more than baseball but less than basketball. Today's fans would have no trouble following the action in a pro football game played around the turn of the century, though they might find it so dull that they would nod off. (Forward passing was not permitted then, and the game was more of a regulated brawl than a sporting contest.) By the 1930s and 1940s, pro football had evolved into something approaching today's game, except that there were fewer passing plays and less dependence on field goals. Television was not yet a financial factor, though some games were being televised to the growing number of home television sets by the late 1940s. The big money was still far in the future. Players' agents were unheard of. Pro football players were hometown heroes but far from the national icons that quarterbacks and running backs can become today.

Let us look back to the early days through the eyes of a few veterans of the football wars.

Like most young men who grew up in the South during the 1930s, Kenneth (Ken) Kavanaugh did not even know that professional football existed when he enrolled at Louisiana State University in 1936 after graduating from Little Rock High School. The NFL had nine teams at the time, all in the Northeast and Midwest, and there was so little national interest in it that southern newspapers ignored the league.

Kavanaugh—a 6-foot, 3-inch, 205-pound end with great speed— had a sterling career at LSU. He was named to the All-Southeast Conference team three times and finished seventh in the Heisman Trophy balloting in his senior year. During his sophomore year, he got a letter from the Paterson Panthers, a New Jersey team in the minor American Association, inquiring about his interest in a pro career—the first inkling he had that he could get paid for playing football.

Although he did not know it, the Chicago Bears drafted him in the second round of the 1940 NFL draft. That summer, Kavanaugh was playing first base for the St. Louis Cardinals' farm team in Kilgore, Texas, when he got a call from George Halas, owner and coach of the Chicago Bears. Kavanaugh remembered his initiation into contract negotiations in the NFL:

> I'd never heard of George Halas. I didn't know anything about him. He said, "I'm George Halas." I said, "So?" He said, "Chicago Bears; it's a professional football team." George wanted to know if I was going to come to Chicago to play in the *Tribune* College All-Star game. [The game, promoted by *Chicago Tribune* sports editor Arch Ward, was played annually from 1934 to 1976 at Soldier Field and pitted the NFL's reigning champion against college stars.]
>
> I said "No, because I'm playing baseball right now. I'm under contract to the St. Louis Cardinals, and our season is going to run past the All-Star game date." The next day I got another call. It was from Arch Ward. He said, "You're going to have to play in the All-Star game," and I said, "No, I don't have to." He said, "If you're going to play professional football you have to play in the *Tribune* All-Star game."
>
> I said, "Well, I don't know if I'm going to play football," and I hung up. Skip a day or two. Halas calls back. He has Arch Ward on the phone with him. They said, "Would you like to play football?" and I said, "Yeah, I'd like to but I can't." They said, "Well, see if you can get out of your contract." So I told them I'd try to see if I could.

Ken Kavanaugh was able to end his baseball season early so that he could play in the All-Star game. He continued:

The All-Stars were practicing at Northwestern University near Chicago, and George Halas came around to talk to me. I think he offered me $100 a game. I said no, I'm not going to play for any $100. Halas came back a week later and said, "I'll give you $200 and that's as far as I can go." I said no again, and then he came back again and went up to $250 a game. I thought, well, I'll get 300 out of him. In those days, you didn't know what to ask for. I didn't know what anybody was making on the Bears.

Halas said, "There's no way I can pay you 300." I said, "Okay, I've got to go to practice anyway." The next day, he's again up in my dormitory room at Northwestern. I just stayed at $300 a game. I said, "You can talk all you want to, but that's it." And he said, "Okay, but nobody makes that kind of money around here."

Kavanaugh's rookie-year wage of $300 a game put him among the elite of the NFL. "We had All-Pro linemen who were making $100, $150 a game in 1940!" Kavanaugh said he found out later. "I didn't know it when I signed that $300 was a lot." The per-game wage was only for league games; the players earned nothing from exhibitions. So Kavanaugh's actual pay for 1940 was $3,300 for eleven games, plus $873 as his share of the Bears' pot for beating the Washington Redskins, 73 to 0, in the NFL championship game.

Over most of the first half century of professional football, the pro sport and its players and coaches were denigrated by college and high-school coaches. Pro football was anathema to college coaches, even though they themselves earned a living from the sport.

In 1924, Amos Alonzo Stagg, one of the great innovators as a college coach in the early days, deplored professionalism: In an open letter "to all friends of college football," Stagg wrote:

It seems like a matter of little consequence for one to attend the Sunday professional football games—nothing more than attending any Sunday event—but it has a deeper meaning than you realize, possibly a vital meaning to college football. Intercollegiate football will live only so long as it contributes to the well-being of the students; that is while the influences of the game are predominantly on the side of amateur principles, right ideals, proper standards and wholesome conditions.

For years the colleges have been waging a bitter warfare against the insidious forces of the gambling public and alumni and against over-zealous and short-sighted friends, inside and out, and also not infrequently against crooked coaches and managers who have been anxious to win at any cost, and victory has not been completely won. And now along comes another serious menace, possibly greater than all others, viz., Sunday professional football.

Two years after Stagg's blast at pro football, Herbert Reed, a former football coach and writer for the *New York Evening Post*, predicted the imminent demise of professional football in the pages of the weekly magazine *Outlook*. Football fans, Reed wrote,

> know that while there is often great skill in the passing and kicking, the game is not played as hard and as wholeheartedly as the amateur brand. And the other element that demands a "show" will be satisfied with nothing less than All-American stars. When these fail to appear, the professional game will drop back to normal, which means in most cases an attendance averaging between 4,000 and 8,000.
>
> What will kill professional football on a large scale is ostracism.

Even after World War II, when professional football was growing in status, though not yet in financial terms, there was still a stigma attached to the pro game, according to Harold (Hal) Lahar. A guard from the University of Oklahoma, Lahar started with the Chicago Bears in 1941 for a wage of $140 a game. After Navy service during World War II, he joined the Buffalo Bills of the All-America Football Conference (which also spawned the Cleveland Browns and San Francisco 49ers, Lahar said,) and spent three seasons with them before going into coaching.

> When I started with the Bears in 1941, if you played pro football, you had two strikes against you in the colleges as a football coach. The concept of professional football players was kind of like a bunch of bums. On the Bears we had all kinds of guys who were surgeons, dentists, lawyers, all kinds of people. They had intelligence, lots of it. We had the other kind of guy too.
>
> Pro football was still not quite respectable in the late 1940s. Even in the high schools in southern Louisiana, where I applied to be a high-school coach, they raised an eyebrow when they heard I had been a pro. It had started way before my time. Gradually they overcame it.

A smattering of African-American athletes dotted professional football rosters during the first third of this century. For unknown reasons, they disappeared from the NFL from 1933 to 1946. A handful of black players were, however, in minor leagues during that period.

Pro football was by no means alone in barring black participation. Basketball was also segregated. Worst of all was organized baseball, which had not welcomed black players since 1898.

But a new era for African-American athletes began dawning in October 1945 when Jackie Robinson, an accomplished all-around athlete, was signed by the Brooklyn Dodgers baseball team to play the 1946 season with its International League farm club in Montreal. (Robinson had spent the 1945 baseball season with the all-black Kansas City Monarchs. In 1941 he had played pro football with the Los Angeles Bulldogs of the Pacific Coast Football League.) Robinson had a triumphant year

as Montreal's second baseman and was promoted to Brooklyn in 1947
to begin his Hall of Fame career.

The arrival of Jackie Robinson and a handful of other black players
in hitherto lily-white organized baseball had a liberating effect on football too. In 1946 the Los Angeles Rams of the NFL hired black stars
Kenny Washington and Woody Strode, and the Cleveland Browns of
the new All-America Football Conference put fullback Marion Motley
and guard Bill Willis on their roster. The number of black players in
pro football increased—but very slowly—over the next several seasons.

Jackie Robinson was the cynosure of all eyes in the sports world.
He endured more abuse and enjoyed more hero worship than any black
athlete in American history, not excepting long-time heavyweight boxing champion Joe Louis. Perhaps because pro football was far behind
baseball in sports fans' affection, there was a comparatively dimmer
spotlight on the black pioneers in football, but they were besieged by
the same vocal and physical abuse Robinson encountered.

In 1949, when Penn State halfback Wally Triplett joined the Detroit Lions, he was one of only a half dozen black players in the NFL.
He remembers:

> Initially, black players had to overcome some prejudice. You had south-
> ern guys on the Lions, guys from all over. I didn't live with them or any-
> thing. On the field they had their quirks, but I couldn't care less. I was
> really bent on establishing myself, and I made some good friends.
>
> It was more or less accepted that opponents would call racial re-
> marks and get in some kicks and punches. You'd hear "nigger" a number
> of times. Some of the black players would resent it, but you're trying to
> win a ball game; you'd just take it. It just made me want to do better,
> that's all.
>
> Some teams took extra delight in getting that extra kick in and that
> extra punch. I can remember being down in the pile waiting for the of-
> ficial to blow the whistle. Is he going to blow the whistle or not? In the
> meantime, you're feeling these kicks. When they did it to me, I knew it
> was racial because along with it I'd hear some names and stuff. Back
> then, you didn't have face guards. You bled all the time.

George Halas, owner and coach of the Chicago Bears for many
years and one of the founding fathers of the NFL, was known as a tough
man in contract negotiations—and not only with Ken Kavanaugh. In
short, he might have been called a tightwad. But he had another side,
as explained by quarterback Bob Snyder, who spent four years with
the Bears:

> He was something, God love him! We never got paid for pre-season
> games, and we had to buy our own shoes. I said to him one day, "You
> know, George, the other teams provide shoes for their players." And he
> said, "Well, Bob, you went to Ohio University and you probably used one

brand of shoes, and this guy went someplace else and they used Rawlings shoes, and this guy over here went someplace else where they used Wilsons. I don't want to get you guys' feet all screwed up." What he didn't want to do was pay for the shoes.

But Halas was awfully good about certain things, too. On one occasion, I lost a baby boy on the morning of a Green Bay game in 1939. I didn't tell anybody except my roommate, Ray Nolting, a halfback, but as the game went on, the word about my baby got around the squad. I kicked a field goal and we won, 30 to 27.

I'm making a hundred and a quarter a ball game. Halas didn't have any money; believe me, he was struggling. George kept back 25 percent of your salary after every game to make sure the players would have money to go home with after the season. When the season was over, I walked into the office to get my money, and when I checked it outside I found there was an extra check for $1,000. So I went back and told the secretary that I didn't have a bonus arrangement with George. She said she didn't know anything about it, so I went in and asked him. And he said, "Oh, that will help on the burial of the little kid." That was George Halas.

Albert H. (Hank) Soar is one of the few men who have had a part in the major leagues of three spectator sports: football, baseball, and basketball. From 1937 to 1946, with one year out for service in the army during World War II, he was a fullback for the New York Giants. In the 1947/1948 basketball season, he coached the Providence Steamrollers in the Basketball Association of America, one of the forerunners of the NBA. And for many years, he was a baseball umpire in the American League.

During Soar's football-playing days, there were no messenger guards, no coaches high up in the stadium suggesting plays by telephone to the bench, and little coaching from the sidelines. In fact, there were very few coaches—just a head coach with one or two assistants. Like many other veterans of the early football wars, Soar deplores some of the developments in the game and remembers how it was in 1939:

Today, guys up in the boxes call down to tell them what plays to use. What the hell do they know about what you're doing on the field? I can't understand that. It drives me nuts when I see that. A guy who never played quarterback in his life is up there calling plays!

We called our own plays out there, both on offense and defense. I remember a game against the Washington Redskins—it was in 1939, I think. It's late in the game and, if we win, we go to the championship game.

Now Sammy Baugh, their quarterback, could thread a needle with that ball. Talk about quarterbacks today—none of them could carry Sammy's jockstrap!

I'm playing safety. Sammy was throwing his short passes, bang, bang, bang, and I'm watching the clock because I *knew* what Sammy was going to do. I know he's going to fake another short one and pull back and throw that long one. I *know* he is going to do this.

And I'm looking at the clock and Steve Owen, our coach, hollers at me, "For Chrissake, Hank, watch the ball! Never mind looking at the clock!"

I said, "Shut up! Can't you see I'm busy out here?"

And then Sammy did it. He threw a long one, and I intercepted it. I hollered at Steve, "Does that satisfy you? Can I look at the clock now?"

In the days before no-cut contracts and a players' union, a professional football player's job was precarious. He was paid by the game, not by the season, and every year he faced tough competition for a place on his team's final roster.

It might seem that Frank Maznicki, a swift halfback out of Boston College, should have had no worries about making the cut in later years after leading the NFL with his rushing average of 6.4 yards a carry in 1942, but he did. Maznicki played for the Chicago Bears and Boston Yanks until 1947, with three years out for service as a navy pilot during World War II. At every training camp, he sweated out the final cut. Maznicki remembered:

You'd go to training camp and there would be sixteen or twenty other backs there. They were only going to keep six halfbacks and three full-backs, something like that. There were sixty-five players, and they were going to cut down to thirty-three. That was the toughest thing.

I was always worried because a lot of good football players were there. I wasn't a superstar. You have to worry all the time. They could cut you on a Tuesday after a game, and you got no pay after that. That would be it.

But my years in football were nice. The only thing that wasn't fun was the pre-season start, with all those candidates for jobs. Once they made the cuts and you had made the team, then it was okay.

When Maznicki was sent to the Boston Yanks by the Chicago Bears in 1947, his salary jumped from $4,700 to $10,500. The reason for the hefty increase was that a player war was raging between the NFL and the upstart All-America Football Conference. Despite this bonanza, Frank Maznicki left pro football at the end of that season to teach and coach football back in his home town, West Warwick, Rhode Island. "I had always wanted to coach," he said, "and when the job opened up here, I said I might as well take it now." He taught physical education, physics, and football at West Warwick High for thirty-seven years. Maznicki became such a legend in Rhode Island schoolboy football that the street he lives on was renamed Coaches Court in his honor.

Pro football players have always earned more during the football sea-son than the average workingman, but their wage did not enter the stratosphere—contracts in the hundreds of thousands of dollars a year—until the 1980s. A journeyman pro in 1950 earned around $6,000, but that was about double the wage of the average Joe.

So players did not have the financial incentive to hang on in the NFL for as long as possible, especially if they were eager to start another career or had been offered a tempting business opportunity. Most players were in the game because they loved it and enjoyed the life of a professional athlete.

One such enthusiast was Don Doll, a defensive back from the University of Southern California who played for the Detroit Lions, Washington Redskins, and Los Angeles Rams from 1949 through 1954 and then coached in college and the pros for more than thirty years. He retired as a player at the early age of twenty-seven and later regretted it:

> I loved to play the game. I enjoyed practice just as much as I enjoyed playing the game. At Southern Cal, a friend and I used to have a competition as to who would be the first one out on the practice field.
>
> If I could play again, I would. Emphatically yes! This time I would play until they dragged me off, and they could bury me right there. I quit too early. I was twenty-seven.
>
> But, you know, I never got a raise in six years and that's why I quit. In my first year with the Lions, I got a salary cut even though I had had a good year. I just missed Rookie of the Year by a few points behind a kid by the name of Joe Geri with the Pittsburgh Steelers. I had twelve interceptions that year, but I got a salary cut. In my third year I got my salary back up to where it was in my first year, but I never got a raise after that. After my last season, I asked for a $500 raise from the Rams and they wouldn't give it to me, so I went into coaching.

As Don Doll's reminiscence suggests, money is at the heart of pro football, but it's not the whole story. There is also the thrill and satisfaction of hard competition, the pride in doing something supremely well, and the camaraderie that comes from being a member of a team with a common goal—victory.

2

IN THE BEGINNING

Professional football almost certainly began in the Ivy League, of all places, during the late 1880s. Today when the Ivies are represented on the football field by student athletes—with the emphasis on student—that may seem unlikely, but it is not. American football was born in the Ivy League, and far and away the best teams were found among the Ivy until the turn of the century.

The premise that the first professional football players were on college teams runs counter to prevailing opinion. Most football historians believe that professionalism first surfaced among athletic association teams in Pittsburgh in the early 1890s. Irrefutable evidence that William W. (Pudge) Heffelfinger, an All-American guard who graduated from Yale's Sheffield Scientific School in 1891, got money for a game in November 1892 is found on the walls of the Pro Football Hall of Fame in Canton, Ohio. The evidence is an expense sheet of the Allegheny Athletic Association for a game against the Pittsburgh Athletic Club stating that Heffelfinger, undoubtedly the greatest player of his day, was paid $500 cash as a "game performance bonus for playing." (That $500 payment, incidentally, was an astonishing amount for a single game at that time and for many years later. It equaled the annual salary of a schoolteacher in the later years of the nineteenth century.) We will return later to the football scene in Pittsburgh during the Gay Nineties.

American football evolved as an offspring of rugby and soccer (with rugby the dominant parent) in matches beginning in 1869 between teams representing Yale, Harvard, Princeton, Rutgers, Columbia, and McGill University of Montreal. The first games for eleven-man teams with rules and methods at least distantly related to those of today's football were played in 1880.

By the late 1880s, there were only a handful of college teams, chiefly in the East, but the game was spreading rapidly. Notre Dame fielded its first varsity team in 1887, and the University of Southern California did so the following year.

Where football had taken root, it was already the major fall sport on the intercollegiate scene. In 1888, less than a decade after the first game that somewhat resembled today's football, the Yale–Princeton game on Thanksgiving Day drew 15,000 fervent rooters to the Polo Grounds in New York City. The big game was almost as much a major social occasion as an athletic contest, according to Parke H. Davis, an early chronicler of football. For three days before Thanksgiving, fashionable hotels in midtown Manhattan rang with college cheers, and the blue of Yale and the orange of Princeton brightened the costumes of students and old grads on the city streets.

At midmorning on game day, a parade of horse-drawn conveyances carrying the fans started on the long drive to the Polo Grounds in northern Manhattan. "The coaching parade was a feature that was second only to the game itself," Parke Davis wrote in *Football: The American Intercollegiate Game:*

> A full year in advance every drag in the city was engaged, and by the day of the game [so was] every omnibus, coach and other vehicle capable of transporting a half dozen or more men upon its roof, for no one rode inside. [A drag was a stagecoach with seats both inside and on top.] Flaunting from the tops hung great blankets of blue or orange bunting. Style required the attachment of at least four horses and as many more as the finances of the passengers permitted, the horses being no less ornately and abundantly caparisoned than the coach. . . .
>
> At the field a space was reserved for the coaches directly overlooking the field of play, and here, still upon their coach-tops, these coaching parties lunched.

Talk about fashionable tailgate parties!

College football players became heroes to their fans, and the intense desire for victory by both undergraduates and alumni led inevitably to the blurring of the line between amateurs and professionals in sport. This was especially true in the Ivy League because of its pre-eminence in football. As pro football historians Bob Braunwart and Bob Carroll put it in *Pro Football; From AAA to 1903:*

> Quality football—first-rate football—IMPORTANT football—was the exclusive preserve of four schools: Harvard, Yale, Princeton, and a school that was just coming up to football par with the first three, Pennsylvania. It was not sectional chauvinism at work when 129 out of 132 All-American berths between 1889 and 1900 were filled by players from those four schools. The best players were really there.

In 1889 there were well-founded charges that football players in the Ivy League were receiving financial incentives that were not available to ordinary students. The first true pro—a player who accepted a wage for playing—probably was among them. (Incidentally, it could have been Pudge Heffelfinger, who had an All-American year at Yale.)

The evidence comes from a bitter dispute over eligibility of Ivy League football players in the fall of 1889 that led to withdrawal of Harvard from the Intercollegiate Foot-Ball Association, the predecessor of the National Collegiate Athletic Association (NCAA) in governing college football. The dispute arose while Princeton was enjoying an undefeated football season. Just before Princeton's big game with Harvard, two veteran players—one a Princeton graduate student and the other a man who had earlier played at Penn—were added to the Princeton roster. With their help, the Tigers whipped the Crimson. The argument over the two latecomers soon festered into a "You're another" mode and simmered throughout the winter.

In March 1890, the dispute was rehashed in excrutiating detail in a special eight-page supplement to the daily *Princetonian.* The student newspaper published in full the charges and countercharges by both colleges on eligibility questions, on whether athletes had received monetary inducements, and on various proposals for doing away with the evils of professionalism in sport.

The heart of the matter is contained in a long paragraph in a statement by Harvard's athletic committee, which was made up of faculty members, alumni, and undergraduates. The committee wrote:

> The withdrawal of Harvard from the Intercollegiate Foot-Ball League [Association] was due to the fact that the intense competition within that League had led to objectionable practices in all the colleges, which, as was proved at the meetings held in New York on Nov. 4 and 14, Princeton could not be brought to abandon by amicable agreement. The chief of these objectionable practices are—first inducing good players to enter college, or to return to college mainly for the purpose of engaging in intercollegiate contests; and secondly, putting on teams good players who are not in reality amateurs, but have received compensation for the practice of their sport. In many cases, this has gone no further than the acceptance of board, travelling expenses, and perhaps a money allowance for incidentals. Present players on various college teams—in Princeton, Yale and Harvard alike—have accepted such pecuniary advantages. *But in other cases it has included the acceptance of money for playing particular games*, the acceptance of a salary for teaching athletics, and the practice of athletics for a livelihood. According to the invariable practice of amateur organizations in England and America, any one of the three acts last named debars the person concerned from further participation in amateur sports. (Italics added)

Because Harvard's statement was not contradicted by Princeton's reply, we may assume that the Tigers found no fault with it. And so, it is clear that Harvard and Princeton admitted in the spring of 1890 that at least some of their players had accepted money for playing particular games—in short, that they were professionals.

Actually, all the charges contained in Harvard's statement were prima facie evidence of professionalism in the context of the times. The purists of that era frowned on any indication that an athlete competed for any reason other than love of the sport. But times were changing, as Ronald A. Smith has shown in *Sports and Freedom: The Rise of Big-Time College Athletics*. He notes that rowing crews and track and field men were vying for valuable prizes as early as 1852 and that other athletes were competing against professionals—another no-no—soon afterward. The Yale baseball team, for example, played professional teams in 60 percent of its games from 1868 through 1874. Smith also notes that in the nineteenth century, college teams sold tickets for their games, maintained training tables for athletes, and had professional coaches—all signs of professionalism in the minds of the purists.

Colleges were also recruiting talented athletes from the prep schools, though in this practice the athletic teams trailed their more intellectual brothers. Smith writes:

> The recruiting of athletes, however, was predated by half a century by the recruiting of sub-freshmen for college literary societies. Literary and debating societies formed around the ferment of the American Revolution and were the first organized extracurricular activities. It was important to competing literary societies to recruit preparatory students to enhance their society in the eyes of others.

When the first players were paid, football was very different than it is today.

The field itself was different. It was 110 yards long from goal line to goal line—10 yards longer than at present—and 53 yards wide, 1 foot narrower. There was no end zone. The area beyond the goal line was called "in goal," but it had no rear boundary. There was no need for one because forward passing was prohibited. The goal posts were 18½ feet apart, as they are today, with the crossbar 10 feet high, but they stood on the goal line, not 10 yards back.

The only essential piece of equipment was the ball, a rubber bladder encased in leather. It was a copy of the rugby ball; in fact, rugby balls imported from England often were used in the early days of American football. The ball was a cross between today's football and basketball—fatter than modern footballs and blunt at the ends. Sportswriters who fancied florid prose often called an American football a "prolate spheroid."

As in rugby, the players' bodies were largely unprotected. The players wore no helmets, though those who feared broken bones could buy a "nose mask" made of rubber. For one year during the 1890s, there was a vogue for long hair, ostensibly to protect the head. Spalding advertised special skullcaps made of woven silk that were said to protect ears and hair. Ears were especially vulnerable in football's early years because of the clutching, grabbing style of tackling that was prevalent then. In 1891 James A. Naismith, the inventor of basketball, devised earmuffs—the forerunner of helmets—while playing center for the football team at the School for Christian Workers in Springfield, Massachusetts. (One of his teammates was Amos Alonzo Stagg.)

Canvas jackets or vests were worn over team jerseys or sweaters. The jackets, called "smocks," allegedly for their inventor, L. P. Smock of Princeton, were tight-fitting in the hope that tacklers' hands would slide off them. But in some cases, their value for that purpose was negated by leather straps that were sewn to the shoulders like suitcase handles. The straps were attached to help a runner's teammates pull him through the opponents' line, a tactic that was permitted by the rules.

The earliest football shoes were high-tops with hard leather spikes that were screwed into metal plates in the sole. Shin guards of hard leather were sometimes worn under thigh-high wool stockings. Football pants were knicker-length and made of padded canvas or a cotton fabric called "moleskin."

Nineteenth-century football players were very small by the standards of today's college and professional teams. In the Yale–Princeton battle for the national championship in 1888, the biggest man on the field weighed 203 pounds. The average weight was 171 pounds for linemen and 151 for backs. However, despite their small size, the early players were highly aggressive and not above a sneak punch or kick. Reporting on the game, the *New York Times* said:

> There was apparently no bad blood between the teams, but football is not a game calculated to develop gentleness of spirit or superlative resignation to accidental annoyances. Therefore in this very first scrimmage it became apparent that the practice of turning one cheek when the other is smitten was not to be adhered to or even entertained for a moment. As the game progressed, this fact became more potent. The eye of the umpire was the only thing they feared, and when his attention was diverted the surreptitious punches, gouges, and kicks were frequent and damaging. In this particular, Princeton was more effective if not more aggressive. She succeeded in knocking the breath out of at least five Yale men to the extent of having the game stopped until the unfortunates could recover, whereas Yale failed to lay out an opponent so effectively. Possibly the young gentlemen from New Jersey were tougher, for it must be confessed that the spirit of unfair play was not monopolized by either side.

The favorite methods of damaging an opponent were to stamp on his feet, to kick his shins, to give him a dainty upper cut, and to gouge his face in tackling.

Until 1894, when a linesman was added to the officiating crew, there were only two officials: the referee and the umpire. The referee was supposed to follow the ball and the umpire to watch for foul play. These officials had their hands full trying to detect rule violations and deciding how far a ball carrier had advanced. The team on defense tried to push a ball carrier backward, and the runner had to shout "Down!" to end the play.

The team with the ball had to make 5 yards in three downs to retain possession. The field was marked with chalk lines at 5-yard intervals, but there was considerable guesswork in determining whether a team had moved 5 yards after three downs because there were no measuring chains and line sticks. John W. Heisman, for whom the Heisman Trophy is named, remembered:

> The referee kept track of distance by just dropping a handkerchief where he guessed the ball was last put into play. The players of both sides would slyly try to move that handkerchief while some teammates engaged the referee in a discussion of the rules. So we varied action by kicking a handkerchief as well as a football.

Games consisted of two forty-five minute halves, compared with today's thirty minute halves in the college game and thirty minutes in the pros. But even though all players played both offense and defense and substitutions were infrequent, the longer game time did not necessarily mean more action than exists today.

Football historians Bob Braunwart and Bob Carroll, in their monograph on the first pros, point out that "time was stopped only for scores, injuries and arguments. Actual playing time was far less than today. Teams could use a minute and sometimes two between plays." They also write: "Arguments were an important part of strategy. A clever captain, seeing his team winded by their endeavors, could always pick some wrangle with the officials and give his boys a five- or ten-minute breather. With the slow play and interminable arguments, games often stretched into the gathering autumn dusk."

As befits a sport that had soccer as one parent, kicking was important in football's early days. A field goal was worth 5 points when the first professionals appeared. A touchdown counted as only 4, with 2 points added for a kicked goal after a touchdown. A safety was worth 2 points, just as it is today.

Because the ball was a fat oval with blunt ends, drop-kicking for a field goal flourished. To drop-kick, the kicker dropped the ball point down, and just as it rebounded he met it with his toe and sent it over the crossbar. The drop-kick faded from football's scoring repertoire in the early 1930s, when the ball was made slimmer and more pointed at the ends to enhance passing. The slimmer ball was much harder to drop-kick because its rebound was less true. (However, the last successful drop-kick in the pros occurred on a broken play in 1948, long after the last drop-kicker had retired. Joe Vetrano, the San Francisco 49ers' place kicker, was forced to improvise when holder Frankie Albert couldn't handle a bad pass from center. Vetrano picked up the ball and drop-kicked the point.)

In the early days, games began with a kickoff, just as they do today, but because there was no rule that the ball had to travel at least 10 yards, the kickoff sometimes was an offensive play. The kicker would merely nudge the ball forward and then pick it up and pass it to a teammate to carry forward.

That practice gave birth in 1892 to the flying wedge, the most dangerous of the mass momentum plays that were developed in the early years. The flying wedge was the brainchild of Lorin F. Deland, a Boston businessman who had never played football. He suggested the play to Harvard's captain, and it was first used in the big game against Yale.

To start the second half of a scoreless game, Harvard prepared for the kickoff by sending nine of its players back about 25 yards in a V shape. The kicker stood over the ball. The eleventh Harvard man was behind him. On the signal, both legs of the V began running at full tilt toward the kicker. Just as the V reached him, the kicker tapped the ball, picked it up, and lateraled it to the runner behind him, who was enclosed by the onrushing V. The play is said to have gained about 20 yards before Yale broke the wedge and made the tackle. Within months, the flying wedge was a staple in the offense of most teams.

The wedge principle of momentum was used in plays from scrimmage too. At the University of Pennsylvania, coach George W. Woodruff was the prime creator, according to Parke Davis. "He introduced the flying principle into all interference, causing the interferers to start before the ball was put in play and the latter to be snapped just as the interference struck the opposing line," Davis writes. "Around this feature a great number of variations were evolved which came to be known as mass momentum plays."

One variation, used by Yale, was a flying wedge from scrimmage rather than a kickoff. It took advantage of the fact that no set number of linemen were required on the line of scrimmage. All the linemen except the center and guards dropped back into the backfield and formed a wedge with the backs 15 yards from the center. The center did not snap the ball until the point of the wedge arrived. "It is needless to say that the impact was such that the objective point usually remembered it for years," Davis wrote.

Coach Amos Alonzo Stagg, another innovator, had devised momentum plays even before the wedge was born in 1892. Two years earlier, he had created an "ends back" play for Springfield College. Both ends dropped into the backfield, and just before the snap they rushed toward the line to make running blocks on the defenders. "Guards back" and "tackles back" plays used the same principle of momentum.

The basic offensive formation, however, was the T, with seven linemen on the "rush line" and four backs. The quarterback stood just behind the center, or snapper-back. Behind him were two halfbacks and the fullback. At first, the quarterback did not receive the ball on a handoff from center. Rather, he was back a yard or two. In the 1880s, the center snapped the ball to the quarterback by pressing down on the ball with his foot so that it would roll end over end into the backfield. But by 1890, the center was passing the ball back between his legs. The quarterback was forbidden to run with the ball, so he either lateraled or handed off to one of the other men in the backfield.

Until 1888, tackling below the waist was prohibited. That made open field running easy, and both the line and backfield men were spread out. The quarterback got the ball from center, lateraled to a halfback or fullback, and they were off to the races. The result was an open game somewhat similar to rugby. But in 1888, tackling was allowed between the waist and knees, though not below the knees. Long runs became more difficult. Linemen lined up nearly shoulder to shoulder. The aim was to exert maximum force at the point of attack.

Plays were called by shouted signals. Huddles were not used. The quarterback or captain would call, "Play sharp, Charlie," or "Look out, Sam," indicating that one or another back was to hit the line or sweep the end. In later years, letters of the alphabet and numbers were used for signaling plays.

When a touchdown was scored, netting 4 points, the scoring team had a choice of ways to try for the goal after the touchdown and add 2 points. The ball could be brought straight out onto the field from the point where the runner crossed the goal line for the try for the extra 2 points. If the runner had crossed the goal line near the sideline, the place kicker had a very bad angle unless he went back 30 yards or more for the try. The alternative was to punt the ball from the goal line at the point where he had crossed it to a teammate standing about 5 yards in front of the goal posts. That receiver could then drop-kick for the goal; the opponents were not permitted to try to block the kick until the ball was in the air.

Football as it was played in the Gay Nineties would be achingly dull and boring to today's fan. Without forward passing it was one-dimensional, with line plunge following end run, following line plunge, with only an occasional downfield lateral thrown in for excitement. But the game thrilled at least some spectators, as the *New York Times* reported in 1890: In a story attempting to educate readers to the fine points of football technique, the *Times* writer gushed about a play that had occurred in 1885, when there was more open field running:

> No man who saw Lamar of the Princeton team make his wonderful run the full length of the field in the Yale game at New Haven in November 1885 will ever forget that feat. It was the greatest football play ever made in this country, and the enthusiasm that the yellow-legged player awakened as he alternately dodged eleven men, jumped and tore down the field with the ball tight-clasped in his arms will not die as long as memory lasts. No climax in baseball, no hairbreadth victory at the oars, no long-drawn-out love sets at tennis can begin to compare with the splendid prowess of this strong man as he fought his way past his eleven opponents and rushed victoriously to the coveted goal.

College football players enjoyed the thrills of the sport, too, and wanted to continue playing after graduation. They found teams to play on in the athletic associations that had sprouted in most large cities in the latter half of the nineteenth century. Those athletic associations were the incubators of professional football.

3

THE CRADLE OF PROFESSIONALISM

The first fully professional teams grew out of rivalries between the athletic associations that proliferated in America's cities during the late nineteenth century. These athletic clubs had the obvious purpose of providing facilities and playmates for athletes and wannabees in track and field, boxing, wrestling, cycling, gymnastics, and football. They also had a less obvious purpose: to give ambitious young men a toehold on the social ladder by putting them in touch with well-connected men who also enjoyed sports competition.

Athletic clubs were the lowest rung of the social club ladder, writes J. Thomas Jable, author of the most definitive monograph on the infancy of professional football: "Membership in them was generally the first step toward gaining admission in the more exclusive Union Leagues and University Clubs or the top-level Metropolitan Men's Clubs."

The athletic club ideal was amateurism. At the time, there was a faint odor of disrepute over big-league baseball players and a veritable stink over prize fighters. Even the physical directors of those athletic clubs that owned gymnasiums were looked down on by social-climbing members.

In their desire for social status, some athletic clubs began to put greater emphasis on social events than on sports. Their membership requirements became more restrictive, which kept the riffraff out and made the clubs more socially exclusive. The clubs found, though, that what they may have gained in social cachet they lost in sports victories. Since more people prefer to be associated with winners than with losers, the clubs did an about-face and sought good athletes, offering them special athletic memberships. The athletes could use the clubs' facilities, but could not hold office or even vote in club elections. By accepting athletes but making them second-class citizens, the socially conscious clubs had the best of both worlds—social prestige and winning teams.

It was not long before the athletic clubs had to sweeten the pot to hold on to the best athletes and keep them from jumping to rival clubs. Sometimes the lure was expense money well beyond the actual costs of travel to games and meets. Sometimes it was trophies or medals that could be turned into cash.

One way of doing it was explained in 1934 in the first study of pro football's history. It was written by Harry March, once the president of the New York Giants and an entertaining, though not very reliable, historian:

> [I]n 1890–91, there were a number of athletic clubs in and around New York, composed of well-known college men who played on various teams without thought of monetary consideration. These teams included the Manhattan Athletic Club, the Orange Athletic Club in Jersey, the Crescent Club in Brooklyn, the Staten Island Club, and the Knickerbocker, which was a descendant of the Manhattan.
>
> Snake Ames, Phil King, Parke Davis, until his death early in June, 1934, chief statistician for the Intercollegiates (and our authority for this particular phase of the transition) and Furness—all of Princeton—played on these teams, as well as many Yale men, whom Mr. Davis courteously forgot. The boys played for only expenses and a "trophy"—all strictly amateur.
>
> Now, here is the catch. The day after the amateur was presented with the "trophy," which was usually a pretty fine gold watch, one who cared to follow him would find him threading his circuitous way to some well-known pawnbroker where the watch was placed in "hock," the usual sum received thereby being a "sawbuck"; in plainer words, twenty smackers. Then the player—still strictly amateur—somehow ran across the man who managed these amateur games and sold him the pawn ticket for another twenty dollars. By some special senses of divination, second sightedness or mental telepathy, the promoter found himself urged toward the same pawn shop and under irresistible impulse, retrieved the pawned watch, paying therefore a small interest and twenty dollars. Then, after the next game, the player received as his "trophy" the same gold watch which went through the same identical experience.

The Amateur Athletic Union (AAU) had been founded in 1888 to try to do away with such chicanery, but had little success in stopping it among the athletic clubs and YMCAs that were its chief components. Most of the offenders at the time of the AAU's formation were track and field athletes; football was not yet an important sport among athletic clubs. But the young sport was on its way to prominence, especially in western Pennsylvania.

In the Pittsburgh area, which J. Thomas Jable and other football historians view as the cradle of professionalism, the sport appeared in 1890 in four athletic clubs, two or three colleges, and at least one college prep school. The busiest team among the athletic clubs was the Allegheny Athletic Association (AAA), based in the city of Allegheny, which today is Pittsburgh's north side. The AAA played six games that year, winning three, losing two, and tying one.

Their opponents included athletic club teams from Detroit and Cleveland, a local prep school named Shadyside Academy, Western University of Pennsylvania (now the University of Pittsburgh), and an "all-star" team made up largely of members of another local athletic club, the East End Gyms. (The Gyms, later known as the Pittsburgh Athletic Club, were the AAA's archrival.)

The AAA's sixth game, against Princeton Prep, was the most revealing about the state of football in Pittsburgh in 1890. The Princeton Prep team was made up of divinity students at the university and was basically the Princeton scrub team. The Prep eleven did have Hector W. Cowan, a star tackle who had played for the Princeton varsity for five years and was named to the first All-American team in 1889, but it was otherwise undistinguished. If there was any doubt that athletic clubs had a long way to go to match Ivy League football teams, it was dispelled as Princeton Prep whipped the AAA by 44 to 6.

Even so, the AAA was the class of the Pittsburgh area in 1890. Not so in 1891, when the Pittsburgh Athletic Club (PAC) still known as the East End Gyms, entered gridiron competition. The East Enders enjoyed an undefeated season, beating Shadyside Academy, the Altoona and Greensburg athletic associations, and four college teams. They could not, however, entice the AAA into a match for local supremacy. The AAA had a mediocre year, with two wins, two losses, and a tie, which may have accounted for their reluctance to accept the East Enders' challenge.

Things were different in 1892. Both the AAA and the East End Gyms, now called the Pittsburgh Athletic Club, were optimistic about their outlooks for the season. The PAC forgave the AAA for luring away several of their stars during 1891, and the PAC overlooked the AAA's decision not to meet them that year.

So they scheduled a game for Friday, October 21, at the PAC's field in Pittsburgh. (Most athletic club games that year were played on Saturdays.) The PAC tuned up for the big game by beating Western University (Pitt), the Greensburg Athletic Association, and their own scrubs when the scheduled opponent for October 15—the Johnstown Athletic Association—failed to show up. The AAA got a later start on the season and had had only one game before the Columbus Day test with the PAC. (In that game, the AAA whipped a college team—Indiana Normal School in Pennsylvania.)

When the PAC–AAA match finally took place on Columbus Day, it proved to be inconclusive in establishing supremacy, ending in a 6 to

6 tie. The game did, however, make it plain that football was a good draw in Pittsburgh. More than 3,000 wildly enthusiastic rooters saw the contest. Jable wrote:

> Gate receipts totaled $1,200 which the teams divided equally. Of greater importance, however, was the public's response to the game which formally established football in Pittsburgh. Football's acceptance and support by the Pittsburgh public increased the number of applicants seeking membership to the two athletic clubs. Taking an interest in football, local rooters applied for membership in the athletic clubs in order to identify more closely with their favorite team. In the weeks following the AAA–PAC contest, PAC admitted 100 new members to its organization, while AAA acted on a comparable number of applications.

But the tie game did not end arguments over which was the better team, so a rematch was scheduled for November 12 at the AAA's Exposition Park. In the days leading up to that battle, hard feelings between the two clubs were exacerbated when it was revealed that the PAC had used a ringer in the tie game. PAC captain and quarterback Charles Aull, who had played for Penn State the previous year, had brought in Penn State center A. C. Read to anchor the PAC line under the alias Stayer. Aull had led the AAA to believe that Stayer was an old friend he just happened to meet on the street and persuaded to play because the PAC's regular center was disabled.

Within days after the rematch was scheduled, Pittsburgh's sporting circles were awash with rumors that both the AAA and the PAC were seeking the services of some of the country's best players. The prime targets of the recruiters were said to be William W. (Pudge) Heffelfinger, an All-American guard from Yale who was acknowledged as the best player in the game, and Knowlton L. (Snake) Ames, a former Princeton halfback who, like Heffelfinger, was on the first All-American team in 1889. Both were playing that season with the Chicago Athletic Association team.

While the rumor mill was flourishing, a local newspaper called the *Alleghenian* published an interview with one of the nation's strongest advocates of amateurism. He was Caspar W. Whitney of *Harper's Weekly*, who selected the All-American teams from 1889 to 1896 in addition to promoting amateurism.

"I am of the opinion," Whitney told the paper, "that the condition of amateur sport just at present is very critical. The desire on the part of clubs to secure points in the games and the anxiety on the part of colleges to overcome their rivals have induced the managers of both athletic clubs and college clubs to do things that are very unbecoming and subversive of the best interests of amateur sport."

Whitney didn't know the half of it. The day after his interview appeared, the *Pittsburgh Press* reported that George Barbour, an officer of the PAC, had allegedly offered Heffelfinger $250 and Ames $100 to play for his team, a scandalous proposition for purists. Barbour stoutly denied the rumor, though he did admit to being interested in other players, among them halfback "Rags" Brown, whose Johnstown, Pennsylvania, Athletic Association team had recently disbanded.

Both the AAA and the PAC continued to blow smoke over the rumors, promising to field virtually the same teams that represented them on Columbus Day. AAA manager Billy Kountz, who also played guard, asked rhetorically in the *Pittsburgh Press:*

> Why shouldn't we have the same team[?] All of the men who lined up at the East End grounds on Columbus Day are anxious as can be to try it over again. . . . In fact, I think we will play the same team as we did before, and if the East Enders play the same team, I think we will be able to beat them without any trouble. Our boys are getting stuck on themselves, and you may be sure we will not put up an easy team that day. We want the game and will not neglect any precaution to win the game.

Few believed Kountz's disclaimer. Fueled by the rumors of ringers on both sides, interest in the rematch was growing by leaps and bounds. It was reported that the AAA's fans already had bet between $5,000 and $10,000 on their team, even though they had to give odds. The day before the game, when three stars from the strong Chicago Athletic Association team were seen around Pittsburgh, the PAC fans canceled their bets and said that they would make no more wagers until they saw who took the field.

A crowd of 5,000 had been expected for the showdown, but snow and low temperatures on game day inhibited fair-weather fans, and only about 3,000 spectators turned out at Recreation Park. Most were as curious to see who would take the field for both teams as they were about the game's outcome.

The visiting PAC team appeared on the field first for limbering-up exercises, and lo! among them were Simon Martin, a center from Lehigh who had played for the Steelton [Pa.] Athletic Club, and Rags Brown, a halfback from Johnstown. While Martin and Brown would undoubtedly strengthen the PAC, they did not strike fear into opponents' hearts.

When the AAA team came out, the PAC rooters fell silent, for there were three gilt-edged ringers: Pudge Heffelfinger; Ben (Sport) Donnelly, a brawling end from Princeton; and Ed Malley, a big tackle and shot putter from Michigan.

The PAC players promptly left the field to return to the horse-drawn omnibus that had brought them from Pittsburgh. From that sanctuary, they called all bets off and offered to play an exhibition game. Oliver D. Thompson, an old Yalie and teammate of Walter Camp who was the power behind the AAA team, refused to agree that bets were off.

After a short interval, the referee awarded the AAA a victory by forfeit, 6 to 0. The *Pittsburgh Press* reported:

> Confusion dire reigned all this time and it seemed as though the best advertised and most promising event of the foot ball season was about to end up in a farce. The Allegheny men claimed they had only followed the East Enders' example in that they had got these three men. It was cited that on Columbus Day the East Enders had played a State College man at center under an assumed name and the A's made a virtue of the fact that they had not complained at the time.

Thompson also said that he could prove the PAC had tried to sign Jessie Riggs, an old Princeton player, as well as Heffelfinger and Snake Ames, for this game. In addition, Thompson noted that the PAC had Simon Martin and Rags Brown, neither of whom was an AAA club member, in uniform and could also call on Clarence Lomax of Cornell, who was on the grounds but not in uniform, if desired.

In short, Thompson admitted that the AAA had three ringers. But, the *Pittsburgh Press* reported, "Mr. Thompson came to the conclusion that the Allegheny management had been successful where the East End manager had failed."

To keep the crowd from growing too restless, the AAA got a game of sorts going between its second-line players—excluding Heffelfinger, Donnelly, and Malley—and players from Western University (Pitt) who, fortuitously, were on hand. The PAC's George Barbour again offered to play an exhibition game if all bets were called off. Thompson at first refused but, said the *Pittsburgh Press*, "cooler heads prevailed and after much talking and peering the claims of the crowd on both teams became potent and the A's gave in[,] though they declared they would not have done so but for so many people being present who wanted to see the game."

By now it was almost an hour after the announced starting time of 3:00 P.M. With the sun already low in the November sky, it was decided to play thirty-minute halves, making the game a half hour shorter than regulation. As it turned out, darkness was coming on swiftly when the second half started, and the game was ended by the referee after eighteen minutes of second-half play.

After all the preliminary wrangling, the game itself was anticlimactic. The only score came midway through the first half when Heffelfinger scooped up a fumble by a teammate and ran for a touchdown. The distance was variously described by Pittsburgh papers as 15, 25, and 30 yards. Malley missed the try after the score, so the final score was 4 to 0.

Despite the low score, the spectators were treated to plenty of action, though much of it was extracurricular. Jable wrote:

> The low score and stalwart defenses reflected the ferocity with which the game was contested. Pudge Heffelfinger led the way with his vicious method of breaking the wedge. ". . . [W]hen PAC wedged down the field, he (Heffelfinger) ran and jumped at it with full speed, bringing his knees against the mass. The wedge didn't hold long" [reported the *Chronicle-Telegraph*]. "Captain Charley Aull and his brother, Burt, received severe injuries. Aull left the game with a badly injured back after he was crushed beneath a pile of several opponents. Earlier in the game, Burt Aull fell victim to a fierce blow to the head, causing him to retire. "Sport" Donnelly of AAA received a terrific smash in the eye and PAC officials offered no sympathy, contending that Donnelly had played dirty football. Expressing disappointment to the officials for halting the game at the onset of darkness, Donnelly pleaded: "Oh, I wish this game would last just two minutes longer. I just want two minutes to get even" [according to the *Chronicle-Telegraph*].

Thus ended the first game in which there is no doubt that at least one player—Heffelfinger—received money beyond his expenses, though it was never admitted by the AAA. But the AAA's expense sheet for the game, which is now a featured exhibit at the Pro Football Hall of Fame, shows Heffelfinger getting $500 as a "performance bonus." The sheet also shows $75 for expenses for Heffelfinger, Donnelly, and Malley—presumably $25 each. Heffelfinger and Malley left town after the game, but Donnelly stayed on and earned $250 for playing with the AAA against Washington and Jefferson College the following week, thus becoming the second certain pro footballer.

Pudge Heffelfinger never admitted receiving wages for playing football. Nevertheless, he holds a place in the annals of pro football as the first certifiable professional. Until the AAA's expense sheet turned up at the Hall of Fame, it was thought that the first professional had probably been John K. Brallier, a young, talented quarterback who had earned $10 plus expenses from the Latrobe, Pennsylvania, team for a game in September 1895. Brallier, who was not quite nineteen years old at the time, went on to become an accomplished quarterback at Washington and Jefferson College, at West Virginia University, and for several pro teams of the early years. Later, while practicing dentistry in Latrobe, Brallier coached in high schools. The NFL gave him its first lifetime pass for his pioneering play.

Heffelfinger was without doubt the most famous player of the early years, as well as the putative first professional. At 6 feet, 3 inches tall, and weighing about 205 pounds, he was considered to be a giant at a time when most linemen weighed between 165 and 185 pounds. He was born in Minneapolis on December 20, 1867, the son of a shoe

manufacturer who speculated in real estate. He attended Central High
School in that city and played football and baseball there.

In 1888 Heffelfinger matriculated in the Sheffield Scientific School
at Yale, a less prestigious place than Yale College but a part of the
university. During his four-year football career at Yale, the Blues suffered only two defeats. Heffelfinger was on Caspar Whitney's All-
American teams in 1889, 1890, and 1891.

Heffelfinger is credited with originating the pulling guard play, in
which a guard steps back from the line and leads the interference. He
is said to have destroyed opponents' flying wedges by leaping over the
point man in the V and flattening the ball carrier. Over the first half
century of American football, he was a unanimous choice as a guard
on every all-time team selected by experts.

After graduating from Yale, Heffelfinger got a low-level job in a
railroad office in Omaha, Nebraska. He was working there when the
1892 season began and he heard about the liberal expenses being paid
by the avowedly amateur team of the Chicago Athletic Association. He
joined the Chicago Athletic Association, playing with teammates Sport
Donnelly and Snake Ames, until Oliver D. Thompson tapped him for
the AAA team in Pittsburgh later in 1892.

He played only one more pro season. He was again with the AAA
in 1896, the final year of the team's existence. According to historians
Bob Braunwart and Bob Carroll, Heffelfinger and his teammates each
earned $100 per game, a payroll that put the team out of business after
only two games.

Heffelfinger at various times coached at the University of California, Lehigh University, and the University of Minnesota. He also served
as a volunteer coach at Yale. He became a successful businessman in
Minneapolis but maintained some connection with football right up to
his death on April 2, 1954. As an elder statesman of the game, Heffelfinger was critical of modern linemen. He believed, for one thing, that
they should assume a standing position, rather than get down in the
modern three-point stance before the snap, so that they could see
where the play was going. It was a classic case of an old-timer saying,
"That's the way we did it in my day."

Professionalism took root among the Pittsburgh-area athletic clubs in
1893, though the clubs continued to protest their innocence to charges
that they paid their players. Hypocrisy was at high tide.

On January 1, 1893, just six weeks after the brouhaha over the
appearance of Heffelfinger, Donnelly, and Malley in the AAA lineup,
the *Pittsburg Dispatch* published a blurb praising Oliver D. Thompson,
the AAA manager who had hired Heffelfinger, for his untiring efforts
on behalf of amateur athletics. The *Dispatch* said that Thompson and

John Moorhead, another old Yale footballer who was president of the AAA, "have done much toward making amateur sports and pastimes what they are in Pittsburg [*sic*]. For years they labored to get football established here and how well they have succeeded the present popularity of the game will tell.

"But they have always aimed at sports that are pure and ennobling," the *Dispatch* continued. "If all sports and contests were carried on according to their principles there would be absolutely nothing dishonest or dishonorable in the sporting world today. They were athletes for the love of it and they patronize athletics now because of the resultant benefits to athletes."

Perhaps. But among the resultant benefits for several players on the AAA in 1893 were weekly wages for their efforts, according to Braunwart and Carroll. In fact, they believe that the AAA paid at least three of their players for every game that year. So, probably, did the PAC. The Pro Football Hall of Fame has a copy of the first known player's contract, witnessed by PAC manager George Barbour. Alas, the player's signature is ripped across, so it can't be said for sure who he was. Braunwart and Carroll think that it was probably Grant Dibert, a halfback from Swarthmore who had played for the PAC for three years. The contract reads in full: "I hereby agree to participate in all regularly scheduled football games of the Pittsburg [*sic*] Athletic Club for the full season of 1893. As an active player I agree to accept a salary of $50 per contest and also acknowledge that I will play for no other club during PAC games."

In 1894 the Greensburg Athletic Association became the third known team to pay a player something more than his expenses. He was Lawson Fiscus, a farmer's son from Indiana County, Pennsylvania, who had earned the title "Samson of Princeton" for his sterling play as a guard for the Tiger varsity during his one year there. Fiscus had received what were described as "liberal expenses" from the AAA as early as 1891, but in 1894 Greensburg paid him $20 a game plus expenses. Lawson Fiscus's brothers Newell and Ross also were on Pittsburgh-area athletic club teams during the 1890s and were highly regarded as players.

By the time John K. Brallier, for many years thought to be the first pro football player, was paid $10 a game plus expenses in 1895 by the fledgling YMCA team in Latrobe, Pennsylvania, professionalism was common, though unacknowledged, throughout southwestern Pennsylvania. Brallier achieved the distinction of being the first pro largely because he was honest, never denying that he had been paid to play. The Latrobe manager, Dave Berry, like Brallier, thought he was the first football man to pay a player, according to Robert B. Van Atta, the authority on the early pros in Greensburg and Latrobe.

Professionalism flourished in the late 1890s in southwestern Pennsylvania. The athletic clubs continued the charade that their athletes
competed for love of the game, but professionalism was widely assumed in the media. Interest in the game was growing. In 1897 the PAC
and Washington and Jefferson College drew more than 12,000 to their
battle, and in 1899 Washington and Jefferson and the powerful Duquesne Country and Athletic Club, which had succeeded the AAA as
the dominant team in the area, attracted 17,500—at that time the largest crowd ever to see "independent" (that is, professional) players. Such
throngs, though, were the exception; much more common were ad-
missions totaling 2,000 to 4,000.

The small cities of Latrobe and Greensburg did not have the fan
base to draw big crowds, but in terms of enthusiasm they took a back
seat to no one. Van Atta found this newspaper description of Latrobe's
reaction to a victory over Greensburg:

> The town was wild and the din terrific. It started when news of the great
> victory was phoned down and it grew every minute until the climax was
> reached at 10 o'clock when the team came home. Billy Showalter had the
> brass band out and two thousand people packed the streets. [The] [t]own
> was ablaze with red fire and Roman candles and the din was incessant
> and awful. Five hundred tin horns kept up a crash while a skillet brigade
> created a new and strange noise.

The line between amateurism and professionalism remained ex-
ceedingly fuzzy. It was common for a player to spend a season or two
with an athletic club and then play for a college team, or even play on
both sides of the fence in the same season. College teams routinely
scheduled the independents, even when it was widely acknowledged
that they were paying players. Washington and Jefferson College, the
Western University of Pennsylvania (now Pittsburgh), West Virginia
University, Geneva College, Grove City College, and Penn State were
on the schedules of most Pittsburgh-area athletic clubs throughout the
middle to late 1890s.

The AAU did its best to discourage professionalism, but its best
was not very good. In 1896 the AAU ousted the AAA for paying players,
which meant that the AAA cyclists and trackmen could not find opponents from other athletic clubs. They dropped out of the AAA,
whereupon the football players organized a team that was short-lived
but without doubt the best in the region, if not the country. After two
shutout victories on consecutive days over the Duquesne Country and
Athletic Club and its old rival, the PAC, the AAA effectively vanished.
"They'd left an incredible legacy, however," wrote Braunwart and Carroll. "They had the first known pro in 1892, the first regularly salaried
players in 1893, the first completely professional team in 1896, and

they'd gone out—as they wanted—in a blaze of glory. Their final team was undefeated, untied, unscored-upon, and unparalleled in pro football history."

During the late 1890s, the Duquesne Country and Athletic Club, the Greensburg Athletic Association, and the Latrobe Athletic Club were the most consistently successful teams. Most were probably fully professional in that contracts were signed for the full season, not just for a game. Van Atta writes that when the Greensburg Athletic Association team disbanded at the end of the 1900 season, the local paper reported:

> The contracts with the players were carried out to the letter, and . . . they received every dollar that was coming to them. . . . Their pay started on the first day of October . . . [but] with the exception of the local men, none of them reported on time. . . . Not a cent was taken off for the time lost. . . .
>
> When it was impossible to get a Thanksgiving Day game [to replace one canceled by Latrobe], it was decided to disband early, and one week's pay was deducted. . . . Where a contract called for transportation to and from a player's home, it was paid. . . . Where a contract called only for room and boarding, transportation was not paid.

Greensburg had lost two close games that year to the curiously named Homestead Library and Athletic Club. The team, which was undefeated over its short life of two seasons, was apparently bankrolled by the Homestead Works of the Carnegie Steel Corporation, whose founder, Andrew Carnegie, was a noted donor of public libraries in the late 1890s. (A decade later, Homestead, a steel town just east of Pittsburgh on the Monongahela River, became home to the Homestead Grays, one of the most famous teams in the segregated black baseball leagues.)

The Homestead Library and Athletic Club team, with several All-Americans and stars from the Duquesne Country and Athletic Club team, went undefeated and untied throughout the 1900 and 1901 seasons and worked up a serious sweat in only four of its twenty-one games. Unfortunately, Homestead did not do well at the gate, at least in part because of bad weather. The autumns of 1900 and 1901 must have been the rainiest on record in southwestern Pennsylvania if the Pittsburgh newspapers are to be believed. In reporting late in the season of 1900 that all local teams had lost money, the *Pittsburgh Press* lamented that "such a run of miserable weather had never before been encountered." Weather conditions were not much better in the 1901 season. Homestead lost $8,000—a significant sum then even to the Homestead Works of Carnegie Steel, and that turned out to be the last season for the Homestead Library and Athletic Club football team.

The next season, 1902, marked the end of the Pittsburgh area's glory years as the cradle of pro football. The 1902 standard bearers were the Pittsburgh Stars, made up of many of the old Homestead players, plus Christy Mathewson, a former Bucknell fullback who was regarded as the best punter in the game. (Mathewson was already a big-league pitcher, though not yet the best in baseball.) The Stars appear to have been bankrolled by Barney Dreyfus, owner of the Pittsburgh Pirates baseball team.

The Stars were the creation of David J. Berry, a Latrobe newspaperman who had managed the fine Latrobe professional teams of the late 1890s. Berry was also the founding father of the first amalgamation of teams to call itself a league. In September 1902, he announced the founding of the National Football League, with himself as president. That first NFL had no bylaws, no office, and no schedule-making powers. What it did have was three of the strongest teams in the country.

Besides the Stars, the NFL had only two teams, both in Philadelphia and both backed by the city's big-league baseball teams. Berry was unsuccessful in trying to entice teams from New York and Chicago into his league. The Philadelphia Phillies football team was managed by baseball manager Bill Shettsline and coached by Ben F. Roller, a veteran guard from Purdue. The Philadelphia Athletics footballers were backed by the Athletics baseball team (now the Oakland Athletics), managed by baseball manager Connie Mack and coached by C. E. (Blondy) Wallace, a guard from Penn.

The three league teams played one another two or three times, with no team appearing to dominate the others. The Athletics won three games, lost two, and tied one with league rivals while compiling an overall record of 10–2–2. The Phillies were 2–2 in the league en route to a final mark of 8–3. And the Pittsburgh Stars, coached by quarterback Willie Richardson of Homestead fame, were 2–2–1 in the league and 9–2–1 against all competition. The Stars had beaten the Athletics, the team with the best league record, in a game that was advertised as determining the championship; so, not surprisingly, both the Stars and the Athletics claimed the title of "champion."

Not many people cared, though. The "championship" game attracted only 1,800 diehard fans in Pittsburgh. The turnout was so small that Connie Mack demanded his $2,000 guarantee before he permitted his team to take the field. Dave Berry did not have the money, but the president of Carnegie Steel guaranteed payment and the game went on. The Stars and Phillies battled to a scoreless tie. Two days later, the Stars won a rematch, 11 to 0, before a slim crowd of 2,000. So ended the only season of the first NFL.

While they were tuning up for the "championship" game, the Philadelphia Athletics played in the first professional night game. It was held in Elmira, New York. Their opponent was the Kanaweola Cycle

Club team. The *Elmira Daily Advertiser* did not explain how the field was illuminated, beyond saying that electric lights were used. Tradition has it, though, that huge searchlights were placed at opposite ends of the field, so that the players must have spent most of their time squinting into the glare. In any event, the Athletics whipped the Kanaweolas, 39 to 0. There was another first in 1902—the first football "world series," though it wasn't called that at the time. It was a series of games played indoors at New York City's Madison Square Garden in late December. Garden Manager Tom O'Rourke hoped to fill seats over the post-Christmas holiday period, which, in the era before college basketball became a huge draw in New York, was a dull time for the Garden. He invited some of the top college and professional teams, but the colleges declined because the AAU was beginning to cast a jaundiced eye on college teams playing professionals.

The Philadelphia and Pittsburgh teams that made up the late and unlamented National Football League had already disbanded. The Watertown [N.Y.] Red and Blacks, who for several years had been claiming the world championship title mainly for having bested other teams in upstate New York, also turned thumbs down on the prospect of a series in New York City.

O'Rourke was left with two local teams—the Knickerbocker Athletic Club and the Warlow Athletic Club—as well as the Orange [N.J.] Athletic Club, the Syracuse [N.Y.] Athletic Club, and a team labeled "New Yorks," made up of eight old Philadelphia Athletics and four Phillies. The New Yorks were not the only team with ringers; Syracuse signed up Bemis and Hawley Pierce, veteran linemen from the Carlisle Indian School, which was beginning to make a name for itself in football; three backs from the Watertown Red and Blacks; and Glenn and Bill Warner, star linemen from Cornell. (Glenn later gained fame as Pop Warner, one of the most famous coaches in the college ranks.)

A cozy gridiron was laid out in the Garden. Due to space limitations, it was only 70 yards from goal line to goal line—40 yards short of regulation at the time—and about 35 yards wide. The Garden's wooden floor was taken up, exposing ground that was "rather too sticky and holding for fast work," as the *New York Times* described it.

The tournament was scheduled for three nights, starting on December 29. O'Rourke made the mistake of pitting the two best teams against each other for the opener. Syracuse beat the New Yorks, thus ending any possibility of having the best local team in the final contest. The next night, the Knickerbocker Athletic Club defeated the Warlow Athletic Club. Syracuse then rolled over the Knicks, 36 to 0, in the semifinal match. Meanwhile, the Orange Athletic Club had drawn what amounted to a bye, not having to face anyone to get into the championship game, while Syracuse and the Knickerbockers had played two games. Orange is not far across the Hudson River from New York City, so O'Rourke must have kept its athletic club out of competition to ensure a "local" team in the final.

Despite playing its third game in five nights, the Syracuse Athletic Club had no trouble mastering Orange, winning again by 36 to 0. The "world series" had drawn upward of 2,500 fans for each night. The games were only forty minutes long—twenty minutes less than usual—but there were two games each night. A preliminary contest was played by second-line teams in the New York City area, so football fans had a full plate. O'Rourke decided to try the tournament idea again in 1903.

The regular season of 1903 was the last hurrah of big-time pro football in western Pennsylvania until the birth of the Pittsburgh Steelers (né Pirates) thirty years later. The scene of the finale was Franklin, Pennsylvania, a city of some 10,000 on the Allegheny River eighty miles north of Pittsburgh. The Franklin All-Stars were the product of a fierce intercity rivalry not unlike the Greensburg–Latrobe and the Allegheny–Pittsburgh competitions. Franklin's athletic enemy was from Oil City, a somewhat larger town eight miles upriver from Franklin.

Civic pride inflamed the burghers in both cities. For several years, their athletic clubs had been hiring one or two ringers for their football battles. In 1902 Oil City had out-ringered Franklin and won, 10 to 0. Both cities had some wealthy citizens since they are in the heart of the nation's original oil region, and some of them were not averse to betting on the outcome of sporting events.

The result was predictable, but Franklin thought of it first. Why not hire the best players in the land and take all that Oil City money? Not every Franklinite approved of the scheme. In a page-1 letter to the editor of the *Franklin Evening News* on September 30, a football fan named Robert J. Stadtlander deplored the proposal for a professional team. He said that he planned to organize an amateur team made up of local players in Franklin. "We do not see why the public should be asked to contribute $2,500 or $3,000 to import players who represent the city in no sense save in the matter of drawing their salaries," he wrote.

Stadtlander was whistling into the wind. Two weeks later, the *Evening News* exulted, "Hurrah for Professionals!" Franklin, it reported, "will have a football team of the first magnitude." D. A. Printz, who had managed Franklin's amateur teams for three years, was to head the new All-Stars organization. A number of Franklin's business leaders and oil promoters were backers, the most prominent among them being Joseph C. Sibley and Charles A. Miller of the Galena Signal Oil Company.

By October 13, just a week before the first game on the Franklin schedule, the *Franklin Evening News* still had not announced who the

All-Stars players would be, but promised that they would be among the best in the land. The newspaper also appealed for financial support for the team:

> The expenses of the Franklin foot ball team are really enormous and it is hardly likely that the gate receipts will more than pay the expenses of the visiting teams. This means a heavy loss to be met at the end of the season. A few gentlemen have stood for this and in order to lighten their load as much as possible Manager Printz has placed in his show window a foot ball which will be raffled off some time during the season. The winner of this will not only be in possession of a handsome ornament or a harmless plaything for the children, but will have a souvenir of the Greatest Foot Ball Team on Earth. Chances are 25¢ each and it is hoped that they will find a ready sale.

When the All-Stars took the field at Athletic Park in Franklin for the first time on October 21, they turned out to be the pick of the 1902 Pittsburgh Stars and Philadelphia Athletics. Seven were from the Athletics and four from the Stars. Their opponent was an independent team called the Youngstown [Ohio] Giants, which turned out to be a misnomer since the Franklin All-Stars walloped them by 74 to 0. The *Evening News* gloated: "The Youngstown Giants are giants no longer— they are dwarfs, insignificant, diminutive dwarfs—outweighed and out-played, out-classed and out-cast by the Greatest on Earth."

It was the first in a series of mismatches for the All-Stars. Playing twice a week and always at home, the Franklin All-Stars whipped club teams from Pittsburgh; Jamestown, New York; Wheeling, West Virginia; Ellwood City, Pennsylvania; Buffalo, New York; Sewickley, Pennsylvania; and Allegheny College in nearby Meadville, Pennsylvania, by scores varying from 23 to 0 to 74 to 0.

Franklin's only real test in ten regular season games came when they met an independent team, no doubt made up of pros, from Syracuse, New York. The All-Stars defeated Syracuse, but only by 12 to 0, and the upstate New Yorkers had the distinction of being the only team to advance past midfield (the 55-yard line) all season. A Syracuse end named Wier got to Franklin's 33-yard line on a 45-yard play called a "double pass," which must have meant that two laterals were tossed since forward passing was still prohibited.

The All-Stars did not play Oil City in 1903, even though that competition was the reason they had been assembled in the first place. A Franklin fan explained why in an article written some years later that was reprinted in the 1981 *Annual* of the Professional Football Researchers Association. The fan, William R. Smith, wrote:

> Before the season started a schedule between Franklin and Oil City was arranged and a forfeit put up by each team to play a certain number of games. Oil City was over-anxious for the contests and was of the opinion

that they were going to put something over on their rivals. Immediately upon the signing of the contract they started to hotfoot after their players, only to find that Manager Printz had been weeks ahead of them and had signed every man they wanted with the exception of "Doc" Roller. . . . Then the great big yellow streak showed up. Those Oil City "sports" came to Franklin, whined around a while, claiming we had signed all the players they wanted, that they could not get a team together that would give us a decent argument, and then asked to be allowed to withdraw their forfeit. This request was so surprising and unusual, even though coming from Oil City "sports," that it was granted, and this is why we did not wallop the daylights out of them . . . like we have every other season for the past 30 years.

Some of the Oil City sports turned out for the Syracuse game against Franklin. "They all wore the Syracuse colors," the *Franklin Evening News* reported, "but before the game was over they showed their usual streak of yellow by taking off the colors and keeping mum." The *Evening News* added,

> An editorial in the [Oil City] *Derrick* this morning says that the game yesterday afternoon was a "bloody, brutal and disgraceful affair," and that Franklin is gaining for herself a "reputation in football that one of these days she will be sorry for." And still the "yellow" crops out. They weren't "sorry" for what they did last year, we guess.

Unfortunately, the All-Stars were not called on to play Latrobe either. John K. Brallier led the Latrobe YMCA as coach and quarterback to an undefeated season in nine games. There was talk of a match with Franklin but negotiations broke down, presumably because the financial terms were not satisfactory to one or both teams. It is hard to say how they would have matched up. Certainly Franklin had more "name" players, but if comparative scores mean anything, it is worthwhile to note that both teams shut out Ellwood City, Latrobe by 35 to 0 and Franklin by 33 to 0. However, Latrobe just edged out the East End Athletic Club of Pittsburgh 6 to 5, while Franklin whipped the East Enders 23 to 0.

The Franklin All-Stars are of particular interest because we know more about the players than about those of any other pioneering pro team. The reason is that during the season, the *Evening News* printed capsule biographies of the players on the fifteen-man "Greatest Team on Earth." The coach, who also played halfback, was John A. (Teck) Matthews, a Native American whose home was in San Marcos, Texas. Matthews had come north a few years earlier to play football at Kiskiminetas Prep in Pennsylvania. He then entered Washington and Jefferson College in Washington, Pennsylvania, where, according to William R. Smith, he became the greatest player turned out by the college up to that time. Matthews apparently attended classes only during football seasons and then went back to Texas. He also attended the Carlisle Indian School in Carlisle, Pennsylvania, before going to Franklin to coach its mostly amateur team in 1902. Matthews was said to be a speedy and shifty runner who stood 5 feet, 11 inches tall and weighed 197 pounds.

With Matthews in the backfield were halfback J. Paul Steinberg, quarterback John (Jack) Hayden, and fullback H. A. (Bull) Davidson. Steinberg had spent the previous season with Franklin, as had Matthews, and both were local favorites. Steinberg was called the "Twister" because of his elusiveness in the open field. Before coming to Franklin, he had played at Cornell University and with the Syracuse Athletic Association and had been a college coach. Steinberg also played professional basketball. After the one great season of the Franklin All-Stars, Steinberg went to Little Falls, New York, as physical director of an athletic club there.

Quarterback Jack Hayden, who was 5 feet, 8 inches tall and weighed 170 pounds, was a typical tramp athlete of the era. He had played a couple of seasons at Villanova University and then at the University of Pennsylvania and University of Maryland. He moved into the quasi-professional ranks with the Maryland Athletic Club and spent the 1902 season with the Philadelphia Athletics as an admitted pro. Hayden, who was born in Bryn Mawr, Pennsylvania, in 1880, was also a major-league baseball player, playing for three years in the outfield for Connie Mack's Athletics, the Boston Red Sox, and the Chicago Cubs.

Fullback Bull Davidson also came to the All-Stars from the Philadelphia Athletics. He had played for and captained the Penn team for three years before coaching the Maryland Athletic Club and playing for Mack's Athletics.

The left side of Franklin's line came from the Pittsburgh Stars of 1902, while the right side were old Athletics. The left end, Clark A. Shrontz, a 6-foot, 186-pounder, was in his second pro season after three years of stardom at Washington and Jefferson College. He was twenty-three years old. Left tackle John Lang, who also played halfback at times, was 5 feet, 10½ inches tall and weighed 208 pounds. He had played at Susquehanna University in Selinsgrove, Pennsylvania, and at Washington and Jefferson College before moving into the pro ranks with Latrobe in 1900. Lang's substitute when he was in the backfield was veteran W. P. McNulty, who had played for three seasons at Notre Dame, then with the Entre Nous Club team of Paterson, New Jersey, and with the powerhouse Homestead Library and Athletic Club team in 1900/1901.

Left guard Herman Kirkoff (sometimes spelled Kerchoffe and Kirkhoff), was probably the most famous player on the team and certainly the most experienced. He had already played for eight seasons before turning up in Franklin. He had only one season in college foot-ball, with Purdue University, and then played with the Denver Athletic Club, the Chicago Athletic Association, and the Pittsburgh Stars. "Guards back" was a popular play during Kirkoff's career, and he did a fair amount of ball carrying as a result. William R. Smith said the 6-foot, 4-inch, 242-pound Kirkoff would run "down the field with the ball tucked under his arm and half a dozen opposing players hanging onto his back and legs, but he moved along as though nothing was opposing him." Smith called Kirkoff "the greatest guard who ever lived," perhaps because he probably never saw Pudge Heffelfinger.

Center Lynn D. Sweet was only 5 feet, 7 inches tall but weighted 172 pounds and was described by Smith as never having had a peer at center. Sweet played for three years at Bucknell and one year at Penn State before moving into the pro ranks in 1902 with the Philadelphia Athletics. At right guard was Arthur L. Mc-Farland (called Tige, as in Tiger), a native of St. Clairsville, Ohio. Like some of the other early pros, McFarland played first with quasi-professional teams before going to college. He spent two years with the Greensburg Athletic Association team before enrolling at Washington and Jefferson College for two seasons and then moving on to West Virginia University. He came to Franklin after a season with Connie Mack's Athletics. The *Franklin Evening News* writer said that McFarland, who weighed 226 pounds and was 6 feet, 1 inch tall, "is pleasant and good natured at all times . . . plays a clean game always, is opposed to slugging and 'dirty' work, and has won a very enviable place in the hearts of the Franklin public."

The left tackle, Charles E. (Blondy) Wallace, starred at Peddie In-stitute, a prep school, in 1896 and 1897 before playing for three seasons at Penn. He was a free spirit and apparently a saloon denizen who came to Franklin after a year with the Philadelphia Athletics. Wallace was captain of the All-Stars. A few years later, Wallace played and coached at Canton, Ohio, when that was the capital of the pro football world.

Tiny B. D. (Bert) Sutter, who stood 5 feet, 4 inches tall and weighed 150 pounds, was the right end. He had played at Western Reserve Uni-versity in Cleveland and at Washington and Jefferson College. Franklin was his first pro team. Smith said that Sutter "was not in the best of health while in Franklin," so he was often replaced by Eddie Wood, another Washington and Jefferson veteran, who had started in the in-dependents with Latrobe in 1896.

The only hometown boys on the Franklin All-Stars, other than manager Dave Printz, were substitutes—guard W. J. McConnell and halfback Chal Brennan. McConnell later was elected mayor of Frank-lin, and Brennan became street commissioner for the city.

In New York City, Madison Square Garden manager Tom O'Rourke was planning a more ambitious indoor football tournament than he had presented in 1902. Historian Marc Maltby writes that in addition to a tourney for pros, O'Rourke was planning a round robin for the top athletic club football teams in greater New York, a high-school all-star game, and a Gaelic football match. All told, fifteen games would be held in six days at the Garden during mid-December.

The Franklin All-Stars was one of the teams invited for the pro title games. The Orange Athletic Club, the Oreos Athletic Club of Asbury Park, New Jersey, and the Red and Black of the Watertown Athletic Association, perennial claimants of the world's professional championship, were the others. In fact, Watertown, which had declined to play at the Garden in the 1902 tournament, was enthusiastic this time. The Watertown president put up $2,000 for prize money ($1,250 for first place, $750 for second). He even brought along a marching band, Maltby reports.

Remembering complaints about the playing surface for the 1902 tourney, O'Rourke planned to make it better. A six-day bicycle race (a popular sporting event of the era) ended in the Garden on Saturday, December 12. "The football tournament was to begin the following Monday evening," Maltby writes.

> When the bicycle race was completed, O'Rourke's maintenance crew removed the banked track and the Garden floor. Some five hundred loads of dirt were spread and steamrolled in an attempt to avoid the stickiness of the 1902 field. Still only 70 yards long and 35 yards wide, the playing field was ready for Monday's games.

In the feature game on the first night, the Red and Blacks of Watertown squeaked out a win over the Asbury Park Oreos in an unexpectedly tight game. The Red and Blacks pushed over a single touchdown on a disputed play early in the second half. The game was marred by rough play, according to the *New York Times*. "Slugging in the game was a common feature," the *Times* reporter wrote, evidently in surprise at watching a typical pro football game. "Every man on the teams was apparently willing, if not eager, to give a little more than he received, and in the first game of the evening two men were ruled off for flagrant violations of the gentlemanly code for pure sport."

Conduct was no better the next night when Franklin tangled with the Orange Athletic Club. The *Times* reported, "Some of the players used rough tactics and a couple of fights occurred, but no damage was done, as the referee as well as the police interfered when trouble was brewing."

The Franklin All-Stars won by 12 to 0, a score that did not reflect

Franklin's dominance. The All-Stars moved the ball 5 to 8 yards at a clip, but scored only twice on short runs by Bull Davidson and Ben Roller, a halfback who had starred on the Syracuse team that the Franklin All-Stars had beaten earlier in the season.

Two nights later, Franklin and Watertown, the two top teams in the tourney, went head to head. Again the All-Stars were dominant, and again they won by 12 to 0.

Harry March, in his entertaining but not necessarily accurate account of the early days of pro football, said that the officials were dressed in full evening dress, from top hats down to white gloves and patent-leather shoes. "In the very last play of the Franklin–Watertown game," March wrote, "with the contest safely 'in the bag,' the Franklin backfield huddled and agreed to run over Frank Hickey, dress suit and all. [Hickey was a famed Yale end.] They did, soiling him effectively and emphatically. He took it good-naturedly and the Franklin management paid his cleaning and pressing bill."

Scores of Franklin fans were at the game, and afterward, the *Franklin Evening News* reported that "wild enthusiasm is putting it mildly when speaking of the feeling of the Franklin contingent. They cheered themselves hoarse and the happiest man in New York was Manager Printz."

Betting on the Franklin–Watertown game was brisk. "Watertown fans had been putting down bets of $100 to $500 at a clip," said the *Evening News*. "Two men for each side were in the arena and they made all the wagers and the money was put up in the men's names." The *News* estimated that Franklin bettors brought home $4,000.

The All-Stars were feted by New York's Chamber of Commerce at a dinner in the Waldorf-Astoria and given a tour of Tammany Hall, the headquarters of the powerful Democratic organization that ran the city.

Tom O'Rourke was disappointed by attendance at the tournament and never tried it again. The biggest crowd of the week was 2,500 for the high-school all-star game. The tournament of 1903 was the last attempt to go national with pro football for nearly two decades, and it was the swan song of the Franklin All-Stars, the last great team of western Pennsylvania's pioneering days in pro football.

It is likely that western Pennsylvania had the only fully professional teams around the turn of the century, but they were by no means the only football clubs outside the colleges and high schools. By the mid-1890s, independent teams were playing in several parts of the country.

As already noted, there were athletic club teams in and around New York City. Some of them no doubt rewarded players with sinecures or trophies that could be turned into cash. In northern New York

State, independent football clubs were established in the early 1890s in Syracuse, Watertown, and Ogdensburg. They began as amateur teams playing under the banner of athletic associations, but by the turn of the century they were at least semipro and were attracting college stars. Farther west in New York State, Rochester and Buffalo appear to have had amateur teams, but no pros or semipros until the new century dawned.

In Buffalo, several businesses sponsored amateur football teams, according to Marc Maltby. Some of them, he notes, were playing "literally small-time football; these teams averaged only about 130 pounds per man. In fact, the Adam, Meldrum, and Anderson team (sponsored by a department store), in an attempt to schedule games, took out a notice in the local newspaper announcing that it 'would like to take on any second-rate teams in Buffalo.' "

Athletic clubs in Cleveland and Detroit had football teams that visited Pittsburgh several times during the 1890s and did very well. And, of course, the Chicago Athletic Association team that starred Pudge Heffelfinger, Sport Donnelly, and Snake Ames, among others, was at times the best of the era. The Detroit players were apparently amateurs, but elsewhere in Michigan some footballers were not averse to taking money. Maltby writes that in 1895 the Michigan Rushers of Shepardsville, a hamlet near Lansing, and the town team of the nearby village of Ovid agreed to play winner-take-all for the proceeds of passing the hat during the game. He reports that the Rushers won the game and split a total of $3 contributed by the spectators.

Independent football also took hold in Wisconsin during the 1890s. The Racine Athletic Association may have paid football players as early as 1894, and two years later Coach Tom Silverwood had a team in Green Bay that paid its star, Tom Skenandore, an Oneida Indian who had learned to play at the Carlisle Indian School in Pennsylvania, according to Maltby.

In the Far West, athletic clubs had football teams in the San Francisco Bay Area, Portland, Seattle and Tacoma, Los Angeles, and Butte, Montana, during the 1890s. These teams probably were not fully professional, though it is likely that they were paying some players. In 1895, for example, Sport Donnelly, one of the pros for the Allegheny [Pa.] Athletic Association in 1892, was on the roster of the Oakland Reliance Club. Pudge Heffelfinger, Ben Roller, and Herman Kirkoff may also have played in the West. In 1896 the AAU charged that two players for the Butte Athletic Club were professionals and threatened to oust the club from AAU membership, thus depriving it of opponents, at least in theory. In fact, though, Butte apparently continued to find teams to play.

In the South, football was in its infancy among the colleges and was rare among athletic clubs. The Southern Athletic Club of New Orleans fielded a team as early as 1892, and the Birmingham [Ala.] Athletic Club also tried the sport. But independent football in the South was far behind baseball, cycling, track and field, and some other sports in the affections of sports fans at the dawn of the new century.

4

THE COMING OF
JIM THORPE

T he independents and nascent professionals of football's early years used intercollegiate rules for the very good
reason that the colleges were the natural leaders. The colleges had invented the game and supplied most of the stars for the athletic clubs
and other independent teams. It was not until the early 1930s that the
pros were confident enough to stray from the leadership of the colleges.

The rules were changing steadily during the 1890s and drastically
in the first decade of the new century. In 1894 mass momentum plays
such as the flying wedge and various formations in which several men
started toward the line before the ball was snapped were restricted,
and the length of the game was reduced from ninety to seventy minutes.
(In the pros, the time of the second half was often cut short if the game
was one-sided.) A third official, a linesman, was added to the officiating
staff of referee and umpire.

In 1897 the values of scores were changed for the first time since
1884. Touchdowns were now worth 5 points; a goal after a touchdown,
1; a field goal, 5; and a safety, 2. It was not until 1909 that a field goal
was cut to 3 points; three years later, a touchdown earned 6 points.

Putting limits on mass momentum plays had helped to reduce injuries somewhat, but football remained a rugged and sometimes brutal
pastime. In 1905, a typical season, there were 18 fatalities and more
than 150 serious injuries in football games. Many college educators
were deploring football, not only for its roughness but also for its ram-
pant commercialism, the hiring of tramp athletes, and the coaches'
penchant for doing anything that produced a winning team. Several
major magazines blasted the colleges and universities in hard-hitting
articles by writers who were at the same time earning the title of
muckrakers for their exposés of political corruption, graft, and other
wrongdoing. Articles condemning football as a sport for college men

appeared in the *Nation, Outlook, Colliers,* and, most effectively, *Mc-Clure's Magazine.*

In mid-1905 *McClure's* ran a two-part article by Henry Beech Needham that scorched not only Yale, Princeton, Penn, and Columbia but even such prep schools as Andover and Exeter. Significantly, Needham's articles caught the attention of President Theodore Roosevelt, who decided to meet with athletic leaders of the "Big Three": Harvard, Yale, and Princeton. The *New York Times* report of their visit with Roosevelt on October 9 said that the president told them "something should be done to reform the rules, especially in the interest of fair play and the discouragement of rough play, and asked them to undertake to start a movement to that end." Roosevelt, a Harvard graduate, had a personal interest because his son was on Harvard's freshman squad "and has already had cause to know how rough the sport may be, having received a black eye and other bruises in scrimmages," the newspaper reported.

Roosevelt's visitors, including the head coaches from the three major colleges, plus Walter Camp for Yale and one other man from each school, pledged to do their best to reduce roughness and foul play. Camp's agreement was especially important because he had almost singlehandedly created American football two decades earlier and had been its guiding light ever since. It was hoped that the Big Three's example would trickle down to the lesser institutions and lead to general improvement.

Alas, it did not work out that way. In November, a Harvard man was thrown out of a game with Penn for slugging a lineman. Two Yale players mugged a Harvard punt returner who was signaling a fair catch. But the precipitating incident that led to major rule changes in 1906 was the death of a Union College halfback named Harold Moore in a pileup in a game against New York University.

Chancellor Henry MacCracken of New York University swiftly called a conference of educators from nineteen colleges and universities that New York University had played in recent years. The question he placed before them was whether football should be abolished or, if not, how it could be reformed. Thirteen institutions, excluding Harvard and Yale, sent delegates to a conference on December 8. Six of them favored banning the game, two short of a majority. Out of that gathering grew the National Collegiate Athletic Association (NCAA) and some major changes in football rules.

The most important change permitted forward passes, though with so many restrictions that passing did not immediately become an important offensive weapon. The passer could not throw directly over his center; his pass had to be at least 5 yards to the right or left of where the ball was snapped back. In addition, if the pass could not be reached

by a receiver or an opponent, the ball was given to the defending team
at the spot where he threw it. If the ball crossed the goal line and was
not touched, it was a touchback.

Other changes were aimed at eliminating bone-crushing mass
plays. Guards back and tackles back plays were effectively barred. The
two lines were separated by the creation of a neutral zone, measured
by the length of the ball. No longer could linemen crouch nose to nose
before a scrimmage started. Hurdling by ball carriers was prohibited.

Since the major changes were expected to create more open action
and probably longer runs, the distance a team with the ball had to make
in three downs was increased from 5 to 10 yards. (The fourth down
was not added until 1912.) The time of games was reduced from seventy to sixty minutes, with two halves of thirty minutes.

Camp was a stand-patter, opposing the forward pass and arguing
only for the 10-yard requirement for the first down. But his desire to
keep the game much as it had been was overcome by the opposition of
many college presidents, not to mention President Roosevelt.

One result of the new forward pass rule was that the old gridiron
with stripes across the field was changed into a checkerboard. To help
the officials determine whether a passer had thrown the ball at least 5
yards on either side of the center, stripes 5 yards apart were drawn
lengthwise on the field. The checkerboard pattern ended four years
later when rules makers decreed that the passer could throw anywhere
over the scrimmage line but had to be at least 5 yards back when he
threw.

Protective equipment was much improved by 1910. Helmets had
started to appear fifteen years earlier, mainly to save torn ears. Now
helmets, which were called "head harnesses," were readily available,
though not yet in common use. They were made of a stiff leather crown
and had ear flaps; the best ones in the A. G. Spalding & Brothers catalog
cost $4. Shoulder pads covered shoulders and collar bones, and padded
knickers of either canvas or moleskin prevented bruises on the thighs.
The most expensive piece of equipment was shoes, which were high-
topped and fitted with nine cleats; Spalding's best cost $8 a pair. The
canvas jackets worn by players in the 1880s and 1890s were being replaced by more colorful jerseys of worsted or cotton.

With the disbanding of the short-lived Franklin All-Stars at the end
of the 1903 season, teams made up entirely of professionals passed out
of the picture in western Pennsylvania, though some Pittsburgh-area
teams undoubtedly were paying individual players in 1904 and afterward. The best of the surviving teams was Latrobe, coached and quarterbacked by John Brallier, now a practicing dentist in the city. He led
Latrobe to three unbeaten seasons from 1903 to 1905. The team was
all-amateur in 1903, according to Robert Van Atta, but at the end of

the 1904 season the sixteen players divided the team's $500 profit. Latrobe's winning streak did not end until late November 1906, when the Canton [Ohio] Bulldogs hosted Latrobe and whipped them 16 to 0. Canton could not pay its guarantee to the visitors, so the Latrobe YMCA, sponsor of the team, had to pay its bills. "That experience ended pro football in Latrobe," Van Atta writes. From then on, Latrobe teams used only local players. Van Atta adds:

> Dr. Brallier played his last with the 1907 team, which had a winning year. . . . One last incident stems from a visit that year of a team from California, Pa. What was labeled as the California YMCA team was ejected from its rooms at the Parker House for "chasing and frightening a chambermaid," jumping on beds and breaking two of them, and for language "far from what might be asked for from YMCA boys." Latrobe won the game, 38–0. And it turned out that there was no YMCA at California, Pa.

The California team, which sounds like a pickup town club, was not unusual in the first two decades of the new century. Bob Snyder, a quarterback and tailback for the Cleveland Rams and Chicago Bears during the 1930s and 1940s, said that his father had played on such a team in Fremont, Ohio, from 1901 to 1906. "He was what they called a center rush," Snyder said. "They'd pick the eleven or twelve biggest guys in town and they would be the team. My dad's name was Calvin Lewis Snyder. I don't suppose he was that good a football player, but he was a big man—6 foot 2 and 270 or 280 pounds—and he was a tough guy, I guess."

Football historian Marc Maltby writes that in the early years of the century there were three more or less distinct levels of professional competition. The California "YMCA" club was clearly at the bottom:

> At pro football's lowest level were small, semi-professional teams like the Rochester Jeffersons, the Buffalo Niagaras, the Louisville Brecks, the Racine Cardinals and countless others scattered throughout the East and Midwest. These clubs usually had no real management. They were led instead by chosen captains who handled scheduling and financial matters. Players often came from the same neighborhood, and the teams adopted nicknames that reflected that fact: The Rochester Jeffersons took their name from Jefferson Avenue; Buffalo's Niagaras were a westside team from Niagara Street; the Racine Cardinals of Chicago played on Racine Avenue; the Louisville Breck's home field stood on Breckenridge Street.

Such teams used only local players who received a share of the net receipts, either after each game or, more commonly, at the end of the season. Usually it was a pittance but, Maltby writes, "the players were not interested in profit so much as they were in just playing football for their own personal enjoyment."

One step up on the pro football hierarchy were teams sponsored by small athletic clubs or industries. Buffalo's best independent team in the early years of the century was the Oakdale Club, an athletic association in south Buffalo. In Cleveland, Hunkel's All-Stars had the backing of a wholesale liquor business, which paid some of the expenses of the team in exchange for free advertising. The Shelby Blues, a strong team in a town of 10,000 in north central Ohio, was a hybrid. The Blues played under the aegis of the Shelby Athletic Club, but also had support from the Shelby Steel Tube Company, according to Maltby. (From 1902 to 1906, the Blues had on their roster a halfback named Charles W. Follis, who is believed to have been the first black player in pro football; it is known that Shelby paid him during his last three years on the team.)

The pinnacle of the pro football pyramid was occupied by the top teams in northeastern Ohio, especially Canton and Massillon. The dominant team in that area was universally regarded as the professional champion each year. It was not by accident that the NFL was born in Canton in 1920 or that the Pro Football Hall of Fame is located there. When the NFL began, Canton and its sister cities in the "Ohio League" were the heartland of the professional game.

The Ohio League was not really a league at all; it was more a state of mind. Its membership fluctuated somewhat from year to year as the strength of various teams waxed and waned. But Canton and Massillon were always "members." Akron usually had a team in the league too, and often so did Columbus, Dayton, Toledo, and Shelby.

Professionalism arrived in Ohio at the end of the 1903 season, just as it was about to end in Franklin, Pennsylvania. The Massillon Tigers and the undefeated Akron East End Athletic Club, both ostensibly all-amateur, were vying for state honors. Among the Tigers' victories was one over the Canton Athletic Club, which, to Massillon's civic boosters, was the high-water mark of the season; it couldn't get any better than that. The Tigers had lost one game but felt entitled to challenge Akron East End for the "Ohio independent championship," like the "Ohio League" an unofficial title that was bestowed by consensus on the state's most successful team.

Several of Massillon's starters were on the injury list as the December 5 game in Akron drew near. The Tigers had enough reserves to replace the injured, but undoubtedly the team would be weaker than usual. So it should not have come as a surprise to knowledgeable football fans when four veterans of the pro wars in Pittsburgh appeared in Massillon and began practicing with the Tigers. Among the quartet were two brothers, halfback Harry and tackle Doc McChesney, and a 250-pound tackle, Bob Shiring; all three had played for the East End professional team in Pittsburgh during the regular season.

With the help of the ringers, the Massillon Tigers beat Akron East

End and claimed the state title. The final score was 12 to 0 in a game that caused a good deal of bad blood and saw several thousand dollars change hands in wagers. Historian Bob Carroll states that Ohioans were well aware that football players were being imported and paid openly in Pittsburgh and Chicago; they even knew that some hometown players in Ohio were earning a few dollars a game. But, he writes, "What really raised the hackles was the idea of paying good Ohio money to an outsider. That was blatant!" It was also the signal that ringers were needed if a team hoped to be competitive in the Ohio League from now on.

In the following season, seven or eight Ohio teams were paying their players, often ringers from western Pennsylvania. They were paid by the game in amounts ranging from $10 to perhaps $100, depending on their reputation and the management's assessment of how important the game was. As western Pennsylvania teams had found, this could be an expensive proposition if there was a bidding war for imported players. Most crowds at pro games totaled fewer than 1,000 fans paying 35 to 50 cents each. Not many $100-a-game pros could be hired out of such receipts, so as was the case with the Franklin All-Stars in 1903, well-to-do businessmen were called on to help pay the wages of the mercenaries.

This lesson in economics was not lost on pro football managers, and in mid-1904 the call went up for an agreement that would keep players from jumping to another team to increase their wages—in effect, for something approaching a league. It would not be the last such suggestion, but another sixteen years would pass before the NFL came into being in Canton.

Massillon's head start in importing players evidently was too much to overcome for Canton, Akron, and other pretenders to the "Ohio independent championship." The Tigers took that unofficial title in 1904, 1905, and 1906. Counting seven victories after an opening-game loss in 1903, they had won thirty-two straight games before the Canton Bulldogs defeated them, 10 to 5, in November 1906. Massillon had no compunction about running up the score. During that thirty-two-victory string, the Tigers buried the Marion [Ohio] Athletic Club, 148 to 0; the Broadway Athletic Club of Cleveland 88 to 0; and Muskingum College, 96 to 0.

Massillon's loss to Canton in 1906 came in the second of two games between the two powerhouses. In the second game, the Tigers turned the tables on the Bulldogs, beating them 13 to 6. Those two games brought a measure of national attention to pro football for the first time. Grantland Rice, one of the best-known sports writers of the period, was complimentary, and play-by-play reports were telegraphed to major cities.

The day after the second meeting between Massillon and Canton in 1906, Ed J. Stewart, Massillon's manager and the city editor of the *Massillon Independent*, dropped a bombshell, igniting pro football's first scandal. He charged in his newspaper that Canton men had tried to bribe some of the Massillon players to throw the first game. Involved in the attempted fix, said Stewart, was Blondy Wallace, the coach of the Canton Bulldogs.

Bob Carroll, the most assiduous and best-informed researcher on early pro football, has proved that Wallace got a bum rap. The full story is too convoluted and full of questions to recount here, but suffice to say that Blondy Wallace, though no babe in the woods when it came to the high life, made no attempt to fix either game and that both game results were almost certainly on the level. That Wallace has come down in pro football's history as a fixer is due chiefly to the fact that Harry March, in his book *Pro Football: Its "Ups" and Down,"* searched nothing but his faulty memory when, nearly thirty years after the fact, he brought up the scandal and got most of the facts wrong.

In any event, the fix scandal of 1906 put a damper on professional football in Ohio; it did not end it. But on the scale in which players could earn as much for a game as most workers made in a month, pro football was finished for a time in Ohio. In the 1906 season, Canton and Massillon probably had payrolls of $20,000. Those salaries could be justified when the Bulldogs played the Tigers because they drew sellout crowds of 8,000. They were fortunate to attract 1,000 spectators for some of their early-season games because football fans knew they would be blowouts.

As in every other phase of the game, the early professionals trailed the college teams in exploiting the forward pass. This should come as no surprise because the collegiate football powers had a monopoly on innovative coaches. They also had the luxury of daily practice in season, which few pro teams did.

Amos Alonzo Stagg was the premier coach among the pioneers, having originated ends back, tackles back, and other mass momentum plays, as well as the spiral pass (it had to be a lateral before 1906), the man in motion, and hidden ball and sleeper plays. He was also the first to pull the center from the line on defense and make him a linebacker. Glenn (Pop) Warner, who coached at Cornell, Pitt, and the Carlisle Indian School, among other venues, was the inventor of the single and double wingback formations. While at Carlisle, he developed the rolling block, in which the blocker cut down a defender by rolling into his legs. George Woodruff of Penn created the guards back play to devastating effect before mass plays were finally outlawed. And at Clemson, John W. Heisman, who gave his name to the Heisman Trophy, was advocating the forward pass in 1903, three years before it arrived over the opposition of Walter Camp.

Whether the first forward pass was thrown by a collegian or a professional can't be determined with any certainty. But because college teams started their seasons earlier than the pros, it is likely that a college man tossed the first forward pass and an end caught it in early September 1906. Colleges usually began play in early September, while the pros tended to begin either the last weekend of September or the first of October.

The first use of the forward pass probably was by St. Louis University in a game against Carroll College played the first or second week of September. Coach Edward B. Cochems had taken his squad to training camp in July. His sole purpose, Cochem wrote later to the *St. Louis Post-Dispatch*, was to work on forward passing:

> I studied the proportions of the ball and discovered of course that it had been designed to fit the instep of the shoe for kicking and the pit of the arm for carrying. . . . Then I lit on the seven lacings as the only physical part of the ball for finger purchase in throwing the ball on its long axis.
>
> Just before our first practice, I told the players to put their fingers between the two lacings nearest the end of the ball where the diameter was shortest and throw it with a twist of the wrist, on its long axis. . . . In about half an hour Bradbury Robinson, all excited, came back and said, "Coach, I can throw the danged thing 40 yards!"

St. Louis University went undefeated that year. Evidently, Cochem's team was far ahead of the big eastern universities in tapping the potential of the forward pass because a referee for one of the St. Louis games said:

> What struck me most in the work of the St. Louis eleven this afternoon was the most perfect exhibition of the new rules in this respect that I have seen all season and much better than that of Yale and Harvard. The St. Louis style of pass differs entirely from that in use in the East. There the ball is thrown high in the air and the runner who is to catch it is protected by several of his teammates forming an interference for him. The St. Louis players shoot the ball hard and accurately to the man who is to receive it and the latter is not protected. . . . The fast throw by St. Louis enables the receiving player to dodge the opposing players, and it struck me as being all but perfect.

The first use of the forward pass in a professional game (at least in the Ohio League, according to the Professional Football Research Association [PFRA]) may have been thrown on October 25, 1906. The passer was George W. (Peggy) Parratt, probably the best quarterback of the era, who was pitching for the Massillon Tigers. In a game against a West Virginia team at Massillon, Parratt completed a short pass to end Dan Riley (Dan Policowski). Since Massillon ran up a 61 to 0 score on the hapless Mountain Staters, the pass played no important part in the result. In fact, according to the PFRA, "no one got excited about Peggy's short pass; his 65-yard run from scrimmage and 100-yard kickoff return got the headlines." Massillon had played four games before meeting the West Virginians, so it is possible that Parratt had thrown passes earlier in the season.

Peggy Parratt, like another pro pioneer, John Brallier, was an honest man. In 1905 he had been a backfield star for Case University in Cleveland. At the same time, he was playing on Sundays with the professional Shelby Athletic Club team using the alias Jimmy Murphy. When a Cleveland newspaper penetrated his disguise—a helmet and nose guard—the chairman of the Case athletic authority questioned him. Parratt readily admitted that he was taking money for playing football, and he was barred from further participation in Case athletics. Milt Roberts, a PFRA researcher, said that "Parratt thus became the first well-known college football star to be disciplined by his school for playing professional football on the side. Other name players had done the same thing but when questioned about it had winked and denied the charges. To Peggy's credit, he didn't lie."

Subsequently, Parratt played for a Lorain, Ohio, team, Shelby, Massillon, Cleveland, and the Akron Indians until 1916. He was coach and owner of the Indians as well as quarterback.

By the time Parratt played his last game, most of the restrictions on forward passes had been removed. In 1910 a pass no longer had to be thrown outside a point 5 yards on either side of the center. But the passer had to be at least 5 yards behind the line of scrimmage, and the pass could not go more than 20 yards beyond the line. The 20-yard limit on a forward pass was removed two years later in a fairly sweeping revamping of the rules. The playing field was set at the present length—100 yards between goal lines—and 10-yard-deep end zones were added in which passes could be legally caught. A fourth down to make 10 yards was added. The value of a touchdown was fixed at 6 points—1 more than it had been since 1897. (The field goal had been reduced from 4 to 3 points in 1909.)

Although wounded by the scandal of 1906, the Ohio League was far from finished. Even Massillon, the putative victim of the fix attempt, remained in the field. In fact, a team of local players called the All-Massillons claimed the 1907 Ohio state title with a record of seven victories, no losses, and a scoreless tie with the Shelby Blues. Canton, the putative villain of the scandal, also had a team called the Canton Indians and a second called the Canton Athletic Club, which played only one game before disbanding. Over the next few years, several clubs—none bearing the Bulldog name—operated in the Canton area. They were essentially semipro, passing the hat during games and dividing the proceeds at the end of the season.

The Akron Indians and the Shelby Blues, led by Peggy Parratt, were Ohio's best from 1908 to 1911. Neither would have been a match for the earlier Canton Bulldogs or Massillon Tigers. A crowd of 3,000 was considered good. That was less than half of what a Bulldog–Tiger game would have attracted in 1906 and earlier. But of course, because the teams were not paying high wages for imported players, income was more likely to match outgo than in the early heyday of the Canton Bulldogs and Massillon Tigers.

In 1912 the Elyria Athletics were undefeated and claimed the Ohio independent championship. But the most significant event of the year for pro football was the appointment of a twenty-one-year-old gas-company office worker named Jack Cusack as the unpaid secretary-treasurer of the new Canton Professionals, made up largely of local men who played on the basis of splitting the profits, if any. Cusack was instrumental in restoring football in Ohio to its former high level and in bringing Jim Thorpe, the world's greatest all-around athlete, into professional football. Thorpe brought instant prestige to the Canton team and thus to Ohio football.

Cusack apparently never played organized football, even in high school, but he was an avid fan and an astute businessman. In his first year as manager, the Canton Professionals (renamed the Bulldogs a couple of years later when it became clear that the name carried no negative baggage) won six games and lost three. Not bad, but not good enough for Cantonites, who were used to winners.

Cusack decided that he had to hire some college stars, which meant paying salaries because college grads tended to prefer guaranteed wages to speculative profit sharing. That could be a problem. Games against patsies might draw only 500 spectators at 50 cents a ticket, which would not pay many salaries. For games against powerful Akron, Canton might attract 2,500, and when Elyria or Shelby came in, the count might be 1,500—better, but no bonanza.

Cusack believed that to control escalation of salaries, it was necessary to stop players from jumping from one team to another in midseason. Such stability would also heighten the interest of fans because the public could be reasonably sure of seeing the same players all year. So Cusack engineered what amounted to a secret agreement among the Ohio League's managers to keep players tied to one team. He told author Bob Curran:

> I was brightly aware that if professional football was to be a success we
> had to live down the scandal of 1906 and gain the public's confidence in

the honesty of the game, and I felt that this could be done only with proper understanding among the managers and backers of the various teams. It was my theory that if we could stop players from jumping from one team to another, it would be a first step in the right direction. Therefore, the managers (unknown to the players) made a verbal agreement that once a player signed with a team he was that team's property as long as he played, or until he was released. This helped to gain added respectability, and also aided us in keeping the salaries down.

By 1915 Cusack had assembled a strong team for Canton. Equally important for the Ohio League, some Massillon businessmen decided to back a strong pro team. Canton and Massillon scheduled two games for late November as the climax to their seasons. Cusack immediately tried to strengthen his lineup and signed several All-Americans, including Carlisle Indian School tackle Bill Gardner; end Hub Wagner from Pitt; Earle (Greasy) Neale, who was the coach at West Virginia Wesleyan; and Neale's assistant coach, John Kellison, a tackle.

Canton won four of its first five games, losing only to the Detroit Heralds, 9 to 3, in Detroit. Just before Canton's first meeting with Massillon, Cusack scored a coup by signing Jim Thorpe, the best football player in the game, for the very high price of $250 a game. (It was not a record; Pudge Heffelfinger had gotten $500 and Sport Donnelly $250 for games in 1892.) Thorpe was a punishing runner, a booming punter, the best drop-kicker and place-kicker of his time, a tough blocker, and a sterling defender. Thorpe was the part-time backfield coach at Indiana University. He had been an All-American at the Carlisle Indian School and had won both the decathlon and the pentathlon at the 1912 Olympic Games in Stockholm.

Fortunately for Cusack, Bill Gardner, an old teammate of Thorpe's at Carlisle, was on his roster. Cusack sent him to visit Thorpe in Bloomington, and Gardner brought back the good news. Cusack said later that some of his friends thought Thorpe's salary would bankrupt the Bulldogs.

They were wrong. Canton–Massillon games were always good draws, of course, but in the two games of 1915, with Thorpe as the main attraction, both games were sellouts: 6,000 in Massillon and 8,000 in Canton—about five times as many spectators as the Bulldogs had averaged for their first five games. Clearly, Cusack knew what he was doing.

Thorpe was not, however, an instant superstar in the pro game. Massillon shut out the Bulldogs, 16 to 0, in the first game. The Tigers' lineup was full of ringers, mostly playing under assumed names. But two of them, Knute Rockne and Gus Dorais of Notre Dame, used their real names. Two years earlier, the Notre Dame stars had popularized the forward pass in a 35 to 13 drubbing of Army. The battery of quar-

terback Dorais pitching to left end Rockne was so successful that the
West Pointers were demoralized. At the time, Notre Dame was well
regarded in midwestern football circles, but it was not the powerhouse
it would become in the 1920s under Rockne's coaching. (In 1915 he
was an assistant coach for Jess Harper at Notre Dame.)

In the first game, Thorpe broke free of tacklers twice, but slipped
while trying to evade the safety man and failed to score. "He was the
only man feared by the Massillon defense," the *Canton Repository* reported. The star of the game was Massillon's Gus Dorais, who drop-
kicked three field goals and passed to a substitute end named Kagy to
set up the Tigers' only touchdown.

For the second match between Canton and Massillon, Cusack
brought in two more All-Americans—Robert Butler of Wisconsin and
Earl Abell, a tackle from Colgate—plus Charlie Smith, a black tackle
from Michigan Agricultural College (now Michigan State).

The Bulldogs pulled out a victory over the Tigers, but they needed
help from a spectator to do it. Cusack had the happy chore of dealing
with an overflow crowd at Canton's League Park, the city's baseball
stadium. He put the overflow as standees in the end zones. A special
ground rule said that a runner who went into the crowd after crossing
the goal line had to be in possession of the ball when he emerged. "As
things turned out," Cusack later wrote, "this proved to be a lucky break
for Canton." That was a considerable understatement.

It was a tough, close battle. Thorpe drop-kicked a field goal from
the 18-yard line and place-kicked another from the 45. The Bulldogs
clung to their 6-point lead in the fourth quarter when Massillon's Gus
Dorais began connecting with his forward passes. With just minutes to
go, he hit his end, named Briggs, at Canton's 15-yard line, and Briggs
high-stepped into the standing-room-only crowd in the end zone. There
he fumbled, or so it appeared. In any case, the ball popped right into
the hands of Canton tackle Charlie Smith, who had been pursuing
Briggs. Since Briggs did not bring the football out of the crowd, the
referee ruled a touchback and no score. Briggs protested vehemently:
"I didn't fumble! That ball was kicked out of my hands by a policeman,
a uniformed policeman!" Briggs said he even saw brass buttons on the
cop's coat.

It was pointed out that Canton had no uniformed police officers at
the time, so Briggs's insistence was attributed to hallucinations. Fans
of both the Tigers and the Bulldogs swarmed onto the field. The officials
were unable to clear the field for the last three minutes of play. In his
Pioneer in Pro Football, Cusack continues the story:

> The Massillon team and its loyal supporters demanded that the game
> officials settle the matter conclusively by making a statement on the re-

feree's decision, and at last they agreed to do so—on the condition that the statement be sealed and given to Manager Langford of the Courtland Hotel, to be opened and read by him thirty minutes after midnight. This arrangement was made in order to give the officials plenty of time to get out of town and escape any wrath that might descend upon them from either side. Tension remained high throughout the evening, and the hotel lobby was filled with a bedlam of argument until Manager Langford read the statement at 12:30 A.M. It backed Referee Conners' touchback decision, saying that it was proper under the ground rules, and the Canton Bulldogs and Massillon tied for the championship.

Ten years later, Cusack wrote, the mystery was solved. He was reminiscing about the old days with a friend who was a streetcar conductor. The conductor, it turned out, had been among the standees in the end zone when Massillon end Briggs fell into the crowd. The conductor, who said he had been wearing his brass-buttoned uniform, promptly kicked the ball out of Brigg's hands and into Smith's waiting arms. "Why on earth did you do a thing like that?" Cusack asked. "Well," the conductor replied, "it was like this—I had thirty dollars bet on the game and, at my salary, I couldn't afford to lose that much money."

Jim Thorpe played with the Canton Bulldogs until 1920 and lent his name and prestige to the new NFL that year by assuming the title of president. It is not too much to say that Thorpe lifted professional football out of the minor sports among the truss ads on the nation's sports pages to a position of some respectability. Pro football was hardly prepared to challenge baseball, college football, or boxing for sports fans' favor, but it was no longer just a line score from Canton, Akron, or Massillon.

When he joined the Canton Bulldogs in 1915, Jim Thorpe was at the height of his physical prowess. He was twenty-seven years old, having been born with a twin brother on May 28, 1888. His twin, Charlie, died at the age of eight. Both of their parents were part Native American, with forebears from the Sac and Fox, Pottawatomi, and Kickapoo tribes. Their father, Hiram, a farmer with land near the village of Prague in Oklahoma Territory, also came from Irish stock and their mother had French antecedents. They gave James Francis Thorpe the Native American name Wa-Tho-Huck, which means Bright Path.

The Thorpes followed some Native American customs but spoke English at home. Thorpe's early education was at Indian Agency schools near Prague. He became an avid hunter, often trekking thirty miles a day following his father in the field. Jim, like most Native American boys of the day, loved to play Follow the Leader. At school, he showed early potential as an athlete in races and jumping contests.

As a youth, Thorpe was sent to the Haskell Indian School at Lawrence, Kansas, and subsequently to the Carlisle Indian School in Pennsylvania. He entered Carlisle, which had students ranging in age from twelve to twenty-three, at seventeen. As was the custom, he spent parts of the first two years living off campus with a local white family to learn the ways of white society. Carlisle's curriculum was more like that of a vocational high school than a college, but the school competed with the top college teams in several sports. Harvard, Army, Navy, Pennsylvania, Columbia, Minnesota, and California all appeared on the Indians' schedules during Thorpe's years there. Many of Carlisle's players besides Thorpe played professional football in the late 1910s and early 1920s.

Thorpe got into a few of Carlisle's games as a substitute in 1907. In 1908 he was a regular and developed a reputation as a fine runner and kicker. In the spring of 1908, Thorpe joined the track team and quickly earned fame as a jumper and hurdler. He left Carlisle at the end of that school year because his five-year term had ended.

In 1911 his football coach at Carlisle, Glenn S. (Pop) Warner, persuaded him to return and begin serious training in track for the 1912 Olympics in Stockholm—and, not incidentally, to play some more football. Carlisle had excellent teams, losing only one game in 1911 and one in 1912. Thorpe was named to Walter Camp's All-American team in both years.

He started training for the Olympics in the spring of 1912, with his eye on competing in the decathlon and pentathlon. Thorpe was already an excellent jumper and hurdler and a good shot-putter. He concentrated on learning how to pole vault and to throw the hammer, discus, and javelin, all skills that would be required for those two major events.

That summer, Thorpe reached the pinnacle of amateur athletic achievement when he won both the decathlon and the pentathlon in Stockholm. In the pentathlon, Thorpe placed first in the long jump, the 200-meter and 1,500-meter races, and the discus throw, and third in the javelin throw, which he had only recently tried for the first time. He finished the pentathlon far ahead of the favorite, Ferdinand Bie of Norway.

The ten-event decathlon is regarded as the supreme test of a track athlete since it includes all aspects of track and field. Thorpe was again dominant, placing no worse than third in any event and winning the shot put, high jump, 110-meter hurdles, and 1,500-meter run. At the awards ceremony, King Gustav V of Sweden said to Thorpe, "Sir, you are the greatest athlete in the world." Thorpe replied with a grin, "Thanks, King." Thorpe said later that it was the proudest moment of his life.

Soon after Thorpe's last football game for Carlisle, the sporting world was rocked by the revelation that in the summer of 1909, Thorpe had played pro baseball with Rocky Mount in the Carolina League. What's more, he did not even use an alias, which was a common subterfuge by college players who wanted to earn a few dollars by playing ball. In those days of very strict rules against professional athletes in the Olympic games, having been paid to play baseball was a grave transgression. Thorpe asked for mercy, or at least understanding, in writing to the AAU:

> I was not wise in the ways of the world and did not realize this was wrong, and that it would make me a professional in track sports. . . . I hope I would be partly excused because of the fact that I was simply an Indian school boy and did not know all about such things. . . . I hope the Amateur Athletic Union and the people will not be too hard in judging me.

It was a vain hope. The AAU demanded that he return the medals he had earned in Stockholm, as well as gifts he had received from the Swedish king and Czar Nicholas II of Russia. The action inflicted a lifelong hurt on Thorpe, though he put a good face on it and never publicly criticized the AAU or the International Olympic Committee (IOC). Until his death in 1953, Thorpe continued to campaign for the return of his Olympic medals. Twenty-nine years after he died, the IOC returned his medals, giving them to Thorpe's children and restoring his records at the 1912 Olympics.

Shortly after the medals were taken away in 1913, Thorpe signed a contract to play baseball for the New York Giants. A right-handed thrower and batter, he had a strong arm and speed, but he was just a middling outfielder and hitter. Thorpe was good enough to spend parts of six seasons in the big leagues with the Giants, the Cincinnati Reds, and the Boston (now Atlanta) Braves. His lifetime batting average was .252 in 289 major league games. A good indication that he was a fast base runner is the fact that while he hit only seven home runs and twenty doubles in 698 at bats, he had eighteen triples.

While baseball was the most lucrative occupation for a professional athlete in Thorpe's day, football was his first love. He stood 6 feet, 1 inch tall and weighed 190 to 200 pounds—ideal for a pro halfback or fullback in that era. Thorpe was a complete football player—a shifty yet punishing ball carrier; a good blocker; a superb punter, drop kicker, and place kicker; and a tough defender. He may have had equals in each of these skills, but no one could match Thorpe as an all-around player. He loved to hit hard and be hit.

Harry March, whose history of the pro game was described as "something of a historical novel" by Jack Cusack, wrote that Thorpe enhanced his capability for punishment by using illegal shoulder pads.

The pads, said March, were pieces of corrugated metal, padded next to his skin but unpadded between the metal and his jersey. Cusack indignantly denied it. "Maybe they felt like that to the men the big Indian tackled or knocked aside on his terrific plunges through the line, but the only metal involved was just enough interior ribbing to hold the layers and felt padding in place," he said. "They were constructed of hard sole leather, riveted together, and their legality was never questioned while Thorpe played for me."

Thorpe had great pride in his prowess as an athlete, as indicated by an anecdote involving Notre Dame coach Knute Rockne. Rockne, who had earlier played professionally for the Fort Wayne Friars and coached semipro teams in and around South Bend, was thirty years old and in his second year as head coach of the Fighting Irish in 1919. He and Gus Dorais were with the Massillon Tigers for their epic battles with the Canton Bulldogs and Jim Thorpe. Rockne was a skillful end and pass catcher, but at 145 pounds he was no physical match for Thorpe.

The story was that Rockne stopped Thorpe several times on end sweeps. Thorpe showed no reaction. The next time Thorpe swept left end, he flattened Rockne, knocking him out. When Rockne came to, Thorpe is supposed to have told him, "That's better, Knute. These people want to see Big Jim run."

Years later, Rockne gave a slightly different version, according to his biographer, Jerry Brondfield, who quoted Rockne as saying that Thorpe never

> actually said it that way. It was more like: "I'm glad you're slowing down, Rock. Now the people who are paying to see me run can get their money's worth." The fact was that Thorpe was still the greatest runner in the game and I no longer had the legs and stamina I thought I had. He was getting around me on almost every sweep and I decided right then and there that I was going to hang up my cleats for good. And I did.

With Thorpe as their pièce de résistance, the Canton Bulldogs dominated the Ohio League from 1916 to 1919—the years leading up to the formation of the NFL. Only in 1918, as World War I was ending in victory for the Allies, did the Bulldogs lose out. The Dayton Triangles were the champions that year, but because few teams could play full schedules and the talent was diluted by war service, the 1918 title was not highly prized.

During the second decade of this century, the Ohio League was generally considered to be the major league. Among the strong teams were the Toledo Maroons, Cleveland Erin Braus, Cincinnati Celts, Shelby Blues, Elyria Pros, and Youngstown Patricians. But perhaps the best of the bunch overall after Canton, Massillon, and the Akron Indians were the Columbus Panhandles, a rock 'em, sock 'em outfit that never won an Ohio League title but often challenged the big boys.

The Panhandles, named for a division of the Pennsylvania Railroad, were notable because over their life from 1904 to 1926 seven brothers and a son of one of them wore Panhandle colors. Like most of the Panhandle players, the Nesser brothers worked for the railroad and had never been to college. The best of them was probably Ted, who stood 5 feet, 10 inches tall and weighed 230 pounds. He played halfback, center, tackle, and guard and was usually the Panhandle coach. John, a quarterback and lineman, was the oldest Nesser on the team. The next oldest, Phil, who was 6 feet, 2 inches tall and weighed 225 pounds, was a tough tackle and guard. Fred, an end, tackle, and fullback, carried 250 pounds on a 6-foot, 5-inch frame. He was a professional boxer as well as a football player.

Another 250-pounder was Frank Nesser, a fullback, guard, and tackle, who did the punting, drop-kicking, and place-kicking for the Panhandles. Like Jim Thorpe, he thought there was nothing unusual about a 70-yard punt, and he was credited with a 63-yard place-kick. (It should be noted that such long punts were often the result of a quick kick over the safety's head that bounced and rolled 20 or 30 yards after hitting the ground.) Frank Nesser was also an accomplished passer. He played professional baseball for six years during his football career.

Al Nesser played in the pros for nearly twenty-five years as a rough end, guard, and center in the Ohio League and during the first decade of the NFL. He finally retired after playing the 1931 season with the Cleveland Indians of the NFL.

Raymond, the youngest Nesser brother, was on the Panhandle roster but did not play often. Ted Nesser's son Charlie joined the Panhandles in 1921; Ted was still active, making them the only father and son who ever played together in the NFL.

The Columbus Panhandles played most of their games on the road, for the very good reason that most of them were railroad employees and could ride the trains for free. That meant that their traveling expenses were fairly low (and they sometimes lodged in haylofts to save money). Finding time to practice together was a problem, though, because their first duty was to the railroad. As Bob Braunwart and Bob Carroll wrote in the PFRA's *Coffin Corner* in 1979, the Columbus Panhandles, who spent their final four years in the NFL, were very good sandlotters and the last of the breed in the big leagues:

> The Panhandles gave professional football's rag-tag days the Nessers, a hard-as-nails attitude, and colorful stories. They symbolized pro football's past. By 1920, the day when a whole team of rugged sandlotters could compete on an equal footing with college-trained pros was over.

Many sandlotters still played useful roles with good pro teams, but the key men had earned varsity letters at colleges.

The Columbus Panhandles also gave pro football a leader in the person of Joseph F. Carr, their founder and manager for two decades. The year after the NFL was formed in 1920, Joe Carr became its president and guided the league through its formative years.

The last year of the Ohio League—1919—was the first year in which a black player starred on a major team. There had been several blacks on Ohio League teams going back to Charles Follis with the Shelby Athletic Club in 1904, but not even Follis, a very good halfback, could match the luster of Fritz Pollard, an All-American at Brown University.

Pollard was signed by the Akron Indians in the latter half of the 1919 season while he was head coach at all-black Lincoln University in Oxford, Pennsylvania. It appears that he was recommended by Clair (Mike) Purdy, Pollard's teammate at Brown, who was in the Akron backfield that year. The Indians were having a mediocre season and hoped to add punch to their lineup for their second meetings with Canton and Massillon. They had lost once to both teams.

In his debut, Pollard scored Akron's only touchdown as the Indians lost to Massillon, 13 to 6. The *Akron Beacon Journal* said, "In running back punts he was sensational while from the backfield position he carried the ball many times for long gains." The Massillon Tigers had threatened to "get Pollard," a speedy and shifty runner weighing only 150 pounds, but the threats did not materialize, according to the newspaper. Pollard said later that he was paid $200 for the game. He later claimed to have demanded $500 a game for the remaining three contests on Akron's schedule; if he got it, he probably would have been the highest-paid player in professional football.

For the big game between the Indians and the Canton Bulldogs at Akron, Ohio newspapers touted the matchup of Fritz Pollard with Jim Thorpe, called by the *Beacon Journal* the "two greatest backfield men in professional football," which may well have been true. However, Thorpe was not the only backfield star with the Bulldogs. Canton also had fullback Pete Calac and halfback Joe Guyon, both from the Carlisle Indian School, as was Thorpe.

Several ringers—college stars playing under false names—joined Pollard with the Indians. The Pollard–Thorpe matchup never really materialized, as Canton dominated the Indians by winning, 10 to 0. Thorpe did not even enter the game until the fourth quarter. His chief contribution to the Bulldog cause was a touchdown-saving tackle of Pollard at Canton's 22-yard line.

Akron's last game of the season was against the Rock Island Independents in that Illinois city. Only 1,700 fans turned out in freezing cold to see their favorites whip the Akron Indians, 17 to 0, on an icy field. Pollard's speed and elusiveness were of little use on such a field. He slipped on a frozen puddle and fumbled. The ball was recovered by the Rock Island center on the Indians' 5-yard line. It led to the Independents' first touchdown. It was an inauspicious end to Akron's season, but Pollard would return to become one of the stars of the fledgling NFL.

The 1919 Akron Indians, with or without Fritz Pollard, were not the best in the Ohio League, but they were far from the worst. The trouncing they got from the Rock Island Independents made it plain that good football was not the exclusive province of Ohio teams as the second decade of the century came to a close.

Rock Island was probably the best team in Illinois that year despite the presence of the Chicago Racine Cardinals, who after several metamorphoses are today's Arizona Cardinals. The Chicago Racine Cardinals were born as the Morgan Athletic Club just before the turn of the century. They started as one of the city's semipro clubs that slugged it out for local supremacy. The Cardinals drew their name from South Racine Avenue, the South Side neighborhood where most of the players lived. Chicago newspapers sometimes confused the Cardinals with a team from Racine, Wisconsin, which did not help them at the gate. Neither did the fact that the University of Chicago, coached by Amos Alonzo Stagg, was a major football power and got the lion's share of the ink on Chicago's sports pages each fall. Stagg, incidentally, was death on professional football. "A real man would never turn to professionalism," he said.

In 1919 the Chicago Racine Cardinals played six games, all in the Chicago metropolitan area. They won three, lost one, and tied two. One of the ties was with the Hammond [Ind.] All-Stars, located in a city on Lake Michigan just south of Chicago. While the Chicago Racine Cardinals were pleased with a crowd of 2,000 at high-school fields, the Hammond All-Stars could attract up to 10,000 fans for a game at Cubs Park (Wrigley Field) with the Canton Bulldogs. Two of the Hammond standouts—George Halas and John (Paddy) Driscoll—would go on to play large roles in the infant NFL.

Hammond was not the only Indiana incubator of professional football. In fact, Indiana was probably second only to Ohio in the overall quality of its teams. South Bend had several strong semipro teams that benefited from coaching by Notre Damers Knute Rockne, Gus Dorais, Hunk Anderson, and Slip Madigan. Pine Village, the Fort Wayne Friars, the Wabash Athletic Association, and, immediately after World War I, the Fort Wayne War Vets were strong teams too.

The class of the pro teams in Michigan was the Detroit Heralds, though they had a poor year right after the war, winning only one game in seven. They played home games in Navin Field, the Detroit Tigers' baseball park. In Wisconsin, there were no major professional teams but plenty of semipros. One brand-new Wisconsin team in 1919 was the Green Bay Packers. The Packers were founded by Earl L. (Curly) Lambeau, a twenty-one-year-old former halfback at Notre Dame who had been expelled for playing professionally on Sundays. Lambeau, a Green Bay native, had been a high-school hero there. The new owner-coach cajoled his employer, the Indian Packing Company, a meat packer, into paying for twenty football jerseys, a dozen footballs, and some shoulder pads. The company also permitted the use of its property for a practice field. For home games, Lambeau arranged to use Hagemeister Park, an open field with no fence and, of course, no seating arrangements. The playing field was ringed by ropes, and the "gate" receipts were collected by passing the hat. It was an inauspicious start for what would become a solid franchise in the NFL, but Green Bay's arrangements were not at all unusual for the time.

In the East, there were a lot of semipro teams after the war, but few professional clubs of high quality. In New England, the best was the Providence Steam Roller, organized in 1916 by three members of the sports department of the *Providence Journal*. One of them was sports editor Charles Coppen. Another was a young Pearce B. Johnson, a part-time sportswriter, who recalls how the team got its name:

> In our very first game we played the Providence Pros. Between the halves, one of our owners, Charles Coppen, was getting a hot dog and he heard somebody remark, "Gee, they're getting steam-rolled," meaning the other team. We were ahead by a big score. He liked that remark, so he gave the team the name Steam Roller after that.

The name Steam Roller became a tradition for Providence sports teams. It was used from 1946 to 1949 by the Providence entry in the Basketball Association of America, one of the parents of the National Basketball Association, and by the city's team in the indoor Arena Football League in 1988, as well as by the football team in the NFL in the late 1920s.

By 1919, the Steam Roller footballers were so popular that they were outdrawing hometown Brown University by two to one, according to the *Evening Bulletin*. That seems unlikely, since the Steam Roller's average crowd was only about 3,000. Players' wages were much lower than in Ohio and Indiana, about $10 or less a player, so the team did not bring in many high-paid ringers. College men who did play for the Steam Roller usually used aliases.

The New York City metropolitan area had several semipro teams in the World War I era, but only one of them moved on to prominence. That was the Staten Island Stapletons, named for a neighborhood in the smallest of New York City's five boroughs. The Stapletons began to play in 1915 with local players who earned $10 a game. By 1929, they were good enough to join the NFL.

In 1919 the Stapes almost had an intracity rival when the owners of the New York Giants baseball team announced plans to start a football team to play in the Polo Grounds, home of the baseball Giants (now San Francisco Giants), on Sundays. The Polo Grounds was often the site of college games on Saturdays. Charley Brickley, described by the New York Times as "the greatest drop kicker in the history of the sport," was named general manager and coach. Brickley was a Harvard star who had kicked five field goals against Yale in 1913. The announcement said that the idea for a pro team in New York had grown out of a plan to select an all-star team to oppose the Canton Bulldogs at the Polo Grounds. "The Canton game is now the outstanding feature of a tentative schedule, but plans are under way for games with professional elevens at Cleveland, Chicago, Massillon and with the strong elevens which are organized annually at Bridgeport, New Haven and other nearby cities," the Times reported.

Prospective players for the Giants included stars from collegiate football powers in the East and Midwest. One of the players mentioned, Alfred G. Gennert, a former Princeton center, indignantly rejected the idea of playing professionally. In a statement to the Times a few days later, Gennert said,

> I have never been approached on this subject by any representative of the National Exhibition Company [owner of the baseball Giants and the football team] or any other professional club, and the use of my name in this connection is wholly unwarranted and inexcusable. I would not play football for money on Sunday, or any other afternoon. I believe that any attempt to professionalize football is a direct attack on the best traditions of the game and should be resented by all loyal devotees.

Brickley called the team's first practice for Sunday, October 5, and took the quarterback position himself for signal drills and a light scrimmage. Two other practices were scheduled during the week to get ready for the first game against the Massillon Tigers at the Polo Grounds. But it was not to be. The day after the Giants' only practice, City Corporation Counsel William Burr said that there could be no football games on Sunday. A recent city law had ended the ban on Sunday baseball, and Brickley and the National Exhibition Company had assumed—not unreasonably—that if Sunday baseball was all right, football would be too. Not so, said Burr. The repeal did not apply to Sunday football.

Since the Polo Grounds was booked for most Saturdays that fall, the Giants expired without having played a game. It would be six more years before a team called the New York Giants took the field.

In upstate New York, there were two fairly strong pro teams right after World War I: the Buffalo Prospects, led by Ernest (Tommy) Hughitt, an old Michigan quarterback; and the Rochester Jeffersons. They played each other twice—one ending in a scoreless tie, and the other in a 20 to 0 victory for Buffalo. But they did not play Ohio League teams, so it is hard to judge their quality. Two years earlier, the Jeffersons had gone to Canton and absorbed a 41 to 0 stomping by the Bulldogs, but Jeffs manager Leo Lyons had strengthened his club since then.

There were blue laws against Sunday football in some Pennsylvania cities too, so pro teams were scarce in areas where major college teams played on Saturdays. The predecessors of the Philadelphia Eagles were the Frankford Yellow Jackets, a team born in 1919 in Frankford, then a suburb of Philadelphia but now a part of the city. The founding organization was the Frankford Athletic Association, which gave the team lavish support. For the first few years, the Yellow Jackets played semipros in the Philadelphia area and the clubs in coal-region towns north of the city, including Pottsville, Shenandoah, Coaldale, and Gilberton. A field with seats for about 10,000 was built for the Yellow Jackets. When they joined the NFL in 1924, the Yellow Jackets often played two games a weekend, one at home on Saturday and the other away on Sunday.

It was clear in 1919 that pro football was outgrowing the Ohio League. Ohio still had most of the strongest teams, but no longer had a monopoly on the best in the pro game. Most of the Ohio teams were losing money because they could not draw enough fans to pay the top stars at the going rate of $100 a game and up. The use of college players by the pros was still rampant, too.

In short, there were problems galore for Ohio League managers. The beginnings of a solution would come in 1920.

5

THE BIRTH AND INFANCY OF THE NFL

George S. Halas, founder and long-time coach of the Chicago Bears, is often referred to as the "father of the NFL." Halas was there at its beginning, and there is no doubt that he exercised great influence in pro football circles for well over sixty years, but he does not deserve this title.

The men who conceived of and developed the first viable organization for pro football teams (they called it first a "conference" and then an "association") were several businessmen in northeastern Ohio. Chief among them was Ralph E. Hay, a twenty-nine-year-old Hupmobile auto dealer in Canton who took over management of the Canton Bulldogs from Jack Cusack in 1918. The Bulldogs did not play in that war year, and Cusack pulled up stakes in Ohio and entered the oil business in Oklahoma. Under the leadership of Hay and Jim Thorpe, the 1919 Bulldogs were undefeated and tied only by the Hammond All-Stars in a scoreless game. Naturally, they claimed the "U.S. Professional Football Championship." As owner–business manager of Canton, Hay was a power in pro football circles.

Vague talk about the need for a professional football league had been common in Ohio, and probably elsewhere, for fifteen years by the summer of 1920. The first step toward realization of the dream came on August 20 in the auto agency offices of Ralph Hay. Whether he or someone else suggested the meeting is not known. On hand were representatives of teams in Canton, Cleveland, Akron, and Dayton. The *Canton Evening Repository* reported the next day that they had formed the American Professional Football Conference with their four teams and had admitted teams from Buffalo and Rochester, New York, that had applied to join by letter. Hay was elected secretary, the *Repository* said. The *Akron Beacon-Journal* also had a story about the meeting in Canton but made no mention of a new conference, stating only that a working agreement had been reached to curb the jumping of players from team to team and the use of college men. The *Dayton Journal* reported flatly that a league had been formed.

The team managers evidently instructed Hay to get in touch with managers of other strong clubs in the Midwest and western New York State and invite them to a second meeting in Canton on September 17. Among those invited was George Halas, who was organizing a semipro football team to represent the A. E. Staley Manufacturing Company, a starch maker in Decatur, Illinois.

Halas, who was born and raised in Chicago, was a three-sport star at the University of Illinois, from which he graduated in 1918 with a civil engineering degree. He played end on the football team under renowned coach Bob Zuppke, was captain of the basketball team, and played outfield for the baseball team. In January 1918, Halas was commissioned an ensign in the U.S. Navy and was assigned to the Great Lakes Naval Training Center, which had a powerful football team. It was chosen to play in the Rose Bowl. Halas earned the "most valuable player" designation in the Rose Bowl game on January 1, 1919, as Great Lakes beat the Mare Island Marines, 17 to 0.

Halas was mustered out of the Navy in March 1919, four months after World War I ended. He was given a contract by the New York Yankees baseball team that spring and played twelve games as a speedy but light-hitting outfielder, batting .091 before being farmed out to St. Paul of the American Association for the rest of the year. That fall, he worked in the bridge-design department of a railroad and played end on Sundays for the Hammond All-Stars. Halas was 6 feet tall and weighed 182 pounds, a fairly average size for an end of that period.

In March 1920, A. E. Staley offered Halas a job in his business if he would also organize a company football team to advertise Staley's. Another condition was that Halas would play for the company baseball team, which was managed by Iron Man Joe McGinnity, winner of 247 major league games in a ten-year pitching career beginning in 1899. Halas accepted happily, and by midsummer he had corraled several college stars for the Staley football team. The lure was jobs in the starch factory, football practice on company time, and extra pay for playing. One of his signees was an All-American end from Nebraska named Guy Chamberlin. He had played for the Canton Bulldogs in 1919, which may explain how Ralph Hay had heard about Halas and his prospective Decatur Staleys and sent him an invitation to the meeting in Canton.

Twenty-five-year-old George Halas and Morgan O'Brien, a Staley company engineer and football fan, represented the Staleys when the managers of ten pro teams showed up at Hay's auto agency on September 17, 1920. Hay and Jim Thorpe represented the Canton Bulldogs. The Akron Indians had died after the 1919 season, as had the Massillon

Tigers. Both expired due to severe financial anemia. Massillon had no representative at the meeting, but two Akron businessmen, Frank Nied and Art Ranney, were on hand with promises to field a good team in the Rubber City. The fourth of Ohio's Big Four, the Cleveland Tigers, which had picked up many of Massillon's stars, had manager Jimmy O'Donnell and coach Stanley Cofall, a former Notre Dame quarterback, at the meeting. Carl Storck of the Dayton Triangles, who had attended the earlier meeting, was back. Newcomers were Leo Lyons of the Rochester Jeffersons; A. A. Young, manager of the Hammond Pros; Walter H. Flanigan, manager of the Rock Island Independents; Chris O'Brien, a businessman and veteran manager of the Chicago Racine Cardinals; and Earl Ball of the Muncie [Ind.] Flyers.

The group of fourteen men was too large for Hay's office, so they convened on the auto showroom floor. Some sat on the running boards of the cars and drank beer from buckets. Despite the informality, they also transacted some business, though not much dealing with the ostensible purposes of the new organization. In August, the *Canton Evening Repository* had reported that the purpose of the American Professional Football Conference would be

> to raise the standard of professional football in every way possible, to eliminate bidding for players between rival clubs and to secure cooperation in the formation of schedules, at least for the bigger teams. Members of the organization reached an agreement to refrain from offering inducements to players to jump from one team to another, which has been one of the glaring drawbacks to the game in past seasons.

The minutes of the September 17 meeting make no mention of addressing those problems. However, newspaper articles indicate that the managers agreed not to use college players and to honor contracts, which would have the effect of ending player jumping.

What the conferees did do, according to the minutes, was to change the name of the organization to the American Professional Football *Association* instead of *Conference*. At this far remove, it seems like a distinction without a difference, and the managers did not explain their thinking. In any event, they did not call it a "league," which implies a tighter bond than either "conference" or "association."

Jim Thorpe was elected president of the new APFA, not for his untested administrative skills but for his name. The managers calculated that they needed a universally recognized figurehead for instant credibility, and they were right. The *New York Times* and most other newspapers outside Ohio headlined their brief notices of the association's birth by citing Thorpe's election; the *Times*'s tiny one-column headline, for example, read "Thorpe Made President."

A membership fee of $100 for each club was established, but as far as is known, no one came up with any money. Years later, Halas was quoted as saying, "I doubt that there was a hundred bucks in the room."

Thorpe appointed a three-man committee to draft a constitution and by-laws for adoption in 1921. A motion was approved calling for all clubs to send A. F. Ranney, the new secretary, a list of all players they used during the 1920 season by January 1 so that clubs could sign the same men for 1921 if they wished. Another motion called for all clubs to add to their letterheads "Member of the American Professional Football Association."

The minutes say that a Mr. Marshall of the Brunswick-Balke Collender Company, Tire Division, gave a silver loving cup to be presented to the team "awarded the championship by the Association." As researchers for the Professional Football Research Association have noted,

> The phrase is significant because it indicates the title was to be determined by a vote of the members instead of a mathematical won–lost formula. In other words, as had been done in the Ohio League, the championship wouldn't necessarily go to the team with the best won–lost record if the members believed another team had shown itself to be stronger.

As it turned out, at the end of the APFA's first season, the championship title did go to the team with the best won–lost record, but it took a vote of the membership the following April to confirm it.

When the NFL was born, football on the field was similar to today's game in some respects, but vastly different in others. Even the field was different. It was 100 yards long with 10-yard-deep end zones, just like today's gridiron. But the goal posts stood on the goal line rather than on the end zone back line, making field goals and extra point tries easier. There were no hash marks. The next play began where the last one ended, even if the ball was a foot from the sideline. If a ball carrier was knocked out of bounds, the ball was placed at the point inbounds where he went out. The result was that the team had to waste a play just to get the ball into operating territory. All linemen would line up on the field side of the center, and everybody knew in which direction the play had to go. Hash marks were not introduced until 1933 and at first were only 10 yards from the sideline.

Forward passing had been permitted for fourteen years, and most of the original restrictions had been removed. But the passer still had to throw from at least 5 yards behind the line of scrimmage, which greatly reduced the possibility of deception. In addition, if a pass fell incomplete in the end zone, it was a touchback and the defenders were given the ball on their 20-yard line. Consequently, the forward pass was not a full partner with the run in a team's offensive arsenal. The average NFL team in the league's first season probably passed five times in a game, perhaps even less if they led all the way.

George Halas's Decatur Staleys lined up in the T-formation he had learned at Illinois, but they were the only ones to use the T. It had been the original formation when American football began diverging from rugby in the 1880s. It was usually referred to as "regular" formation because it was so common. But by 1920, most teams, both college and professional, had adopted other offensive formations designed to bring maximum manpower to the point of attack in the running game.

The most common was the single wing formation, devised by Glenn S. (Pop) Warner in 1906 while he was coaching the Carlisle Indian School team. Warner explained his thinking in a letter quoted in Allison Danzig's *Oh, How They Played the Game:*

> Defensive tackles had always been difficult to keep out of the offensive backfield because they generally played outside the offensive ends and therefore could not be blocked in on wide plays. I figured that one back could be used to very good advantage by placing him in a position where he could outflank the opposing tackle and still be in a position where he could run with the ball, as on reverse plays. I therefore started using the formation which is known as the single wing formation. . . . In later years I carried the idea a step further by placing both halfbacks in position close to the line and wide enough to outflank the defensive tackles. I therefore believe I should be credited with originating and first making use of the wingback system of play, both single wing and double wing.

Warner does not mention his line's alignment, so it must have been balanced with a guard, a tackle, and an end on each side of the center. But most later coaches who adopted the single or double wing used an unbalanced line, with both guards on one side—the strong side—of center. The aim was to concentrate blockers where the ball carrier intended to go.

In the single wing, the key man was the tailback, usually a halfback and the best athlete on the team. He handled the ball on most plays and did virtually all the passing and punting, as well as most of the running. The tailback lined up about 5 yards directly behind the center. The center passed the ball between his legs, as he does in today's punt formation. A yard in front and to one side of the tailback was the fullback. He sometimes ran with the ball on short yardage plunges, but he was primarily a blocking back in the single wing. The quarterback—usually the play caller—was about 1 yard behind the strong side guard. He was also a blocking back. The wingback, usually a halfback, lined up outside the strong side end and 1 yard back from the line. He blocked, received passes, and ran the reverse. In the double wing, the chief difference in backfield alignment was that the fullback moved to wingback on the weak side of the line.

Some college teams developed offenses utilizing shifts that required the defensive team to adjust quickly. The most famous was Knute Rockne's Notre Dame box. The Irish lined up in a conventional T and then, on signal, shifted quickly into a trapezoid, with a halfback behind center and the other halfback outside his end. The line was balanced. The rules said that all players had to hold their new position for a full second before the ball was snapped. But Halas recalled, "At Notre Dame, the one-second pause frequently was not much longer than the blink of an eye."

Shifts required exquisite timing to be effective, and in the 1920s few pro teams had the time to devote to practicing it. So shifts were not common in the pros.

Most teams' offenses were very conservative, especially in their own territory. If they got the ball on their 20-yard line, they might well punt on first down without having run a play. They waited for the other team to make a mistake and then tried to capitalize on it. Occasionally, a punt returner who caught the ball near his own goal line would punt it right back without attempting to run.

Unless a team was near the opponent's goal, a punt on third down was almost a given. The idea was that if there was a bad pass from center or the punter fumbled, he could fall on the ball and still have a fourth down to kick. On third down and long yardage, teams with a talented tailback might give him the option of passing to an end in front of the safety man if the safety went back to field a punt or quick-kicking over his head if he stayed closer to the line. That way, the offensive team could either complete a short pass play for a first down or gain 50 yards in field position if the punt sailed over the safety's head and took a favorable bounce or two.

Forward passing was still considered a desperation move. Linemen were not prohibited from heading downfield on a pass play, so the defenders had to find the eligible receivers (backs and ends) among them.

The huddle was just starting to appear in college games. Amos Alonzo Stagg said that he had his team huddle in an indoor game in 1896, but Bob Zuppke of Illinois apparently was the first to use the huddle regularly in 1921. All the pros used coded signals, which today are called "audibles." In most signal systems, each hole between linemen was given a number. Each backfield man also had a number. The signal caller, usually the quarterback, would call out a series of numbers, among which would be the number of the back who was to carry the ball and the number of the hole that would be the point of attack. The linemen and backs blocked accordingly.

No coaching was permitted from the sidelines. Substitutes who came into the game were not permitted to speak to anyone before the next play. The quarterback and/or team captain necessarily had to devise strategy and choose plays without help from the coach.

In the early years, NFL teams generally had sixteen-man rosters. Since the players played both offense and defense and there were no specialists, that was enough. The five substitutes usually included two or three backs, an end, and an all-purpose lineman. Starters could be almost sure of playing at least three quarters, and many played the whole sixty minutes week after week.

The players were, on average, much smaller than today's NFL performers. When Halas's Staleys moved to Chicago in 1921 and played their first games at Cubs Park, the starting line averaged 206 pounds and the backfield, 174. The biggest man was the 6-foot, 2-inch, 234-pound tackle Ralph Scott; the smallest was the 5-foot, 8-inch, 152-pound quarterback Pete Stinchcomb. Both men would be deemed too small for their positions in pro football today.

Some of today's leviathans, however, might not have been able to make it in the old days. A 300-pounder would have had to have been an unusual athlete to play a full sixty minutes, as the old-timers did, though if truth be told, the old-timers didn't necessarily go all out on every play. Linemen might relax somewhat if the play went away from them, and a little more time probably elapsed between plays. The recollections of players from those days are full of stories of playing games on consecutive days, which today would be considered impossible. Arda Bowser, a fullback who was one of the last surviving players from the NFL's early years, told writer Emil Klosinski that he had played games *four* days in a row. In 1922 he was on the roster of the NFL champion Canton Bulldogs at a wage of $150 a game. His test of endurance, however, began in Philadelphia on Thanksgiving Day, when he played sixty minutes for the non-league Frankford Yellow Jackets. The next day, he headed for Pennsylvania's coal region to play with the semipros in Mount Carmel. Again, he was in the game for sixty minutes. On Saturday, he returned to Philadelphia for another full day's workout, and then hopped a train for Canton and a Sunday game with the Bulldogs.

Players were expected to furnish most of their protective gear. Some teams provided helmets, socks, and heavy wool jerseys but not much else. Other teams expected the player to bring his own helmet (if he wore one), as well as shoes, shoulder pads, padded pants, elbow pads, thigh guards, knee and shin guards, and a nose guard if he fancied the idea. Not many players did.

The equipment was marginally better than it had been ten years earlier. The best helmet sold by A. G. Spalding & Brothers (which persisted in calling helmets "head harnesses") now had elastic webbing in the crown to absorb blows. Some simpler headgear was of leather so soft and pliable that a player could fold the helmet and stick it in his pocket. Football pants were usually canvas padded with felt and fiber pads. The wool jersey absorbed sweat and on a hot or rainy day could just about double in weight over the course of a game.

The first year of the NFL (né the APFA) was inauspicious—and that is an understatement. From a few days after the organizational meeting on September 17, 1920, until the owners got together the following spring, the APFA was never mentioned in public print.

League standings were never published either, for the very good reason that the APFA did not think in terms of standings or won–lost percentages. From the start, the APFA intended to choose its champion by vote of the members after the season ended, as had been done in the Ohio League. This is not as irrational as it sounds. Each team set up its own schedule, and if a team fattened its record by playing only weak teams and avoiding strong ones, the won–lost percentage would not be a fair measure of the team's strength.

So it was not until April 30, 1921, that the Akron Pros, who had compiled an 8–0–3 record, including two victories over nonleague teams, were given the Brunswick-Balke Collender loving cup emblematic of the "world's professional football championship."

In recent years, members of the Professional Football Researchers Association have painstakingly re-created the APFA's 1920 season; before their work, it was believed that no winner had been designated. As noted earlier, no standings for APFA teams were ever published, but if they had been, this is how they would have read. The results include games against non-APFA teams.

	W	L	T	Percentage	Points—Opponents
Akron Pros	8	0	3	1.000	151–7
Decatur Staleys	10	1	2	.909	164–21
Buffalo All-Americans	9	1	1	.900	258–32
Chicago Racine Cardinals	6	2	2	.750	115–43
Rock Island Independents	6	2	2	.750	201–49
Dayton Triangles	5	2	2	.714	150–50
Rochester Jeffersons	6	3	2	.667	156–57
Canton Bulldogs	7	4	2	.636	208–57
Detroit Heralds	2	3	3	.400	53–82
Cleveland Tigers	2	4	2	.333	28–46

	W	L	T	Percentage	Points—Opponents
Chicago Tigers	2	5	1	.286	49–63
Hammond Pros	2	5	0	.286	41–154
Columbus Panhandles	2	6	2	.250	41–121
Muncie Flyers	0	1	0	.000	0–45

The researchers are not certain that the Chicago Tigers, the Columbus Panhandles, and the Detroit Heralds should be included among the charter member teams, but since each played several APFA teams, they are assumed to have joined the association.

Newspaper reports of games did not always include attendance, and when they did it was often an estimate, no doubt rounded up to the next 100. However, using the available published attendance figures, APFA teams drew an average of 4,241 spectators in 1920. Probably the largest crowd—17,000—attended a game between the Canton Bulldogs and the Union Athletic Association of Phoenixville, Pennsylvania, at Baker Bowl in Philadelphia. The Unions were made up largely of Buffalo All-Americans and defeated the Bulldogs, 13 to 7. (The Unions and All-Americans were virtually identical the whole season. Because of Pennsylvania's blue laws, the Unions could not play in Philadelphia on Sundays, so they booked their games for Saturdays. Thus the All-American players could play for the Unions in Philadelphia on Saturdays, and then hustle to Buffalo for a Sunday game. The All-Americans played all home games, including the one at the Polo Grounds in New York where the Canton Bulldogs were listed as the visitors.)

Canton had played the Buffalo All-Americans earlier at the Polo Grounds before what could have been a bigger crowd than in Philadelphia. Newspapers variously estimated the crowd at 10,000 to 25,000. The All-Americans nipped the Bulldogs on a blocked punt by guard Adolph (Swede) Youngstrom, one of five real All-Americans in the Buffalo lineup. He batted down a Jim Thorpe kick, scooped it up at Canton's 10-yard line, and ambled into the end zone.

Membership in the APFA may have alleviated slightly the problems it was designed to eliminate—player jumping, the use of college players, and rising salaries—but not by much. Salaries apparently rose on average, though stars were mostly in the $150-a-game range. Paddy Driscoll, the quarterback of the Chicago Racine Cardinals, was reputed to be making $300 a game, but the only other star who might have matched that was Jim Thorpe. The owners had agreed in September not to use another APFA team's player, but that didn't stop George

Halas from hiring Driscoll for an important game in December against, the Akron Pros. The Staleys and the Pros played to a scoreless tie, ending Halas's hopes for the "world championship," since his team had lost one game while Akron was unbeaten.

Three of the teams that are listed as charter members of the NFL had folded by season's end. The Muncie Flyers did not last past their first game, and the Cleveland Tigers and Detroit Heralds finished the season and then expired.

Nevertheless, the APFA survived the 1920 season and began planning for the next season in April 1921 at a meeting in Akron. They took several steps to ensure the association's survival, the most important being the election of Joseph F. Carr, manager of the Columbus Panhandles, as president. Carr's good judgment and willingness to make decisions carried the NFL through the shoals of adolescence. Carr was still president of the league when he died in 1938.

If Jack Cusack was responsible for reinvigorating the professional game in Ohio in 1915—and he was—then Joe Carr should be credited with bringing the beginnings of order out of the shambles of the APFA in 1921. If nothing else, he spoke optimistically about professional football's future at a time when most teams were financially on the ropes. His enthusiasm apparently carried over to the election of new officers. Jim Thorpe was not a candidate for reelection—he was not even at the meeting and had little interest in executive duties—so the owners chose Carr to succeed him. Carr said later that it "was much against my will, and while I was out of the room."

Carr had little executive experience other than running the Columbus Panhandles and serving as a minor league baseball executive. As far as is known, he never played organized sports, but obviously he loved them. He had only a fifth-grade education. In 1893, when he was thirteen years old, Carr became an apprentice in a machine shop to help support his family. At the turn of the century, when he was twenty, Carr became a journeyman machinist for the Panhandle Division of the Pennsylvania Railroad. He organized and managed a good semipro baseball team, using Panhandle Division employees, and named it the Famous Panhandle White Sox because he was a fan of Charles Comiskey, owner of the Chicago White Sox in the new American League. He also began writing sports for the *Ohio State Journal*, a Columbus daily, specializing in boxing.

In 1925 Carr became president and secretary of the new American Basketball League. No doubt he achieved this position through the influence of George Halas, who owned the Chicago Bruins in the league. Carr himself knew nothing about basketball and had seen very few games when he took the president's post.

When he assumed leadership of the APFA in the spring of 1921, he was essentially an unknown quantity as an administrator. He wasted no time in establishing his authority and gaining the respect of the owners.

The committee that had been appointed the previous September to draw up a constitution and by-laws had produced nothing, so Carr named three men, including himself, to do the job. He also warned the owners not to approach players from other teams unless the players had been declared to be free agents, and he proposed that the league have a standard player's contract patterned after the one used by baseball leagues.

Carr established the idea of territoriality—that is, that a member team could not schedule games in another member team's territory. From his office in Columbus, Carr issued standings for the first time so that teams and their fans would know where they stood. In 1921, though it was not yet a tightly knit league, the APFA was more cohesive than it had been in 1920.

At the end of the season, Carr faced the first major crisis of his regime. As many other teams had done before them, the Green Bay Packers, who were in their first season in the APFA, hired undergraduate college players using assumed names for some games. Carr felt that an example was required. He declared that Green Bay's action was not only a violation of the rules, but a breach of trust for the fans. In January 1922, he ordered the Packers to turn back their franchise, which had been held by the Acme Packing Company, successor to the Indian Packing Company. Packer coach-manager Curly Lambeau wanted the franchise back. He had the $50 required to buy a new franchise, but he had no way to get to Canton, where the APFA managers planned to meet in June 1922. He mentioned the problem to Don Murphy, son of a Green Bay lumberman. Packer historian Chuck Johnson explains:

> "I'll think of something," Murphy said. "And when I do, maybe I'll go with you—if you'll let me play in next year's opener."
>
> Lambeau knew that Murphy was not a professional football player, but he raised his eyebrows and nodded in agreement.
>
> Murphy got the traveling money by selling his cream-colored Marmon roadster for $1,555. Lambeau and Murphy went to Canton, bought back the franchise and the Green Bay Packers prepared for the 1922 season. Murphy played tackle for the first minute of the opening game, then "retired" from professional football.

The new, better-organized, and more cohesive appearance of the APFA under Carr was reflected in several ways in 1921. For one thing, final standings were issued, and only games against other teams in the APFA were counted. For another, the cost of membership in the association dropped to $50 from $100, but in 1921 the assessment was real.

In 1920, apparently nobody had paid the $100. Each team also paid $25 to cover the association's expenses.

In all, twenty-one teams had franchises in the APFA in 1921. The association's geographical scope broadened to include New York and Washington, D.C., in the East, Minneapolis in the West, and Louisville in the South. The new team in New York was Brickley's Giants, coached and managed by Charley Brickley, the old Harvard dropkicker. The Washington entry was named the Senators, after the capital's team in baseball's American League, which had Walter Johnson but not much else and was invariably toasted as "Washington, first in war, first in peace, and last in the American League." The team in Minneapolis was the Marines, which had long been a regional power in the Upper Midwest. The South's representative, the Louisville Brecks, were mostly sandlotters like the Columbus Panhandles.

Eight of the twenty-one franchise teams were not included in the final standings. One—the Muncie Flyers, who had played only one game in 1920—dropped out after two games, both losses, in 1921. The other seven apparently were ignored in the standings because they did not play the required number of games with association teams. The required minimum number of games seems to have been six. Not meeting the test of playing at least six games against APFA teams, and thus not eligible for the final standings list, were the Evansville [Ind.] Crimson Giants, Hammond Pros, Louisville Brecks, Minneapolis Marines, Brickley's Giants of New York, Tonawanda [N.Y.] Kardex, and Washington Senators.

The 1921 championship race had three contenders: the defending champion Akron Pros, who again had the brilliant halfback Fritz Pollard, plus Paul Robeson, the black All-American end from Rutgers; the Buffalo All-Americans; and the Decatur Staleys, who wound up in Chicago early in the season en route to becoming the Chicago Bears. A. E. Staley, the starch manufacturer in Decatur, told Staleys' coach George Halas that business was bad and he would have to drop his sports teams. Staley suggested that Halas take the team to Chicago, with its much larger base of football fans. "I'll give you $5,000 to help you get started," Staley said. "All I ask is that you continue to call the team the Staleys for one season."

Halas and his business partner, Ed (Dutch) Sternaman, an old Notre Dame star who was a Staleys halfback, agreed that it was worth a try. So after playing two early October games in Decatur, the Staleys moved to Cubs Park in Chicago and played the last ten games of the 1921 season there, attracting crowds ranging from 2,000 to 10,000. The largest crowd was for the Cleveland Tigers game, presumably because Jim Thorpe was the Tigers' player-coach. However, old Jim did not play against the Staleys because of lingering injuries. The Chicago Staleys beat the Tigers, as well as eight other APFA teams, losing only to the Buffalo All-Americans and playing to a scoreless tie with the Chicago Racine Cardinals in their last game.

The Staleys had whipped the All-Americans by 10 to 7 in their second meeting, giving both teams a record of 9–1 (not counting ties). But following the general rule that the second meeting counted for more than the first in establishing supremacy, the Chicago Staleys claimed the championship. The Buffalo All-Americans disputed that, saying that the second game with the Staleys was just a post-season exhibition. The All-Americans had made the mistake of scheduling this "exhibition" for Sunday, December 4, the day after beating the tough Akron Pros in Buffalo. The association's executive committee decided in January 1922 that the champion was the Chicago Staleys.

The Chicago Staleys ended the 1921 season with either a profit of $7 (Halas's version) or a loss of $71 and change (other reports). Pro football was still a nickel-and-dime business. There was occasional financial chicanery, if Jack Cusack is to be believed.

Cusack suffered a severe case of malaria in early 1921 while working in Oklahoma and decided to return to his old home in Canton to recuperate. His good friend Jim Thorpe had gone to Cleveland to play for the new Indians football team there and had taken his fellow Native Americans and Canton Bulldogs teammates, Joe Guyon and Pete Calac, with him. Thorpe asked Cusack to come to Cleveland and look out for his financial welfare, for he thought he was being cheated. Cusack found that he was indeed. In "Pioneer in Pro Football," Cusack explained:

> It did not take me long . . . to learn something about the unusual methods of bookkeeping being practiced. When playing in baseball parks, difficulties rarely arose over the take since the baseball management handled the gates with their own crews, and it was a simple matter to check the gate stiles at openings and closings. Then the baseball men would deduct their percentage for use of the park and give the rest to the football teams in accordance with contracts presented.
>
> However, in parks under the control of the home team, the check on receipts often posed some difficulties. In some instances, the tickets were of the roll variety such as those used at movie theaters, and these required a count before and after the game in order to arrive at the amount of money taken in. Also, the agreements between teams sometimes failed to designate the number of complimentary tickets issued, and those often complicated the business of making an accurate check.
>
> As the representative of the players, I insisted on checking the tickets wherever Cleveland played, and for this purpose I always took sufficient help to man the gates, along with an ample supply of gunny sacks. I

counted all of the tickets into the sacks, then checked the roll figures, and this simple method of audit paid off for the players. On two different occasions I found discrepancies running from $900 to $1100, and complimentary tickets totalling 800 to 900, far in excess of the number that should have been allowed. In both instances, after strong and vivid argument, I succeeded in collecting our share of the deficiencies.

In June 1922, the team managers, meeting in Cleveland, changed the name of their organization to the National Football League. The new name reflected reality. Under the firm guidance of Joe Carr, the teams were no longer a loose amalgamation aimed merely at keeping salaries down, stopping the jumping of players, and discouraging the use of undergraduates on league teams. Not that those problems were solved; far from it. But at least the managers now thought of themselves as members of something bigger than their own teams.

The "national" in National Football League was an aspiration, not a fact, in the 1922 season. Brickley's Giants of New York and the Washington Senators did not renew their franchises, so the team farthest east was now the Rochester Jeffersons. There was no transcontinental air travel, of course, so as a practical matter, any city west of Kansas City was effectively out of reach for NFL teams.

As an indication that the owners were thinking in 1922 in terms of stronger ties, they set the length of the official season from October 1 to December 10. (The dates were changed to September 27 and November 30 in 1924.) To be counted in the final NFL standings, a team had to play at least seven but no more than thirteen games against league teams. The owners also established a standard player's contract that included a reserve clause modeled on baseball's. This clause gave the team first call on a player's services for the following season, which meant that he could not jump to another team after the season.

In their effort to hold salaries to manageable levels, the owners set a team salary limit of $1,200 a game in 1922. That may have been a reasonable salary cap for some of the also-rans who could sign guards and tackles for $50 a game and pay others on their sixteen-man rosters perhaps $75. But for the contenders who recruited All-Americans, $1,200 was grossly inadequate, so undoubtedly they sent the league offices players' contracts calling for wages of $100 a game and then paid players another $100 off the books.

Over the league's first five years, there was a great deal of franchise shuffling. Teams were born in medium-size midwestern cities such as Racine, Wisconsin; Evansville, Indiana; Duluth, Minnesota; and Kenosha, Wisconsin, where they flourished for a season or two and then became a footnote in NFL history. But there were also some solid building blocks for the NFL's future—the Chicago Cardinals, Green Bay Packers, and Chicago Bears.

The Bears got their name in 1922 when George Halas and Dutch Sternaman became the official owners. Up to then, the A. E. Staley Company had held the franchise, even after the team left Decatur and became the Chicago Staleys in 1921. The Chicago Bears Football Club was incorporated in May 1922 by Halas and Sternaman. Bears historian Richard Whittingham wrote:

> They paid the $20 fee and a franchise tax of $13.34 and listed only one other person on their board of directors—ironically enough, Paddy Driscoll of their crosstown rivals, the Cardinals. It was all part of a deal to get Driscoll into a Chicago Bear uniform. He was just about the best player in the league, and he was a consistent plague on Halas and Sternaman's team. The ploy, however, did not work. Joe Carr, NFL president, ruled that Driscoll was the property of the Cardinals and the Bears had no right to him unless the Cardinals agreed to it. They didn't of course.

The Chicago Bears' management might overreach occasionally, but they were a pillar of orthodoxy in the NFL's early years. The Bears were a perennially strong team and played a punishing, bone-crushing brand of football. The roughest player without doubt was center George Trafton, a Notre Dame alumnus who was an all-league choice eight times in his thirteen seasons ending in 1932. Once in Rock Island, after an especially rough game against the Independents, Trafton had to flee for his life to get out of the stadium.

"Two years later," wrote Richard Whittingham in *The Chicago Bears,*

> when the Bears reappeared in Rock Island, the game was again an especially physical one and the crowd grew almost as ornery as it had the time before. When this game ended and George Halas was handed $7,000 in cash—the Bears' share of the gate receipts—he gave the money over to Trafton for safekeeping. "I knew that if trouble came," Halas said, "I'd be running only for the $7,000. Trafton would be running for his life."

The only element of the story that seems improbable is that any visiting team ever netted $7,000 from a game in Rock Island.

Despite the steady development of such solid NFL franchises as the Bears, Cardinals, and Green Bay Packers, there was still plenty of room for the occasional oddity. Surely the strangest team that ever took the field in an NFL game was the Oorang Indians of LaRue, Ohio, a hamlet of 900 near Marion, the home of the sitting U.S. president, Warren Gamaliel Harding. The Oorang Indians, who were in the NFL in 1922 and 1923, were essentially shills for an Airedale puppy–breeding business in the village. Commercial tie-ins were not unusual in the NFL's early years, as witness the Staley starch company's sponsorship of the soon-to-be Chicago Bears. But Airedale puppies?

The Oorang Indians were the creation and property of Walter

Lingo, a LaRue citizen whose Oorang Kennels was the largest mail-order puppy business in the nation, if not the world. Besides being an Airedale fancier, Lingo was an admirer of Native Americans, and he decided to combine those two interests by sponsoring an all-Indian football team that would advertise his puppies.

He invited Jim Thorpe, who was thirty-five years old and had spent the previous season as player-coach of the Cleveland Indians (or Tigers), to recruit players for the Oorang Indians. Thorpe did, and the Indians took to the road in 1922, playing two games in Marion and twelve elsewhere. The Indians were a bad team even by the low standards of some of the NFL's pioneer teams. Over two full seasons, they won only four league games and lost many by huge scores, even though they had two great players in Joe Guyon and Pete Calac, as well as Thorpe. Bob Braunwart, Bob Carroll, and Joe Horrigan of the Professional Football Research Association offer one reason for their lack of success:

> The team found it difficult to take their football seriously because the team owner was far more interested in the pregame and halftime activities than he was in the game itself. They gave exhibitions with Airedales at work trailing and treeing a live bear. One of the players, 195-pound Nikolas Lassa, called "Long-Time Sleep" by his teammates because he was so hard to wake up in the morning, even wrestled the bear. There were fancy shooting exhibitions by Indian marksmen with Airedales retrieving the targets. There were Indian dances, fancy tomahawk work, knife and lariat throwing, all done by Indians. "The climax," explained Lingo, "was an exhibition of what the United States' loyal Indian Scouts did during the war against Germany, with Oorang Airedale Red Cross dogs giving first aid in an armed encounter between Scouts and Huns in no man's land. Many of the Indians and dogs were veterans of the war—the Oorangs up front."
>
> After such a workout, Thorpe's players must have looked upon the game as purely a secondary matter.

Thorpe's old team, the Canton Bulldogs, dominated the league during the two-year life of the Oorang Indians. Led by player-coach Guy Chamberlin, late of the Chicago Staleys and the NFL's best end, the rejuvenated Bulldogs were undefeated in both years. The runners-up in both seasons were George Halas's Chicago Bears. The Canton Bulldogs were an artistic success but a financial disaster. Their Lakeside Park, a minor league baseball stadium, was not big enough to handle the crowds that were needed to cover their salary costs. So in 1924 the Bulldogs were sold to sports promoter Sam Deutsch, who owned the Cleveland Indians football team. He renamed the team the Cleveland Bulldogs, invited ten of the Canton players to join the team, and deactivated the Canton franchise in the NFL. Seven of the Canton players, including player-coach Guy Chamberlin, joined the Cleveland Bulldogs. They won the 1924 NFL championship. They played a tie and lost once to the Yellow Jackets of Frankford, Pennsylvania. The Yellow Jackets were in their first year in the league and gave it a solid base in the East for the first time. They showed their quality by winning eleven games, losing two, and tying the Bulldogs. That was good enough for a third-place finish behind Cleveland and the Chicago Bears. Because of Pennsylvania's blue laws, the Yellow Jackets could not play at home on Sundays, so they usually scheduled a home game for Saturday and an away game for Sunday; as a result, for several years the Yellow Jackets played the most games of any NFL team.

At the league's summer meeting before the 1924 season got under way, Dutch Sternaman, co-owner of the Chicago Bears, made a motion that the league's official season begin on September 27 and end on November 30. He also proposed that the official standings be determined by won–lost percentages of all games between those two inclusive dates. The motion passed easily, to Sternaman's regret the following January when the Bears had to relinquish a claim on the championship because a crucial victory on their record was played after November 30.

On November 30, the Cleveland Bulldogs had the best league record, 7–1–1. The Chicago Bears were second, with 6–1–4, and the Frankford Yellow Jackets were third, with 11–2–1. The Bears invited the Bulldogs to Chicago for a game on December 7 that Chicago newspapers, no doubt with prodding from George Halas, announced would be for the championship. Not surprisingly, the Bulldogs saw it as an exhibition and were thus not unduly alarmed when they lost the game, 23 to 0. Subsequently, the Bears edged the Frankford Yellow Jackets and lost to the Rock Island Independents 7 to 6.

Both the Bulldogs and the Bears claimed the league title, and it was not until the January 1925 meeting that the Bulldogs were officially awarded the NFL championship on the basis of the league's rule that ended the championship season on November 30. It was another example of Joe Carr's firm hand on the NFL tiller.

Professional football was still considered a minor sport in the nation's large cities. In Green Bay, Canton, and other smaller hotbeds of pro football, the local papers covered the pro games exhaustively, but in Chicago, Philadelphia, and Cleveland, teams had to beg for pre-game publicity. Even in the large population centers, crowds of 15,000 were considered good.

The 1925 season would demonstrate that there was a much larger population base for the pro game, given a hero and a plan to market him and the game.

6

GLIMMERS OF GLORY

Harold E. (Red) Grange could not walk on water, but you would have had a hard time convincing the student body at the University of Illinois in 1925. Grange was a 5-foot, 11-inch, 175-pound, swivel-hipped halfback with great speed, shiftiness, and peripheral vision that made him the finest running back of his time. He was called the Galloping Ghost.

In his senior year at Illinois in 1925, Grange destroyed Penn—then a football power—almost singlehandedly. He carried the ball thirty-six times for 363 yards, scored three touchdowns and set up a fourth, and played sterling defense. When the special train bringing Grange and his teammates back to Champaign got there, 10,000 students were on hand to cheer and carry him on their shoulders the two miles back to the campus. Two weeks later, a serious effort was made to place his name on the Republican ballot for the April 1926 primary election for Congress, even though he was only twenty-two years old, three years under the constitutional age requirement. Said one of his admirers, "It would certainly not be a popular move for any Congressman to call attention to Grange's being a few months under the age limit if he were elected by the people of the entire state."

Nothing came of the nominating petition effort, probably because Red Grange was too modest and unassuming to aspire to Congress and possibly because he had in mind more lucrative employment. Grange had first caught the attention of the nation's sports fans in 1924 when he enjoyed perhaps the most spectacular game in college football history. In a game against archrival Michigan dedicating the Illini's new stadium at Champaign, he ran for four touchdowns in the first quarter, scoring each time he touched the ball. He ran the opening kickoff back 95 yards for the first score. He returned another kickoff 67 yards for a touchdown. The other two touchdowns were on runs from scrimmage of 56 and 44 yards. Coach Bob Zuppke took him out then, explaining, "No Michigan man laid a hand on you and I want you to come out unsoiled." However, Grange went back into the game in the third quarter and scored on a 12-yard run; in the fourth, he passed for a touchdown.

After that game, Red Grange was by all odds the most watched and photographed football player in either college or professional ranks. So there was a great deal of interest in whether he would decide to play pro football, which was still stigmatized by Amos Alonzo Stagg and many other coaches. His own coach, Bob Zuppke, was opposed to the pros but not adamant about it. Grange's father said he would support Red's decision, but hoped he wouldn't turn pro.

In November, just before the Illini's final game against Ohio State, the Associated Press reported that the New York Giants, who were in their first year in the NFL, had offered Grange $40,000 to play the last three games of their season. Dr. Harry March of the Giants' front office said that the club would make an offer after Grange graduated, but had nothing on the table then.

Commenting on the story, Major John L. Griffith, head of the Big Ten, said that he hoped Grange would not turn pro. "Grange needs perfect, well-timed interference to enable him to get away on his thrilling runs and he will not get this in a professional game," Griffith said. "They will simply hand him the ball and say to Grange, 'There it is; now see what you can do.'" Griffith deprecated the professional game. "The college spirit is lacking in professional football," he said. "The players are not willing to risk injury just to enable an outstanding star to make a good showing."

The New York Giants were not the only team interested in Red Grange. Out in Illinois, wily George Halas had been watching the "Wheaton Iceman" (because Grange spent his summers lugging blocks of ice into homes in those pre-mechanical-refrigerator days). Halas had written to Grange without receiving a response; he had phoned him and got noncommittal replies.

In October 1925, a Chicago film distributor named Frank Zambrino told Halas that in Champaign there was a promoter and movie theater manager named Charles C. Pyle who was thinking of trying to manage Grange's post-college career. Would Halas be interested in talking with him if Pyle got Grange under his wing? Halas said that indeed he would.

A few days later, Red Grange and Earl Britton, the Illinois fullback, were watching comedian Harold Lloyd playing in *The Freshman* in Pyle's theater in Champaign when an usher asked Grange to go to the office and meet the manager. Grange complied, and when he walked into the office, Pyle said without any preliminary pleasantries, "Grange, how would you like to make a hundred thousand dollars?" Grange immediately suspected a bribe offer and demurred: "I don't do those things. You'll have to get someone else."

Pyle quickly explained that he had a legitimate offer to propose. Grange would join the Chicago Bears immediately after the last Illinois game at Ohio State. After playing in the remaining two games on the Bears' regular-season schedule, Grange and the Bears would begin a nationwide tour so that football fans all over the country could see the fabled Galloping Ghost.

Grange said it sounded good to him. No agreement was signed so that Grange's amateur standing would not be compromised for his one remaining college game, but on the strength of the star's interest in the proposal, Pyle arranged a visit with George Halas and Dutch Sternaman in Chicago.

They were impressed with the sweeping imagination of the dapper, suave promoter from Champaign. Their interest took wing as Pyle outlined his vision of a tour of the large eastern cities where fans would flock to see Red Grange and for a second, post-Christmas tour of the South and West.

Halas and Sternaman also discovered that Pyle was a hard bargainer. In his autobiography, Halas wrote:

> It was obvious all of us had to share earnings. I could not possibly make a cash offer. I had no idea how much the tour would bring in. I had no spare cash for an advance. I said I thought a two to one split would be about right.
>
> Pyle agreed, much to my surprise. Without a word, a single word. I anticipated at least some discussion. My astonishment may have stirred my generosity, because I then volunteered that the Bears would pay costs. "Of course," Pyle said. I said I hoped Grange would find the arrangements acceptable.
>
> "He will," Pyle said.
>
> A sense of uneasiness came over me. The negotiations had moved too easily. I thought I should begin again. "All right," I said, "it is agreed the Bears will get two-thirds and . . ."
>
> Pyle cut me short. He said, "Oh, no, George, Grange and I will get two-thirds. The Bears will get one-third."
>
> I said that was impossible. After I paid the players and the tour costs, I'd be lucky to break even.
>
> The sweetness went out of the discussions.

They haggled all through the night and into the next afternoon. Finally, Halas and Pyle agreed on a fifty–fifty split of the take, with the Bears paying all tour costs. "Pyle would provide Red. Red would provide the crowds. It was a fair arrangement," Halas concluded.

Red Grange ended his college career on a victorious note as Illinois beat Ohio State before 80,000 fans in Columbus on November 21. The press and public clamored to get at Grange to find out what he would do, but he managed to elude them by leaving the team's hotel via the freight elevator while wearing a black wig to cover his red hair and chewing on a big cigar. Grange took a train by himself to Chicago and checked into a hotel under an assumed name. The next morning, he met with Pyle, Halas, and Sternaman and signed a two-year contract with Pyle, making him his manager.

Finally, it was out. The press was told that Grange would play the last two games of the regular season with the Bears and then barnstorm the East. Grange declined to say how much he would earn. However, the terms called for a $2,000-a-game guarantee against a percentage of the gate for all games. The agreement called for Grange to get 60 percent and Pyle 40 percent of the earnings of the Red Grange/C. C. Pyle Company, with Pyle paying all business expenses out of his share.

It did not take long to demonstrate that the signing was a bonanza for Grange, the Chicago Bears, Pyle, and pro football generally. Grange was scheduled to make his first appearance for the Bears in a game on Thanksgiving Day against their crosstown rivals, the Cardinals. Normally a Bears–Cardinal game attracted a good gate—10,000 fans. Optimistically, the Bears had 20,000 tickets printed. The tickets went on sale on Monday, and within three hours they were gone. Another printing was ordered, and by game time at Cubs Park on Thanksgiving Day there was an overflow crowd of 39,000—the largest ever for a professional game—waiting eagerly for Red Grange's pro debut.

They did not see vintage Grange. The field was muddy, nullifying the Galloping Ghost's talent for changing direction to elude tacklers. He carried sixteen times from scrimmage, netting only 36 yards, and failed to complete any of six passes. Paddy Driscoll, the Cardinals' triple-threat halfback, mostly punted away from Grange to keep him from breaking out on one of his specialties—the punt return. The Chicago *Herald Examiner* reported:

> Driscoll's repeated refusal to risk punting to the Phantom Flier unquestionably saved his team from defeat. Three times during the contest, when it was absolutely unavoidable, Paddy kicked to Grange. Three times he saw "Red" run through his entire team for brilliant and spectacular runs of 25 yards each.
>
> Once he saw "Red" sweep through his entire team, with only himself remaining between "Red" and a touchdown. And Paddy succeeded in running "Red" out of bounds, but he had to reverse the field with him to turn the trick. That uncanny football brain gave Paddy the impulse that "Red" was going to reverse his field, and it saved the game for the Cardinals.
>
> Paddy deliberately refused to punt to Grange and was booed throughout the game by that football mad mob that came to see "Red" run.

There is a story, possibly apocryphal, that Driscoll thought the fans were booing Grange. The story goes that Driscoll asked his wife after the game, "Isn't it terrible the way people booed Red?" His wife replied, "Paddy, they were not booing Red. They were booing you for not giving Red a chance."

Grange, who got a black eye in the game, was quoted by the Associated Press as saying later, "I never played a more expert team of football players. I don't remember how I got the black eye, but I never saw a bit of intentional roughness, and I enjoyed my first professional game immensely."

Three days later, after a heavy snowstorm, 28,000 diehard Chicago fans went to Cubs Park to see Red Grange show his stuff. They were rewarded as Grange carried for 72 yards, returned a kickoff 28 yards, and caught a couple of passes as the Bears nipped the winless Columbus Tigers, 14 to 13.

C. C. Pyle (dubbed "Cash and Carry" by some sportswriters) obviously knew very little about the physical demands of football. He had booked a twelve-day tour of the East during which the Bears and Grange would play eight teams in eight different cities. (It was not uncommon at the time for a pro team to play twice a week, occasionally on two consecutive days. But eight games in twelve days—no.) George Halas and Dutch Sternaman must have agreed to that schedule with misgivings in their minds but dollar signs floating before their eyes.

The tour began in St. Louis three days after the game with Columbus. The St. Louis promoter had assembled a pickup team of semipros and NFL players. They played lambs to the Bears. Only 8,000 spectators braved the 12-degree temperature to see Grange score four touchdowns as the Bears won, 39 to 6. The following Saturday, Grange scored both touchdowns as the Bears beat the tough Frankford Yellow Jackets, 14 to 7, in Philadelphia's Shibe Park. The game, played in a drizzle, attracted 35,000 fans.

The next day came the real revelation. A crowd of 70,000 people jammed the Polo Grounds in New York to see Red Grange and the Bears tackle the New York Giants. It was by far the biggest crowd ever gathered for a professional football game. Nearly 100 reporters from eastern and midwestern newspapers were in the press box; usually the home team was lucky to have one local cub reporter on game coverage.

Grange ran for 53 yards in eleven tries from scrimmage on the muddy field, completed two out of three passes for a total gain of 32 yards, caught a pass for a 23-yard gain, and ran back an intercepted pass for 35 yards and a touchdown. The *New York Times* estimated that he had earned $30,000 for the game. The *Times*'s Allison Danzig had this to say about the significance of the game:

To call these 70,000 spectators football followers needs correction. There were thousands in that tremendous assemblage who probably never saw a game before, who did not have the slightest idea of what the proceedings were all about. They knew only that Grange was out there on the field among the twenty-two young warriors clad in moleskins and they watched to see what were the things he did and how he did them to differentiate him from the twenty-one others and win him such renown.

It is a point of pride with the men most concerned about the future of college football that it is the game of the colleges and for the colleges. It is the great college game, so they say. It was the game of America yesterday, calling to those who never saw a college campus as well as to those who have. And it was Red Grange who made it so.

The Giants game was the high point of the barnstorming tour, as well as a harbinger of the tremendous popularity of professional football in later decades. The Bears got Monday off to lick their wounds before taking an evening train to Washington, D.C., for a Tuesday game. Not one to miss a trick, Pyle stayed in New York to entertain commercial offers for use of Red Grange's name. In an afternoon of negotiations, the Red Grange/C. C. Pyle Company earned $13,000 from a sweater manufacturer, $10,000 from a doll maker, $5,000 each for endorsing shoes and ginger ale, and $2,500 from a cap manufacturer. Pyle declined to have Grange endorse cigarettes for $10,000 until it was agreed that Grange's blessing would read, "I don't smoke but my best friend smokes," according to George Halas. Pyle also approved a starring role in a movie for Grange with a fee of $50,000. Such commercial deals are believed to have netted Grange and Pyle $125,000.

In Washington, Grange and Halas were invited by an Illinois senator to call on President Calvin Coolidge, no sports fan. The senator introduced them: "Mr. President, this is George Halas and Red Grange of the Chicago Bears." According to Halas's account, Coolidge replied, "How are you, young gentlemen? I have always admired animal acts."

Washington's football fans stayed home in droves the next day after a snowfall. Only 8,000 turned out to see the Bears whip a pickup team called the Washington All-Stars, 19 to 0. The next day, the Bears were in Boston to meet the NFL's Providence Steam Roller. Grange, favoring a badly bruised arm that had been kicked in the New York game, gained only 18 yards as the Roller rolled, 9 to 6. The crowd of 25,000 booed Grange and the Bears lustily. The ordeal continued the next day in Pittsburgh, where another pickup team beat the battered Bears, 24 to 0, on another snow-covered field. Grange was in the game for only one play.

Two days later, the Bears were in Detroit to meet the NFL's Panthers. Halas had informed Detroit that Grange would not be able to play, since his arm was swollen to twice its normal size. Six thousand fans got refunds for their advance-sale tickets, and only 6,000 were on hand to see the Bears absorb another licking, 21 to 0. By this time, seven men besides Grange on the sixteen-man squad were injured. Halfback Milt Romney had a twisted ankle; halfback Laurie Wahlquist had a broken toe; fullback Dutch Sternaman had a shoulder injury; his brother Joey, who played quarterback, was suffering from a lame knee; and tackle Ed Healey and center George Trafton had leg injuries. Even coach and end George Halas was not immune; he had a boil on his neck.

Their ordeal was almost over. They returned home to Chicago after the defeat in Detroit and the next day were pummeled by the New York Giants, 9 to 0. It was a cold Sunday in mid-December. Grange suited up but was unable to do much to bring cheer to 18,000 shivering spectators at Cubs Park. Finally, relief. After eight games in twelve days, the Bears could relax for a few days before embarking on the southern and western tour.

Both C. C. Pyle and George Halas had learned lessons from the eastern tour. Pyle learned that you could not expect a football player—even Red Grange—to take hard knocks every day or every other day and function at top efficiency. Halas learned that he couldn't take a sixteen-man squad—the usual complement in the NFL—on a barnstorming tour and play games every day or every other day. So he added a half dozen players for the southern and western jaunt.

The second tour was moderately grueling, but it was a cakewalk compared with the eastern schedule. The Bears played nine games over a month's time. The opposing teams were, by and large, pickup squads that were not calculated to test Grange or the Bears very much. In a fairly leisurely trip in a special Pullman car, the Bears appeared in Coral Springs (a Miami suburb), Tampa, and Jacksonville; New Orleans; Los Angeles, San Diego, and San Francisco; Portland; and Seattle. They lost only in San Francisco to a team called the California Tigers. In Los Angeles, 75,000 spectators saw the game in the Coliseum, topping the previous pro game record in New York by 5,000.

The advent of Red Grange was a financial boon for the Bears. George Halas said that their gate receipts almost trebled, going from $116,500 in 1924 to $297,000 for the 1925 season. The Bears players other than Grange received their regular pay of $100 to $200 a game, but the extra games had doubled their annual wages. "Altogether our costs were $282,226.67," Halas reported in his autobiography. "Sternaman and I paid ourselves $2,600 in 1922 and 1923 and $5,800 in 1924. We raised our pay to $12,000 and gave each of us a $23,000 bonus. The Bears ended with our first worthwhile profit—$14,675.01. We declared our first dividend—$15,000."

Red Grange and C. C. Pyle did even better. Grange is estimated to have earned more than $200,000 from the gate receipts of the tours, plus all those juicy endorsement fees and movie loot.

The signing of Grange right after his last college game had several repercussions. For one thing, it made some college educators even more implacable foes of pro football than they had been. For another, it angered college coaches, who feared that their athletes would be tempted to go into pro football before their final college game.

Even before Grange played his first game with the Bears, both the Western Conference (Big Ten) and the Missouri Valley Conference ruled that anyone who had been connected with pro football as player, coach, official, manager, or agent could not be employed by member universities in any athletic position. "We wish to deal a death blow to professional football," W. G. Manley, faculty representative of the University of Missouri on the Missouri Valley Conference board, told the Associated Press. "While we feel that the professional game is on the decline and will die a natural death, we wish to be instrumental in hastening its demise."

As the Chicago Bears were recuperating from barnstorming in the East, Major John L. Griffith, Big Ten athletic director, denounced professional football and all its works. The Associated Press quoted him as saying, "Football will never become decadent through its spoilation by professionalism." Without mentioning Red Grange, Griffith said, "Most of the professional teams throughout the country were financially broke this year. Their managers grasped at the opportunity to build up the game professionally by obtaining college stars. They played them to extinction because of their greed for gate receipts.

"Everybody saw through the idea," Griffith continued. "The games were not sport; they were 'hippodromed' contests played simply for the money that the promoters would get out of them. Almost overnight, sentiment changed. I have watched these gestures with great interest. I saw sentiment for professional football sprout, bloom, wither, and now I believe it has died."

While the Bears were enjoying southern sunshine, the American Football Coaches Association, the college coaches' organization, cast out anyone who would have any association with the pros in the 1926 season. The resolution, introduced by Hugo Bezdek of Penn State, stated that "no person who actively associates himself in any capacity whatsoever with any professional football team after September 1, 1926, shall be eligible to membership in the A.F.C.A." (In later years, Bezkek evidently repented, because he was head coach of the NFL's Cleveland Rams in 1937 and 1938.)

The resolution, said the *New York Times,*

probably is the most drastic action yet taken against the professional game and undoubtedly means that the gauntlet has been thrown down by the coaches. While membership in the association is not itself essential to securing and holding coaching positions, the organization will no doubt receive full backing from most of the institutions throughout the country.

The NFL made an effort to turn away the wrath of the purists by adopting a rule in 1926 that no college man could be signed until his class graduated. George Halas, having enjoyed the services of Red Grange through the winter, gave his approval.

One of the more curious exhibits at the Pro Football Hall of Fame in Canton, Ohio, is a glistening, coal-black football bearing the legend "Pottsville Maroons, N.F.L. and World Champions 1925." The ball was carved from a chunk of anthracite and given to the Hall of Fame in 1964 by surviving members of the Pottsville club in the NFL's Year of Red Grange.

A fan who checks the league records for 1925 will find that the Pottsville Maroons are listed as having finished in second place behind the Chicago Cardinals. In fact, though, the Maroons had been suspended before the season ended and so technically were not even in the league at the end. Pottsville's fans believed that their team was cheated out of the championship, and even today you can start a hot barroom debate in that Pennsylvania coal-region town if you argue the negative.

Pottsville was a pleasant little blue-collar town of 25,000 in eastern Pennsylvania. Like several other towns in the mining area, it had fielded football teams since before World War I. By 1924 the manager, Dr. John G. Striegel, had a regional powerhouse. Clearly, he was paying major league salaries because one of his stars was Wilbur (Pete) Henry, a cherubic, roly-poly, 245-pound tackle who was cat-quick as a lineman and also perhaps the game's best punter and drop-kicker. (Henry was one of the first players chosen for the Hall of Fame in 1963.)

In the summer of 1925, Striegel applied for a franchise in the NFL. It was granted, despite the fact that Pottsville's Minersville Park was a high-school field with a small seating capacity. A factor in the acceptance may have been the fact that a traveling NFL team could play the Frankford Yellow Jackets in Philadelphia on Saturday (blue laws forbade Sunday football in Pennsylvania) and then run up to Pottsville for a Sunday game. Pottsville was also a Pennsylvania city, but it appears that the Schuylkill County district attorney simply ignored the blue laws without challenge by the commonwealth. Doug Costello, former editor of the *Pottsville Republican* and a Maroon's historian, asks rhetorically, "Who was going to tell anthracite miners that they can't have football on their one day off?"

The 1925 Pottsville Maroons were almost certainly the best team in the NFL. While their names do not resonate today, Maroons like Charlie Berry, a fine pass receiver and later a well-known major league baseball umpire; halfback Tony Latone, a punishing runner; veteran tackle Russ Hathaway; quarterback Jack Ernest; and the Stein brothers, Herb and Russ, a pair of tough linemen, were among the best in the game in 1925. They were coached by Dick Rauch, a Penn Stater who had been an assistant coach at Colgate. Because Striegel insisted that the players live in Pottsville during the season, Rauch had the advantage of leading practice every day, which was not the case with most NFL teams.

Joe Horrigan, Bob Braunwart, and Bob Carroll of the Professional Football Researchers Association have studied the argument that the Maroons were cheated out of their rightful NFL championship in 1925 and found it baseless, in part because of understandable confusion about how the league operated. By 1925, NFL team schedules were pretty well established when the season started—up to a point. For the 1925 season, schedules were set through Sunday, December 6, before the season started. By that time, it was expected that all league teams would have played at least the required eight games against eight different league teams to qualify for the championship race. Weak teams that were losing their shirts could close up shop. Teams with prospects of another good gate or two could continue to play through December 20, and games against league teams would count in the NFL race.

By the end of November, the Pottsville Maroons had won nine games and lost two. The Chicago Cardinals had nine victories, one defeat, and the scoreless tie with Red Grange and the Chicago Bears. Striegel of Pottsville and the Cardinals' manager, Chris O'Brien, scheduled a showdown for supremacy at Comiskey Park in Chicago for December 6.

Cold weather and a snowstorm in Chicago kept down the crowd for the big game, which was billed by Chicago newspapers as "for the championship." The Maroons dominated the Cardinals, winning 21 to 7 and, they thought, making them NFL champions. But O'Brien was aware that he could schedule more games and pass Pottsville's record by beating a couple of patsies. Then the Cards would stand at 11–2–1 to Pottsville's 10–2–1.

Meanwhile, the conquering Maroons went back east and scheduled a nonleague game at Shibe Park, in Philadelphia, with a team called the Notre Dame All-Stars. Among the All-Stars were the most glamorous old college stars after Red Grange, the Four Horsemen of Notre Dame: Harry Stuhldreher, Don Miller, Jim Crowley, and Elmer

Layden. They had been immortalized in their undefeated season of 1924 by Grantland Rice, the era's best sportswriter, who wrote the most famous lead paragraph in sports history:

> Outlined against a blue-gray October sky, the Four Horsemen rode again. In dramatic lore they are known as Famine, Pestilence, Destruction and Death. These are only aliases. Their real names are Stuhldreher, Miller, Crowley and Layden. They formed the crest of the South Bend cyclone before which another fighting Army football team was swept over the precipice at the Polo Grounds yesterday afternoon as 55,000 spectators peered down on the bewildering panorama spread on the green plain below.

Overwrought or not, that lead caught the fancy of sports fans everywhere and made them eager to see the Four Horsemen in the flesh. A game against them sounded like a good payday to Pottsville manager Striegel. Unfortunately for Pottsville, Philadelphia was recognized as Frankford Yellow Jacket territory by the NFL, which meant it was off limits to other NFL teams. League president Joe Carr warned Striegel at least three times to cancel the game against the Notre Dame All-Stars. Striegel went ahead with the game. The Maroons trimmed the All-Stars, 9 to 7, on a last-second field goal by Charlie Berry. An unexpectedly small crowd of 8,000 saw the game. Carr sent a telegram suspending Pottsville, fining the Maroons $500, and forfeiting the team franchise.

Meanwhile, in Chicago, the Cardinals' O'Brien was busily trying to pad his team's record with a couple of easy wins. His purpose appears to have been not so much to win the league championship as to make the Cardinals so attractive that George Halas would want his Bears with Red Grange to play them again. O'Brien had asked for only the standard guarantee, not a percentage of the gate, when the Cardinals played the Bears before 39,000 in Cubs Park, and he was anxious to redeem himself for his lack of foresight. This time he would share in the riches the Bears had been reaping with Grange.

His prospective victims, the Hammond Pros and the Milwaukee Badgers, had already disbanded for the season, but they agreed to play. The Milwaukee Badgers could not get most of their regulars back, so they assembled a makeshift lineup that included four high-school players and suffered a 59 to 0 pounding on December 10. Two days later, while Pottsville was beating the Notre Dame All-Stars in Philadelphia, the Hammond Pros, with most of their regulars on hand, put up a battle before succumbing to the Cardinals, 13 to 0. So the Cardinals had their 11–2–1 record, as O'Brien had hoped, but his scheming went for nothing. Grange had suffered his severe arm injury during the interim and was in no condition to play a game on the last possible day of the NFL season, December 20. O'Brien made no effort to schedule a lesser team for that day.

The Pottsville Maroons had been scheduled to play the Providence Steam Roller the day after their win over the Notre Dame All-Stars. Earlier, the Maroons had been edged by the Roller, 6 to 0 in Pottsville and then given them a drubbing in Providence, 34 to 0. Had they beaten the Steam Roller in the rubber match, the Maroons would have tied for the league title with the Cardinals. But, of course, Carr forbade the Steam Roller to host Pottsville, since the Maroons had been suspended by the league. Thus went their last opportunity for at least a share of the championship.

In the aftermath of the squabble, Carr learned about the use of the high-school players by the Milwaukee Badgers. He fined the Badgers $500; ordered their owner, Ambrose L. McGurk, to sell the club within ninety days; and barred him from any further connection with the NFL. At the same time, Carr banned Art Foltz, a Cardinal player who had recruited the high schoolers, for life. O'Brien, who seems not to have known about Milwaukee's use of high-school players, was nevertheless fined $1,000 and the Cardinals were placed on league probation for one year.

Striegel went to the league meeting in Detroit on February 6, 1926, to plead Pottsville's case. The owners heard him out and then approved Carr's action in ousting the Maroons from the NFL, effective December 12, 1925, when they had taken the field against the Notre Dame All-Stars. The Chicago Cardinals have been carried in NFL records as the 1925 champions ever since. Curiously, though, O'Brien told the owners at the February league meeting that they would not "accept" the title after the owners had voted it to them. The owners then tabled a second vote on the championship question, and never made it formal and official that the Cardinals were the 1925 champions.

In that eventful year of 1925, the NFL had twenty teams. One of them, the Chicago Cardinals, was a charter member and can trace its lineage to today after moving to St. Louis and later to Phoenix. Another, the Chicago Bears, began life in the NFL's inaugural season as the Decatur (Ill.) Staleys and did not take their present name until 1922. The Green Bay Packers had joined the league in 1921.

A fifth franchise in today's NFL, the New York Giants, was created in the year of Red Grange and, like the league as a whole, owes a great deal to him. His appearance against the Giants at the Polo Grounds doubtless saved the franchise.

The Giants were founded by Timothy J. Mara, a well-connected bookmaker, at a time when bookmaking was a legal occupation. Mara was a friend of Governor Al Smith and Jimmy Walker, soon to become New York City's mayor. He was also acquainted with sports figures, including Billy Gibson, manager of heavyweight fighter Gene Tunney.

National Football League president Joe Carr wanted to have a league team in New York and had been trying to interest Gibson in buying an NFL franchise for $500. Gibson didn't bite, but he suggested that Mara might be interested. And so, Mara paid $500 for the right to have a team in the six-year-old NFL. He is supposed to have said, "A New York franchise to operate anything ought to be worth $500."

Mara knew very little about football, but he had the good sense to hire people who did. His first head coach was Bob Folwell, an experienced hand at college coaching, most recently at Annapolis. He also knew that a gate attraction would help, so he hired the veteran Jim Thorpe. At thirty-eight years of age and with a growing drinking problem, Thorpe might not help the team on the field but might bring in the curious. As it turned out, Thorpe played only small parts in three games before leaving New York to return to the Rock Island Independents, with whom he had spent the 1924 season.

In the line, the Giants had All-Americans at tackle in Century Milstead of Yale and at center in Joe Alexander of Syracuse. In the backfield there were fullback Jack McBride of Syracuse and halfback Henry L. (Hinkey) Haines, who had starred at Penn State in 1919 and 1920. In the intervening years, Haines had played for the nonleague Philadelphia Quakers, the Frankford Yellow Jackets of 1923 (before they joined the NFL), and a semipro team in Shenandoah, a coal town in eastern Pennsylvania. In the summers, he played baseball and was in the big leagues in 1923 as a New York Yankee outfielder. He played in twenty-eight games and batted only .160. He was a swift, 5-foot, 10-inch, 168-pound halfback who was a threat to go all the way in an open field.

The city's blue laws against Sunday amusements were no longer a stumbling block in New York in 1925. The Giants and the Cleveland Bulldogs were charged with violating these laws after a Sunday game at the Polo Grounds. Dr. Harry March, the Giants' secretary, was summoned to a city court. Magistrate James Barrett dismissed the charges on the grounds that there was no evidence that the game disturbed the city's peace. "I attend the games myself, so I fail to see any basis for such charges," he said.

The Giants finished their first season in the NFL in fourth place, with a very respectable eight victories and four losses. Their balance sheet was much less respectable, however, until Red Grange came along. The Giants were an estimated $40,000 in the hole after their first ten games. The big turnout for Grange and the Chicago Bears at the Polo Grounds turned that situation around, and the Giants had a profit of about $18,000 at season's end.

Tim Mara had foreseen Red Grange's drawing power. At about the time Grange was getting ready to play his last college game against Ohio State, Mara hopped a train for Illinois to try to sign him for the Giants. He arrived too late; George Halas, C. C. Pyle, and Red Grange had already reached an agreement.

Mara sent home a cryptic telegram: "Partially successful STOP Returning on train tomorrow STOP Will explain STOP Tim Mara." His family was puzzled: What did "partially successful" mean? On his return, Mara told them, "He'll be playing in the Giants–Bears game at the Polo Grounds. Only he'll be playing for the Bears."

If Red Grange was the salvation of the New York Giants and a blessing for the Chicago Bears in 1925, he was something else again in 1926. Halas hoped that Grange would be with the Bears again, and Pyle told Halas that he would be glad to accommodate him—for one-third ownership of the Chicago Bears for the Red Grange/C. C. Pyle Company. Out of the question, Halas responded.

So Pyle, ever the opportunist, secured a lease for Yankee Stadium in New York and asked the NFL owners at their February meeting for a franchise. Mara naturally objected vehemently on the grounds that New York was Giants territory. He foresaw disaster for the Giants if Grange was showcased by another team in New York. Carr had established a precedent on territorial rights in 1925 when he suspended the Pottsville Maroons after they invaded Philadelphia, the Frankford Yellow Jackets' territory, for their exhibition against the Notre Dame All-Stars. That precedent held, and Pyle was turned down for a franchise in New York City.

Very well, Pyle said, we'll start our own league for the 1926 season. Characteristically, Pyle's plans were ambitious. By March, he had established W. H. (Big Bill) Edwards as president of the new American Football League (AFL). Edwards had been a Princeton football star during the last years of the nineteenth century and was in the insurance business. He had served as Commissioner of Street Cleaning in New York City and as Collector of Internal Revenue for the Treasury Department in the years after World War I when the income tax bite was minuscule.

Big Bill Edwards was an imposing figure who was dubbed the "czar" of pro football by the *Literary Digest*. "What Judge Landis is to professional baseball and Will Hays to the motion-picture industry in the United States, sports pages picture as the role of 'Big Bill' Edwards, new president of the American Professional Football League," the magazine reported.

The *Literary Digest* quoted Edwards as wanting to "help preserve high-class football as it is played at the colleges." The game, he said, is "a clean, red-blooded sport—a great character-builder—and it must retain these splendid qualities when played professionally."

Edwards promised that there would be no tampering with college players, who would not be eligible for the AFL until their class had graduated. He said that the league expected to have ten teams playing twice a week, starting right after baseball's World Series, for a total of fifteen games each.

It turned out to be a grandiose vision. The AFL had nine teams, only one of which played fifteen games. The teams were the Philadelphia Quakers; New York Yankees, with Red Grange; Cleveland Panthers; Chicago Bulls; Los Angeles Wildcats, a traveling team starring George (Wildcat) Wilson, All-American tailback from the University of Washington; Boston Bulldogs; Rock Island Independents, who had defected from the NFL; Brooklyn Horsemen, starring Harry Stuhldreher and Elmer Layden, two of the Four Horsemen; and Newark [N.J.] Bears. The AFL intended to challenge NFL teams in some of its biggest markets—not only New York, but Philadelphia and Chicago too. Several NFL veterans jumped to teams in the new league. The most significant defector was Joe Sternaman, Chicago Bears quarterback and brother of Dutch, George Halas's partner. Joey became owner, coach, and quarterback for the Chicago Bulls of the AFL.

The New York Yankees drew well with Red Grange as their poster boy, but the other AFL teams did poorly. One by one the weaker franchises folded, and only four teams—New York, Philadelphia, Chicago, and the peripatetic Los Angeles Wildcats—completed their schedules. The Philadelphia Quakers won the league title with a record of 8–2.

Mara issued a challenge to Pyle to have the Giants and Yankees, who finished 10–5 in the AFL, play a game for the championship of New York City. Terms could not be agreed on, so Mara offered to host the AFL champion Philadelphia Quakers at the Polo Grounds. A game was arranged for December 12, which turned out to be a cold, snowy day. Only 5,000 fans came out to watch the Giants, seventh-place finishers in the NFL, drub the Quakers, 31 to 0.

The AFL was a financial lemon. Even the New York Yankees lost money. It appeared that the magic of Red Grange had dissipated. But the failure of the new league was no boon to the NFL. The New York Giants lost $40,000 for the season in competition with the AFL's New York Yankees, Brooklyn Horsemen, and Newark Bears.

The Chicago Bears, who finished second to the Frankford Yellow Jackets in the NFL standings, were not doing much better. George Halas had strengthened his team by buying Paddy Driscoll for $3,500 from Chris O'Brien of the Chicago Cardinals, at least in part to keep

Driscoll from going to the Chicago Bulls in the AFL. Driscoll helped the Bears to a great start in the season. They opened with three victories and a tie on the road, but then returned home to Cubs Park and attracted fewer than 8,000 fans for a game with the New York Giants.

The following Sunday, the Bears were to play their archrivals, the Cardinals, at Cubs Park while Joey Sternaman's Bulls hosted Red Grange and the Yankees at Comiskey Park. The Bears won, 16 to 0, while the Bulls shut out the Yankees, 14 to 0. In this autobiography, Halas wrote:

> At both of the games, everyone, I am sure, had a good time. But I wasn't happy. Nor, I think, was Joey or even Cold Cash Pyle. Without Red, we drew 12,000. With Red, Joey drew 20,000. Put the two together and what do you have: 32,000. A year earlier, before Grange, we would have been astounded at such a turnout. But coming after the winter tour, 32,000 was dismal for the biggest professional football day Chicago ever had, and perhaps ever would have.
>
> It was the same everywhere. We were back to the small gates, the hard grind, the search for fans, the pinching of the penny. The Maras learned the Red Grange euphoria had vanished. The Giants drew only 3,000 or 4,000. Mara would look through binoculars at Yankee Stadium and say, "There's no one over there, either."

Frankford won the NFL's 1926 championship in a tight race with the Bears and the Pottsville Maroons, who had been invited back into the league to keep them from joining the AFL. Coached by an old Canton Bulldog hero, Guy Chamberlin, the Yellow Jackets finished at 14–1–1, the Bears at 12–1–3, and the Maroons at 10–2–1. But the eighth-place Duluth Eskimos attracted more attention than the league leaders.

Duluth, Minnesota, had had a franchise in the NFL since 1923. The team was called the Kelley-Duluths for a local hardware store. Most of their games were with nearby town teams in the iron-ore range, but they usually managed to schedule four to seven games with NFL opponents, mostly as visitors. Money was tight, though, and to get rid of a sinking franchise the owners gave it to their volunteer secretary-treasurer, Ole Haugsrud.

Haugsrud had been a high-school classmate in Superior, Wisconsin, of Ernie Nevers, the most glamorous player to come out of college football in 1926. Nevers was a triple-threat fullback at Stanford University who not only ran, passed, and punted but also place-kicked and called the signals. He won the heart of football fans everywhere at the Rose Bowl game on January 1, 1925, when he played a stalwart game on two recently healed broken legs against Notre Dame's Four Horsemen. His Stanford coach, Pop Warner, who had also coached

Jim Thorpe, called Nevers the better player because he had more competitive spirit.

During the summer of 1926, while the NFL owners were contemplating with dread the depredations of C. C. Pyle, who had already signed up Red Grange and two of the Four Horsemen for his AFL, Pyle hinted that he had lined up Ernie Nevers too. Ole Haugsrud was doubtful.

He visited Nevers in St. Louis, where Nevers was a rookie pitcher for the St. Louis Browns in the American League. (Nevers, a right hander, pitched for three years for the Browns, winning six and losing twelve; he gave up two of Babe Ruth's sixty home runs in 1927.) Haugsrud had guessed right; Nevers had not signed with Pyle and said that he would play for Duluth if Haugsrud could match Pyle's offer of $15,000, plus a percentage of the larger gates.

On the strength of that commitment, Haugsrud had no trouble lining up a full schedule of games with NFL teams, plus enough exhibition games to keep the Eskimos on the move from September 6 to February 5. The team, which usually was called the Ernie Nevers Eskimos, played only one league game at home in Duluth as it compiled a 6–5–3 record in the NFL. The Eskimos also had fifteen exhibitions, for a total of twenty-nine games. Nevers handled the ball on virtually every play because the coach, Dewey Scanlon, installed Pop Warner's double wing offense, in which the fullback usually received the snap. The Eskimos had several Duluth-area players, but they were more than just a town team; also on the roster were future Hall of Famers halfback Johnny (Blood) McNally and guard Walt Kiesling.

Ernie Nevers was not the box-office attraction that Red Grange had been in 1925, but his presence did add thousands of spectators to games with lackluster teams and thousands of dollars to anemic balance sheets throughout the league. He played all but twenty-nine minutes in the Eskimos' fourteen league games, displaying the endurance that led sportswriter Grantland Rice to dub the Eskimos the "Ironmen of the North."

The 1926 season proved to be the AFL's first and last, as well as a financial trial for the NFL. Of the AFL teams, only the New York Yankees with Red Grange survived the debacle and were given an NFL franchise in 1927—C. C. Pyle's goal all along. But Pyle got his franchise at the sufferance of Tim Mara of the New York Giants. Mara had acquired the franchise of the defunct Brooklyn Lions by paying off their debts, and he leased it to Pyle and Grange on the condition that the Yankees play most of their games on the road. As a result, the Yanks were at home in Yankee Stadium for only four of their sixteen NFL games. The Duluth Eskimos, again starring Nevers, spent the whole season on the road. They won only one NFL game in nine tries, despite heroics by Nevers.

Grange's Yankees did better, finishing sixth in the NFL with a 7–8–1 record. But in their fourth game, a 12 to 0 loss to the Chicago Bears at Wrigley Field, Grange was tackled from the side by Bears center George Trafton and suffered a severe knee injury. He was on crutches for a couple of weeks and missed only three games, but it was the end of his brilliance as a broken-field runner. "I was just an ordinary back after that, the moves were gone forever," Grange told Richard Whittingham for his book, *What a Game They Played.* "In other words, I became a straight runner, one who doesn't try to get away from tacklers but instead opts to run into them. And even if a player's knee gets well, he never gets well up in the head."

In the spring of 1927, the NFL owners addressed the problem of weak franchises and decided to reduce the circuit by getting rid of them. The result was the eviction of ten franchises, including the charter member Canton Bulldogs, Akron Indians, Hammond Pros, and Columbus Tigers, the successors of the old Panhandles. With the addition of the Yankees and the Cleveland Bulldogs, who had been the Kansas City Cowboys the previous year, the 1927 NFL had twelve teams. The New York Giants took the championship, with a record of 11–1–1. In Cleveland, the new Bulldogs, who finished fourth, were giving the league a preview of things to come in the passing of tailback Benny Friedman, a 5-foot, 10-inch, 185-pound All-American who had starred for three years on Fielding Yost's University of Michigan powerhouse teams. Said Yost, "In Benny Friedman I have one of the greatest passers and smartest quarterbacks in history. He never makes a mistake, and as for football brains, it's like having a coach on the field."

As a rookie professional, Friedman thought nothing of passing on first down (gasp!), which was heresy to traditionalists. In thirteen games, he tossed twelve touchdown passes and gained more than 1,700 yards with passes—far higher figures than the league had ever seen. It was a revelation to football men, who could not believe that the fat ball of the time could be passed so successfully.

Friedman said later that he had earned $22,000 for the year, including five exhibitions on the West Coast after the regular season. That figure probably would have made him the highest-paid professional football player, even including Red Grange.

A rule change moved the goal posts from the goal line to the end zone's rear line. The result was a sharp drop in successful field goal tries and points after touchdown. In 1926 the average NFL team had scored about three field goals for the whole season. In 1927 that number dropped to a bit less than two.

Taking a lesson from Friedman, the NFL teams passed more often in 1928, but the champion Providence Steam Roller won with defense rather than a passing attack. The Roller scored only five touchdowns by air in eleven league games, but they gave up only 42 points while totaling 128 themselves. The coach-quarterback was Jimmy Conzelman, a 6-foot, 180-pound veteran who had begun his NFL career in 1920 with George Halas's Decatur Staleys and had played for the Rock Island, Milwaukee, and Detroit NFL teams before arriving in Providence. The tailback in the Steam Roller's single wing was George (Wildcat) Wilson, the old University of Washington star who had played for the wandering Los Angeles Wildcats in the year of Red Grange.

The Steam Roller's home field was by all odds the strangest venue in NFL history. It was the Providence Cyclodrome, a bicycle-racing track built in 1925 that could seat 10,000. The spectators were in bleachers that rimmed the banked wooden bicycling track. The oval track was flat on the straightaways and sharply banked around the turns. A football field fit inside the oval—well, almost inside. One end zone was inside, but the other was shorter on the sides because the oval turn began just 5 yards past the goal line. Spectators' seats were directly along the sidelines, so that a player who was tackled near the boundary would wind up in fans' laps.

The home team dressed in a tiny room meant for two bicycle racers. It had two showers and two lockers, which had to serve the eighteen-man Steam Roller squad. The visitors had it even worse. They had to dress at their hotel and return in uniform after the game to clean up.

The Cyclodrome was a cozy place for both players and fans. There was not a bad seat in the house. From its opening in 1925 until the collapse of the Steam Roller franchise in the Depression year of 1931, the Cyclodrome was its home base. It was not, however, the scene of the NFL's first night game, which was played in Providence on November 6, 1929. That game, between the Steam Roller and the Chicago Cardinals, was played at Kinsley Park, Providence's minor league baseball stadium. Ernie Nevers, the former Duluth Eskimo, was in his first year with the Cardinals, and naturally he was the star of the game. He ran for one touchdown, passed for another, and kicked a field goal as the Cardinals shut out the Steam Roller, 16 to 0. The lights were floodlights about 20 feet above field level. The game ball was painted white and, said the *Providence Journal,* "looked like a huge egg."

That game was played just a week after the stock market crashed on October 29, ending a post–World War I period of prosperity that has been dubbed variously the Jazz Age and the Golden Age of Sports. The crash brought on the Great Depression, with plummeting property values and massive unemployment. At the Depression's depths in 1932, a quarter of the nation's workers were unemployed and home foreclosures were epidemic.

Like most other enterprises, professional football suffered. Many blue-collar fans—pro football's natural constituency at a time when well-educated, more affluent folks followed college football—did not have 50 cents for a game ticket. At the end of the 1928 season, even before the Depression started, the Pottsville Maroons, New York Yankees, Detroit Wolverines with Benny Friedman, and Duluth Eskimos called it quits. In 1929 the Boston Bulldogs (made up largely of the old Pottsville Maroons), Buffalo Bisons, and Dayton Triangle disbanded. The 1930 casualties were the Minneapolis Red Jackets and Newark Tornadoes. In 1931 the Providence Steam Roller, the first-year Cleveland Indians, and the Frankford Yellow Jackets folded. The Yellow Jackets didn't even last to the end of the season; they quit on November 10.

Amid the financial bloodbath of the Depression, the first NFL dynasty developed, if "dynasty" is not too strong a word for a team that wins three straight titles. It was the Green Bay Packers, whose championship teams of 1929, 1930, and 1931 no doubt saved the franchise for the city of 37,500 on Green Bay, an inlet of Lake Michigan. Slim gates and balance sheets splashed with red ink during the Depression years doomed the NFL teams in all other small cities.

The Packers had been a solid team ever since they joined the NFL in 1921, always finishing in the top half of the standings. Tailback Verne Lewellen, a five-year veteran from Nebraska, provided scoring punch and was the league's best punter. Other stars included end Lavie Dilweg; blocking back Red Dunn; fullback Bo Molenda, who came to Green Bay from the New York Yankees; and Jug Earp, a veteran center from Monmouth College. For the 1929 season, coach Curly Lambeau signed three veterans who soon were the best in the league at their position. One was Cal Hubbard, a 6-foot, 4-inch tackle who came from the New York Giants and later was a highly regarded baseball umpire. Another was Mike Michalske, a strong guard who had spent two seasons with the New York Yankees after starring at Penn State. The third was a fabled character named John V. McNally, aka John Blood, who had been a four-sport letterman at St. John's University in Collegeville, Minnesota. He had also played freshman football at Notre Dame.

Blood was a free spirit with a taste for booze but not much success in handling it well, a roisterer after a game who was known for buying the attentions of all the women in a brothel and spending the night in conversation with them. Once when the Packers were aboard a train, Blood enraged a teammate with his gibes. The teammate, a big, strong end, chased Blood through the cars to the platform on the rear car, whereupon Blood climbed to the top of the car and ran to the front of the train, leaping across the precarious chasms between cars until he got to the locomotive. The end, having the good sense not to continue the chase, went back to the Packers' car. Blood had a pleasant conversation with the engineer and fireman while his teammate simmered in silence.

But Johnny Blood was more than a flake. He was also a fleet broken-field runner and probably the best pass receiver in pro football until Don Hutson arrived in Green Bay in 1935.

McNally chose the name by which he is generally known. While he was working as a stereotyper on a newspaper in Minneapolis, he and a fellow worker planned to try out for a semipro football team named the East 26th Street Liberties. They decided to use assumed names, since both thought they might have some college eligibility left. As they rode to the field on McNally's motorcycle, they passed a movie theater where *Blood and Sand*, starring heartthrob Rudolph Valentino, was playing. McNally told his friend, "I'll be Blood and you be Sand." Ever after, John V. McNally was Johnny Blood. Before arriving in Green Bay, the 6-foot, 1-inch, 187-pound Blood had played for four years in the NFL with the Milwaukee Badgers, Duluth Eskimos, and Pottsville Maroons.

The Green Bay Packers breezed through their NFL schedule, winning twelve, losing none, and playing a scoreless tie with the Frankford Yellow Jackets. They gave up only three touchdowns in the thirteen games. The New York Giants were hot on the Packers' heels, with a record of 13–1–1. Their only loss was a 20 to 6 whipping by the Packers. Tim Mara had bought the failing Detroit Wolverines' franchise, primarily to get Benny Friedman for the Giants. Friedman's twenty touchdown passes in fifteen NFL games that season were not surpassed until 1942, when Cecil Isbell threw for twenty-four touchdowns in eleven games for the Green Bay Packers.

The 1929 championship brought delirium to Green Bay. Packer historian Chuck Johnson writes that when the Packers' train was arriving home after the final victory in Chicago,

> five miles from the depot, rooters lighted the train's way in by burning fuses. Soldiers and policemen ran interference for the engine, permitting the train to reach the station platform. Signs and banners of gold and blue were waved aloft, proclaiming "Welcome, Packers" and "Hail Champions." An automobile parade took the Packers to city hall where Mayor John V. Diener presented keys to the city to Lambeau and the players.

The following year, the Packers edged the New York Giants again for the NFL title. Their record was 10–3–1, while the Giants finished 13–4. What may have been the most important game of the season did not involve Green Bay. It was a game for charity that pitted the New York Giants against the Notre Dame All-Stars, including the Four Horsemen and several more recent alumni, coached by Knute Rockne, at that time the most famous coach in the land. The game, at New York City's Polo Grounds, was suggested by Giants' owner Tim Mara to his friend Mayor Jimmy Walker, to aid the city's Unemployment Fund for the Needy. A crowd of 55,000 turned out on a cold December day to see the Giants demolish the old Fighting Irish, 22 to 0. The game raised $115,153 for the unemployed. It also demonstrated to sportswriters and diehard fans of college football that a team of old college stars was no match for a pro team and that the professionals were not just a bunch of undisciplined toughs.

The 1930 season was also notable for the appearance in the NFL of the last small-city franchise (other than Green Bay). It was the Portsmouth Spartans, one more product of a rivalry between two towns. In this case, the rivalry was between Portsmouth and Ironton—both industrial cities on the Ohio River in southern Ohio. Portsmouth had a population in 1930 of 42,000; Ironton, 16,600. During the 1920s, the Ironton Tanks, a semipro team, was consistently one of the strongest teams in Ohio, including NFL teams. The chief reason was that many Tanks players were assured of year-round work if they were trained as teachers. Glenn Presnell, an All-American tailback at Nebraska, was quoted by Richard Whittingham in *What a Game They Played* on why he joined the Tanks in 1928:

> They tried to get players who had earned teaching certificates in college who could teach in the local school system. We had a squad of about twenty-two players, and about sixteen of us taught in the school system in the county there. The reason I took them up on it was because they insured me a job teaching science at Ironton High School and another playing for the football team, the Tanks. The two jobs offered me more money than I would have gotten if I played with one of the NFL teams. The New York Giants had offered me a contract, so did the Providence Steam Rollers and the Kansas City Cowboys and several others, but none came near the amount of money I could make in Ironton with the two jobs.

The Ironton Tanks peaked in 1930, their last year, under coach Earl (Greasy) Neale, when they edged the New York Giants, 13 to 12, and whipped the Chicago Bears, 26 to 13. But they lost twice to their archrivals, the Portsmouth Spartans, who were in their first year in the NFL. (The franchise was moved to Detroit and became the Lions in 1934.)

The Portsmouth Spartans tied for seventh place in the NFL in 1930, with a record of 5–6–3. That was not good enough in the estimation of the Portsmouth National League Football Corporation, which owned the franchise. George (Potsy) Clark, head coach at Butler University, was brought in to coach the Spartans. He quickly established a reputation as a disciplinarian and an advocate of physical conditioning. Clark cleaned house in the roster, dumping all but six veterans from the 1930 team and bringing in several players from the recently disbanded Ironton Tanks. One of them was Glenn Pressnell. Five rookie stars were also added, including Earl (Dutch) Clark, a 6-foot, 183-pound All-American tailback from Colorado College.

The revamped Portsmouth Spartans battled the league's other small-city team, the Green Bay Packers, for the NFL title in 1931. The Packers won it, with a 12–2 mark as against the Spartans, 11–3, but not without a dispute. The Spartans contended that Green Bay had welshed on a game scheduled between the two teams at Portsmouth on December 13. Green Bay argued that the game had been only tentatively scheduled, so they were free to cancel it, which would have given Portsmouth a chance to tie for first place. National Football League president Joe Carr accepted the Green Bay argument, giving the Packers their third straight championship.

The Packers' string ended in 1932, but only because of the vagaries of the league's system of deciding championships by percentage. The final regular-season standings of the top three of the eight league teams are presented in the following table:

	W	L	T	Percentage
Chicago Bears	6	1	6	.857
Portsmouth Spartans	6	1	4	.857
Green Bay Packers	10	3	1	.769

At the time, ties were not counted in figuring percentages. Ties are rare today, but if they occur, they are counted as half a win and half a loss. Today the Packers would have been champions.

The Bears and the Spartans were scheduled for a playoff game at Wrigley Field in Chicago a week after the regular season finale on December 11. Chicago in mid-December is not just the Windy City, but usually the cold and snowy Windy City. That was the case in 1932. The temperature hovered around zero most of the week, and snow fell intermittently through Friday. Bears owner George Halas asked approval from NFL president Joe Carr to play the game indoors in Chicago Stadium, home of the Chicago Black Hawks of the National Hockey League. The Bears had tried it for an exhibition game in 1930 and found the stadium satisfactory, though limiting. Carr gave his approval.

From goal line to goal line, the indoor field was only 60 yards long.

The oval shape of the playing area made the end zones half moons rather than rectangles, and the field was only 45 yards wide, about 10 yards short of regulation. A circus had just completed a run at the stadium, so there was a 6-inch layer of dirt—rather aromatic from elephant and horse droppings—on the field. Some special rules were made for the odd venue. Goal posts were moved to the goal line, but they were only for points after touchdowns; no field goals were permitted. Kickoffs had to be made from the 10-yard line, and touchbacks were returned to the 10- instead of the 20-yard line. Each sideline was bordered by a solid fence just a few feet from the line, so it was decided that if the ball went out of bounds, it would be brought in 10 yards from the sideline at the cost of a down. (At the time, the rules called for starting the next play at the sideline.)

Some 11,000 fans turned out for the playoff game—probably 10,000 more than would have appeared in the icebox of Wrigley Field. They saw a tough defensive battle that was decided on a disputed play in the fourth quarter. The Bears were on the 2-yard line with fourth down coming up, and everyone expected them to send Bronislau (Bronko) Nagurski, their all-NFL fullback, smashing into the line. Quarterback Carl Brumbaugh handed off to the Bronk, and he started forward. But then he stopped and backpedaled a few steps before lobbing a pass to Red Grange in the end zone.

Portsmouth coach Potsy Clark protested vehemently that Nagurski had not been 5 yards behind the line of scrimmage when he threw the pass, as the rules required. It was a judgment call by the referee that Nagurski's pass was legal. The extra point was kicked, and in the waning moments the Spartans fumbled the ball out of the end zone for a safety, so the final score was Bears, 9; Spartans, 0.

The playoff game—the first ever in the NFL—helped to usher in a new era for the pro game.

Slingin' Sammy Baugh, Washington Redskins quarterback from 1937 to
1952, sets up against the Chicago Bears for one of his rifled passes. Baugh
was the most famous—and successful—passer in the pre-television era of
pro football. Baugh was also a fine punter and still holds the records
for single season average (51.3 yards) and lifetime average (44.9 yards).
(AP/World Wide Photos)

Advertisment in the *Foot Ball Rules and Referee's Book* of 1888.

What the well-dressed football player wore in the early 1890's. Helmets had not yet appeared, and A. G. Spalding & Bros. advertised skullcaps as protection for the ears and hair. Shoes were high-tops with small, screw-in cleats. There were no shoulder pads, but jackets of heavy canvas may have been better than nothing. Pants were canvas too, and padded. The best quality jackets and pants were made of moleskin, a strong cotton fabric. Players with tender noses could buy a nose guard for $2.50.

Harvard's flying wedge, the most fearsome of the mass momentum plays, attacking the Yale defenders in 1892. *(Courtesy of Harvard University)*

Yale's flying wedge from scrimmage in 1893. The formation was legal because no set number of players was required to be at the line of scrimmage. The center handed the ball back to the quarterback, who could not run with it. He either handed off or lateraled to another back. *(Courtesy of Yale Athletic Department Archives)*

Pudge Heffelfinger, the first certifiable profes-
sional football player, in his uniform as a Yale
All-American. *(Courtesy of Yale Athletic
Department Archives)*

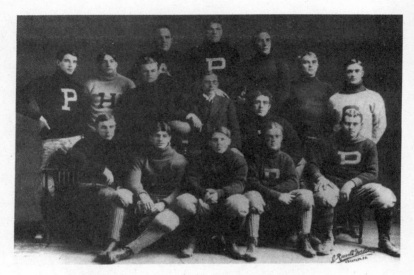

The Franklin [Pa.] All-Stars of 1903, the last western Pennsylvania power-house in the early days. From left, front row: B. D. Sutter, Paul Steinberg, Lynn D. Sweet, Jack Hayden, H. A. (Bull) Davidson. Middle row: W. J. McConnell, Dave Printz (manager), John Lang. Top row: Clark Schrontz, W. P. McNulty, Arthur L. McFarland, Herman Kirkoff, John A. Matthews, Charles E. Wallace, Chal Brennan. *(Courtesy of Carolee Michener)*

Jim Thorpe, the most famous and versatile athlete immediately before and after World War I, shows his drop-kicking form. The photo was taken in 1921 during a game between the Cleveland Tigers, coached by Thorpe, and the New York Brickley's Giants. Thorpe usually wore a flimsy helmet, not the cap he has on here. *(The Bettmann Archive)*

1920 STALEY TEAM

The Decatur Staleys, second-place finishers in the first year of the National Football League (then called the American Professional Football Association). Two years later, they were renamed the Chicago Bears. At center in the front row is coach George Halas, longtime owner and coach of the Bears. His partner in running the team, Dutch Sternaman, a halfback, is second from the right in the top row. Next to him is quarterback Charlie Dressen, who made a name as a big-league baseball player and manager. At left in the front row is Hall of Fame center George Trafton.
(Courtesy of A. E. Staley Manufacturing)

Fritz Pollard, the 150-pound tailback for the Akron Pros, champions of the first National Football League season in 1920. He had been an All-American at Brown University and was the league's first black star.
(Courtesy of Brown University)

Top-of-the-line protective equipment when the National Football League was born. Helmets, usually called "head harnesses," were of felt-padded leather and had a suspension system with a web of fabric straps that helped absorb the force of a blow. Felt-padded shoulder pads cut down on shoulder and collar-bone fractures. Pants were made of either canvas or coarse cotton and were padded with hair or felt.

Joseph F. Carr, who suc-
ceeded Jim Thorpe in 1921
as president of the
National Football League
(then called the American
Professional Football
Association). He served as
president until his death
in 1938 and was largely
responsible for the NFL's
steady progress in its adolescence. *(Courtesy of
Basketball Hall of Fame)*

Red Grange, pro football's
first superstar, and Bronko
Nagurski as his blocker
provided the big punch for
the Chicago Bears in 1930.
Nagurski was a punishing
fullback and a fine line-
backer for the Bears from
1930 through 1937. In
1943, a war year, he
returned to play tackle
for the Bears. *(AP/Wide
World Photos)*

Don Hutson, Green Bay Packers end, receives a pass behind the pursuing Howie Livingston of the New York Giants. Hutson virtually invented the position of wide receiver during the 1930s and 1940s. *(UPI/Bettmann)*

Chicago Bears fullback Bill Osmanski sweeps left end on a reverse for a 68-yard touchdown on the second play of the 1940 NFL title game against the Washington Redskins. The Bears rolled on after that, shellacking the Skins, 73 to 0, in the first pro game on a national radio network. *(AP/Wide World Photos)*

The Cleveland Browns whoop it up after winning their third championship in the All-America Football Conference in 1948. At center, wearing a hat, is coach Paul Brown, shaking hands with owner Arthur (Mickey) McBride. Quarterback Otto Graham, at left rear, has his arm extended. In front of him is tackle-kicker Lou Groza. End Mac Speedie is at Groza's right. Fullback Marion Motley kneels in front of Paul Brown, and end Dante Lavelli grins broadly at extreme right. Over the next decade, the Browns were the dominant team in pro football. *(UPI/Bettmann)*

Paul Brown, of the Cleveland Browns, was the first head
coach to bring scientific methods to coaching and the
first with a staff of full-time assistants. *(UPI/Bettmann)*

Duke Slater, an All-American tackle at Iowa, had the longest tenure of any black player in the NFL during its early years. He played from 1922 through 1931. *(Courtesy of University of Iowa)*

Joe Lillard, carrying the ball for the Chicago Cardinals with Red Grange (77) of the crosstown Bears in pursuit, was one of only two black players in the NFL in 1933. The other Bear in pursuit is unidentified, but may be Hall of fame end Bill Hewitt, who played without a helmet. After 1933, there were no black players in the league until 1946. *(HOF/NFL Photos)*

Above: Marion Motley, carrying the
ball, and guard Bill Willis (right) of
the Cleveland Browns were the first
black players in the All-America
Football Conference.
(AP/Wide World Photos)

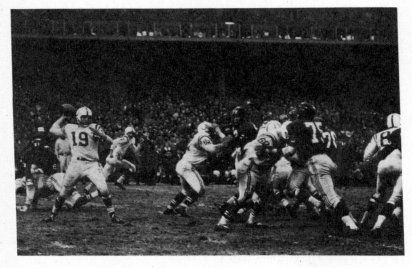

Johnny Unitas, Baltimore Colts quarterback, passing against the New York
Giants in the 1958 NFL title game. *(Hy Peskin/NFL Photos)*

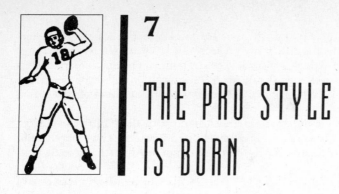

7

THE PRO STYLE IS BORN

During its first forty-odd years, professional football was the raggedy stepchild of the glamorous college game. The pros took their cues about the rules and how to play the game from the college authorities. The major collegiate football powers were far better known and more popular than the top pro teams well into the 1930s, outdrawing the pros in their own localities by five to one.

Harbingers of change appeared in 1933. For the first time, the NFL adopted rules designed to make the pro game more exciting by encouraging forward passing and more field goals in the hope of increasing scoring and reducing the number of ties. The rule changes were introduced because of the lessons of the 1932 playoff game between the Chicago Bears and the Portsmouth Spartans and also because of the peculiar final standings, which saw the Bears winning the championship with only seven victories in fourteen games. (Chicago's final 1932 mark was 7–1–6.)

Undoubtedly, the most important rule change for 1933 resulted from the disputed touchdown pass from Bronko Nagurski to Red Grange that gave the Bears the 1932 title. The hassle led naturally to a question: Why not let passes be thrown from anywhere behind the line of scrimmage? Why not, indeed? The change opened up the game because it allowed for much greater deception in the backfield.

The idea of putting the ball in play 10 yards from the sideline when a play ended within 5 yards of the line or the ball went out of bounds, as was done in the 1932 title game because of the limitations of the Chicago Stadium field, was made a permanent part of the rules. (The college rules were also changed in 1933 to provide for hash marks, so the pros may just have gone along with the intercollegiate rules on that one.) The goal posts, which had been placed at the back of the end zone since 1927, were moved to the goal line in 1933, making field goals and extra point kicks easier. In the 1932 season, only six field goals had been kicked by the NFL's eight teams; in 1933, with ten teams, kickers were successful on thirty-six field goal attempts. The increase in scoring also had the welcome result of decreasing the number of tie games from ten in 1932 to five in 1933, even with the addition of two teams to the NFL.

Another change that enhanced interest in the NFL was splitting the league into two divisions: Eastern and Western. Thus there would be two title races and the need for a championship game to settle matters every year.

Not surprisingly, George Halas of the Chicago Bears was one of the owners advocating the changes. Another was a newcomer to the owners' ranks, George Preston Marshall. He had become part owner of the new Boston Braves in 1932 and sole owner after the Braves ended the season with a loss of $46,000. The Braves had adopted the name of Boston's National League baseball club (now the Atlanta Braves) and had played at Braves Field in 1932. Marshall renamed the team the Redskins and leased the Red Sox's Fenway Park as home grounds in 1933. The team was moved to Washington, D.C., in 1937, when Marshall decided that Bostonians were not turning out in sufficient numbers to see the Redskins play.

Marshall strongly believed that showmanship was necessary for pro football. For the opening game in 1933, the Boston Redskins wore Indian war paint, and in publicity photos they also had Native American headdresses. Their coach was Lone Star Dietz, a real Native American, who had played at the Carlisle Indian School. There is no record that either Dietz or any spectator decried the charade. Later, in Washington, Marshall had a 110-piece Redskins' band decked out in fancy Indian costumes and headdresses to entertain at halftime. There was also a smaller jazz band with a glee club.

The Washington Redskins' band made some trips with the team. Their rooters were encouraged to sing "Hail to the Redskins," with a tune by Washington society bandleader Barnee Breeskin and lyrics by Marshall's wife, movie actress Corinne Griffith. The lyrics ran:

> Hail to the Redskins, hail vic-to-ry,
> Braves on the warpath, fight for old D.C.
> Scalp 'em, swamp 'em. We will take 'em big score.
> Read 'em, weep 'em. Touchdown we want heap more.
>
> Fight on. Fight on till you have won.
> Sons of Wash-ing-ton (Rah! Rah! Rah!)
> Hail to the Redskins, hail vic-to-ry.
> Braves on the warpath. Fight for old D.C.

Time reported that when the Redskins visited New York City for a game to decide the Eastern Division championship in December 1938, 10,000 of their fans marched up Broadway behind the Redskins' band, singing "Hail to the Redskins" with fervor. (Their enthusiasm did not help the 'Skins, who were drubbed by the Giants, 38 to 0.)

The Redskins' band was not the first for an NFL team. The Green Bay Packers had the Packer Band (first called the Lumberjacket Band) as early as 1921. Green Bay fans of the 1930s also had a fight song called "Roll on Packers!" extolling the merits of fullback Bo Molenda, halfback Johnny Blood, and quarterback Red Dunn.

Marshall had inherited a large laundry in Washington at the age of twenty-two and made it even bigger by splashing the slogan "Long Live Linen" all over the capital city. The Boston Redskins were not Marshall's introduction to sports. In 1925, he had sponsored the Washington Palace Five in the American Basketball League, the first attempt to establish a professional basketball league in major cities of the Northeast and Midwest. (George Halas's Chicago Bruins were also members.)

Marshall is generally credited with the idea of splitting the NFL into Eastern and Western Divisions to create a title game at the end of the season. At Marshall's death in 1969, NFL commissioner Pete Rozelle said of him: "Pro football today does in many ways reflect his personality. It has his imagination, style, zest, dedication, openness, brashness, strength and courage."

Such generous praise for Marshall was not universal. Shirley Povich, long-time *Washington Post* sports columnist, feuded with the Redskins owner for many years. "Marshall was easy to dislike," Povich wrote. "He bullied many people. He bragged about being big-league, but he deprived his players of travel comforts to save expenses while reaping huge profits." Later, Paul Brown, founder and coach of the Cleveland Browns, tangled with Marshall at merger meetings when the All-America Football Conference's best teams were being absorbed by the NFL. "He was obnoxious," Brown wrote in his autobiography. "He insulted your intelligence and had a great habit of sleeping most of the day and showing up at the meetings late in the afternoon. . . . By that time all of us were pretty tired and ready to adjourn, but he was rested and mentally sharp. That was when he tried to work some of his little deals."

Marshall was not a favorite of his coaches or players either. End Flavio Tosi, a star at Boston College who joined the Boston Redskins in 1934, remembers: "He would move right into the locker room and criticize the coach, criticize the ballplayers. He threatened to fire everybody. He paid you well [Tosi earned $100 a game], but he wanted to be a coach. He was not a well-liked person by the players during my time."

Marshall liked to tell Redskin players what to do, to the annoyance of those he employed as coaches. In 1936 he installed Ray Flaherty, a former end for the New York Giants, as the Redskins' head coach. The team's star running back, Cliff Battles, told writer Myron Cope about Flaherty's unusual contract provision:

> He had it put in his contract that Marshall would stay off the field. So Marshall had to go upstairs, but he had extensive telephone lines all over the place. He would phone the band and the bench and everything else. Flaherty had a man on the bench who would take Marshall's phone calls, but Flaherty would ignore everything Marshall said.

Cliff Battles had his own—well, battles—with Marshall. He had originally signed a contract calling for $175 a game, or about $2,500 a year—not a bad salary in the Depression year of 1932. By 1937, when the Redskins capped their first year in Washington by beating the Chicago Bears for the NFL title, Battles became the first running back to lead all rushers for a second time. He asked Marshall for a raise of $500, to $3,500. He was turned down in a heated confrontation with Marshall and retired at the prime age of twenty-eight.

Marshall and his Redskins were not the only newcomers to the NFL in the early 1930s. The year 1933 brought into the league Bert Bell and his Philadelphia Eagles and Art Rooney with the Pittsburgh Steelers (né Pirates). Pennsylvania dismantled its blue laws that fall so that pro football games could be played on Sunday, making an NFL franchise more attractive. Bell's team was horrendous throughout the 1930s, but he proved to be a clear thinker who later served the league well as NFL commissioner. Rooney was a good-hearted Irish-American from Pittsburgh who parlayed a talent for betting on the horses into a good living and a stable of horses, as well as an NFL team.

Bert Bell, whose given name was de Benneville, was the scion of a distinguished Philadelphia family. His father had been attorney general of Pennsylvania after serving with Walter Camp on the Intercollegiate Rules Committee for football. One of his grandfathers had been a congressman. Bell played quarterback for Penn from 1915 to 1919, with a year out for overseas service with the Army during World War I. He later coached at Penn and Temple.

The Bell family fortune was wiped out in the stock market collapse of 1929, but when the chance came to buy a Philadelphia franchise in 1933, Bell took it. In partnership with Lud Wray, his teammate at Penn, who had played for the old Buffalo All-Americans in 1920, Bell bought the franchise for $2,500. The money came from his new wife, Ziegfeld Follies girl Frances Upton. In addition to the franchise cost, Bell and Wray agreed to pay off a few of the debts of the Frankford Yellow Jackets, who had surrendered the franchise during the 1931 season.

As president of the Philadelphia Eagles, Bell was a jack of all trades. He was at various times a coach, scout, contract negotiator, press agent, ticket seller, janitor, and gateman for his hapless Eagles. He sold the Eagles in 1940 and was co-owner of the Pittsburgh Steelers with Art Rooney when he was tapped for the commissionership in 1946.

Rooney had been an amateur boxing champion and a semipro football player and coach during his youth in Pittsburgh. Although Rooney denied it, he was said to have started the football team with the proceeds of an excellent day of betting at the track. Despite Pittsburgh's tradition as the cradle of professional football, Rooney's team was mediocre, finishing last in the Eastern Division four times in its first seven years and only once rising to second place.

Ed Skoronski, a Purdue All-American whose home was in Chicago, suffered through a couple of seasons with the Pittsburgh Pirates. (They did not become the Steelers until 1940.) Skoronski, a center and linebacker, played a few games for the Pirates after the college season ended in 1934. The Pirates evidently were not concerned about the league rule that players were supposed to have graduated before they were hired. "It was an unusual situation," Skoronski said. "The center for Pittsburgh was badly injured and I relieved him for four or five games in 1934. Of course, that was my last year in college and I didn't care. I thought I was all through with football. I used to take the train from school on Friday night, practice Saturday in Pittsburgh and play on Sunday.

"I would come in, never practiced all week, and I would practice one day. They treated me royally," Skoronski continued. He was making $125 a game, a top wage for a rookie lineman. "Art Rooney was one of the best owners you'd ever want to meet," he said.

Skoronski returned to the Pirates for the 1935 and 1936 seasons and then was sent to the Cleveland Rams, who traded him to the Brooklyn Dodgers for his final pro season. Skoronski was only twenty-five when he retired from football and became a teacher and football coach at Chicago Vocational High School. "There wasn't any money in football," he said. "We'd play—what?—nine or ten games, and we had to pay our own expenses when we were at home, so a lot of money went for hotel rooms and your food. Of course, when you were travelling, the club would pay all your expenses."

Players were still expected to provide most of their own pads and shoes. "On the teams I played for, the only thing they furnished was a jersey and maybe a helmet," Skoronski said.

Another player who wound up with the Pittsburgh Pirates, more or less by happenstance, was Chester (Swede) Johnston. He was a 5-foot, 8-inch, 195-pound fullback and linebacker who started as a semi-pro and then played with the Green Bay Packers and St. Louis Gunners as well as the Pirates. Johnston, whose antecedents were English and German, was given the nickname "Swede" by a boyhood buddy, and it stuck.

After brief stops to play football at Marquette University and Elmhurst College in Chicago, Johnston headed home to Appleton, Wisconsin, in 1931 and played semipro football with the Oshkosh All-Stars, the New London Bulldogs, and the Wisconsin Blackhawks of Fort Atkinson. In 1932, the Blackhawks visited St. Louis to play the Gunners, and he was asked to stay with the Gunners.

The St. Louis Gunners were one of the country's strongest independent teams, often playing NFL teams on even terms. In their finest season—1933—the Gunners compiled a record of eleven victories, two losses, and three ties. The losses were to the NFL's Cincinnati Reds, by 7 to 0, and the Green Bay Packers, 21 to 0. One of the ties was a scoreless game with the NFL champion Chicago Bears. Over the sixteen games, Johnston scored seventeen touchdowns, many on long runs. The *St. Louis Star-Times* called him a "rip-snorting ball packer."

Partway through the 1934 season, the St. Louis Gunners took over the NFL franchise of the last-place Cincinnati Reds and finished with a 1–2 mark. The club was deeply in debt and called it quits at the end of the season.

Johnston headed back to Wisconsin and caught on with the Green Bay Packers as a fullback and sometime guard. The Packers already had a star fullback in Clarke Hinkle, who had been an All-American at Bucknell, so Johnston became his backup. "Hinkle was the best," Johnston remembered. "He was fast and he was a good punter and place kicker. He was really tough. Sometimes they would take him out and I would go in, and it was an honor to play behind him."

Johnston spent four years with the Packers—1935 through 1938—a time when end Don Hutson was transforming professional offenses. He did it by bringing new meaning to the term "pass receiver." Hutson, who had starred at Alabama, could run 100 yards in 9.8 seconds, which meant that he could outrun most defensive backs. Most important, he was the first receiver to do a lot of faking and feinting and the first to make sharp cuts, not slow curves, in running pass routes.

Hutson was also creative. Pat Livingston of the *Pittsburgh Press* described a play in 1942 in which Hutson used the goal posts to outwit three Chicago Bears backs:

Lining up as a flanker, harassed by three Bears, the cagy old Alabaman ran a simple post pattern, diagonally in on the twin-poled uprights, Bears convoying him, stride by stride.

As the four men raced under the bar, Hutson hooked his elbow around the upright, stopping abruptly, flung his body sharply left, and left the red-faced Bears scrambling around in their cleats. He stood alone in the end zone as he casually gathered [Cecil] Isbell's throw to his chest.

Hutson scored a touchdown on his first play as a professional in 1935, outrunning Beattie Feathers of the Bears on an 83-yard play. By the time he retired in 1945, Hutson was far ahead of everyone in pass catching. His record of ninety-nine touchdowns lasted for forty-four years. He still has the records for most seasons leading all receivers (eight), most consecutive seasons leading the league (five), and most seasons leading the league in touchdowns (eight). Hutson was 6 feet, 1 inch tall but weighed only 180 pounds—light for an end even in the 1930s—and to enhance his speed and maneuverability, he wore slimmed-down shoulder pads and no hip pads at all. To reduce wear and tear on Hutson, coach Curly Lambeau made him a safety on defense.

Hutson joined the NFL at just the right time. In 1934, the year before his debut, the football was given its modern shape. A rule change dictated that the ball at its fattest point could be no less than 21¼ inches or more than 21½ inches around. That was 1½ inches skinnier than the ball was during the 1920s, when Benny Friedman first pointed the way to popularity for the forward pass. It was a passer-friendly ball, but it ended the drop-kick era because its sharper point caused an erratic rebound from the ground.

At Green Bay, Hutson's pass-catching talents were complemented by a talented passer in Arnie Herber and, later, Cecil Isbell. He also benefited from the fact that Curly Lambeau was the most pass-oriented coach in the NFL. But it was Hutson himself who opened the eyes of coaches to the possibilities of a sophisticated passing attack.

Arnie Herber, Hutson's first pitcher at Green Bay, was a hometown boy who made good in a big way. He was a star in football and basketball at Green Bay's West Side High School in the mid-1920s while Swede Johnston was making his name at Appleton High. "While we were in high school," Johnston recalled, "we were playing a basketball game and got into a fight on the floor. Out of the stands here comes Arnie's mother with an umbrella and takes after me with it." All was forgiven by the time Johnston and Herber became good friends on the Packers, and Johnston frequently visited Herber's mother.

Herber joined the Packers in 1930 after a year at the University of Wisconsin and another year at Regis College in Denver. The 6-foot, 200-pound Herber was noted for his long sidearm heaves. "He could throw them far," Johnston said, "and he was accurate. Of course, Hutson could *catch*. If he could touch 'em, he'd get 'em"

In 1939, Johnston was traded to Pittsburgh. He remembered:

> There were about six of us released by the Packers. I was one, Buckets Goldenberg was another. They sent us to Pittsburgh. That's where you wound up when you were through, and that's how I got there.
>
> Buckets Goldenberg, who was also a fullback, said, "I'm not going. I'm staying here." Buckets had started playing some guard, and he got good at that position. He became All-Pro because he wouldn't go. He played four or five more years at Green Bay as a guard.
>
> So I went to Pittsburgh. Several other guys from Green Bay played for Art Rooney there. Walt Kiesling, who had been line coach at Green Bay, was the assistant coach.
>
> We had a nut for a head coach—Johnny Blood. He'd make up plays during a game. I remember one time I carried the ball, and I ran and ran, but there was no place to go, so I just wound up and threw it. There was no pass called for on that play. At halftime Johnny said, "That's the way I want everybody to play." He was an odd one. But you couldn't help liking him.
>
> When I first arrived in Pittsburgh, there was a team meeting and Johnny called the roll. He called out, "Johnston?" and I said, "Yes." Johnny said, "Yes, nothing. Pirates never quit!" Everybody was supposed to answer the roll call with that little speech: "Pirates never quit!" He thought he could keep the team all fired up by doing that, but it didn't pan out.

Blood quit after the Pirates dropped their first three games of the season, and Walt Kiesling was named head coach. Kiesling was not notably successful either, and the 1939 Pirates finished in last place in the Eastern Division with a 1–9–1 record. The next year—Johnston's final pro season—the Pirates became the Steelers and moved up a notch in the standings, finishing ahead of the Philadelphia Eagles.

Despite his depressing experiences with the Pittsburgh team, Johnston looks back on his years in pro football with pleasure: "Would I do it again? Oh, would I ever! I would pay to do it. For one thing, I like all kinds of athletics, especially football. And I like to travel, and one way of traveling is with a football team."

The year before Swede Johnston played in Pittsburgh, the Pirates had shocked the little world of professional football by paying Byron (Whizzer) White, an All-American tailback from the University of Colorado, $15,800 for the season. His fellow owners thought that Art Rooney had lost his mind. It was probably twice as much as any other player was earning.

Whizzer White, who disliked his nickname, was worth every penny as a football player. He had led Colorado to an undefeated season in his senior year and had starred in the Cotton Bowl game despite a 28 to 14 defeat at the hands of a much stronger team from Rice. White was the second choice of voters choosing the Heisman Trophy winner. He was also a basketball star, president of the student body, first in his class academically and valedictorian, and a member of Phi Beta Kappa.

White showed small interest in pro football, but Rooney drafted him anyway. When White learned that he could accept a proffered Rhodes Scholarship as late as January 1939, he decided to accept Rooney's offer of $15,800 for the 1938 season.

Whizzer was not able to lead the Pittsburgh Pirates out of the lower depths of the NFL (they finished last in the Eastern Division, with a record of 2–9). But he led the league in rushing with 567 yards and was named Rookie of the Year and an All-Pro player. After the season, he went to England to study at Oxford with his Rhodes Scholarship. White was back in the United States and studying at Yale Law School in 1940, and played with the Detroit Lions, who had purchased his contract, for two seasons. After World War II and service with Navy intelligence, White took up the law. He was appointed assistant attorney general in the Kennedy administration in 1961. The next year, President Kennedy named him an associate justice of the Supreme Court. Byron R. White served on the high court with distinction for thirty-one years.

White's reputation among pro football players is reflected by the fact that the NFL Players Association named its service award for him, calling Justice White "the personification of the ideal to which professional football players aspire."

The Green Bay Packers and the Chicago Bears won most of the honors during the 1930s in the Western Division of the NFL. The Packers took the divisional title in 1936, 1938, and 1939. The Bears also did it three times—in 1933, 1934, and 1937. If much of the Packers' success can be attributed to Don Hutson, Arnie Herber, and Cecil Isbell, for the Bears much of the credit goes to the strongman Bronislau (Bronko) Nagurski. If ever a pro football player was a legend in his own time among his contemporaries on the field, it is Bronko Nagurski. Even the name seems to suggest power.

And powerful he was. Nagurski left the University of Minnesota in 1930 after earning All-American honors as both fullback and tackle. He was big but not huge—6 feet, 2 inches and weighing 225 pounds—and strong. One story about his strength, no doubt apocryphal, is that his college coach, Doc Spears, discovered Nagurski when "I was driving by a farm and I noticed this big, strong farm boy plowing a field. I stopped to ask directions and the boy picked up the plow and pointed with it."

From 1930 to 1937, Nagurski was the piledriver in the Bears' offense, usually getting the call for a line plunge when a few yards were needed. Statistics were kept somewhat sloppily in those years, but they suggest that Nagurski averaged nearly 5 yards a carry. He could also complete short passes, as the Portsmouth Spartans discovered in the NFL title game in Chicago Stadium in 1932, when his pass to Red Grange for a touchdown won the game. Nagurski was a punishing linebacker, too. During World War II, he came out of retirement in 1943 and played a more than respectable tackle and linebacker for a thirty-five-year-old. He also filled in at fullback and still had that old power. New York Giants fullback Hank Soar remembered:

> He was the first fullback I ever saw who ran the ends. In those days, fullbacks were guys who just bucked in the middle. We were playing the Bears in the Polo Grounds one day. Ken Strong was playing defensive halfback and I was playing safety. Now Strong was no lightweight—he was up around 210 pounds. Nagurski came around the end, and he was close to the sideline. Strong came over, and he didn't try to tackle him—he barreled into him, trying to knock him out of bounds. The next thing you know, Strong had bounced off and landed back in bounds. I guess Bronko hadn't broken stride.
>
> Then it's my turn. I barreled right into him—bang! When I woke up, he was crossing the goal line. I didn't even move him *that* much.
>
> They always tell the story about the wives of Nagurski and Cal Hubbard, the old tackle—he was a baseball umpire like me, by the way—crashing together like freight trains. Mrs. Nagurski said, "When those two guys got on a football field, I used to close my eyes. Wouldn't look at it. I didn't dare to watch the trains come together—boom! It rattled the whole stadium."

When Soar first joined the New York Giants in 1937, they had already won three of the four Eastern Division titles and one NFL championship since the league was split in 1933. The Giants would add two more divisional titles and another NFL championship by the time the decade was over. Only the Boston (and Washington) Redskins interrupted the Giants' string. The Redskins took the Eastern Division laurel in 1936 and 1937 and won the NFL championship in the latter year.

The Giants' NFL championship victory over the Chicago Bears in 1934 has been immortalized as the "sneakers game." The scene was New York's Polo Grounds, which was more like a rough skating rink than a football field. Freezing rain and a temperature of 9 degrees made for treacherous footing.

Giants end Ray Flaherty told coach Steve Owen that when he was in college at Gonzaga in Washington, the team had played in basketball shoes when the field was in a similar condition. Assistant equipment manager Abe Cohen was sent in search of sneakers. He found them at Manhattan College. By the time Cohen got back to the Polo Grounds, the Bears had built a 13 to 3 lead a few minutes into the third quarter on a touchdown by Nagurski and two field goals. In their sneakers, the

Giants scored four touchdowns and won going away, 30 to 13. Bears coach George Halas shouted for his players to stomp on the Giants' feet, but to no avail. Halas, the Bears players, and most sportswriters credited Cohen and his sneaker run for the New York victory.

Many years later, Ken Strong, who had scored two of the four Giants touchdowns, told writer Bob Curran:

> Actually, the sneakers weren't that much of a factor. By the end of the third quarter and through the fourth quarter, they didn't make much difference. The Bears still led . . . with eight minutes to play. The Bears had started with new pointed cleats made of Bakelite, I believe. By the end of the first half they were nubs. That did make a difference. If they had new cleats for the second half, they would have walloped us.

Among the important developments of the 1930s was the institution of the annual draft of players whose college eligibility was ending. The player draft was suggested by Bert Bell of the Philadelphia Eagles. He proposed that teams choose in the reverse order of their place in the standings of the previous season. As perennial also-rans, his Eagles would be the first or second selector in most years. Nevertheless, the idea was supported by George Halas of the Bears and Tim Mara of the Giants because they understood the need to foster competition.

The first draft was held on February 8, 1936. Two of the first three players selected never played in the NFL, largely because they believed that they could do better financially in other pursuits. They were half-back Jay Berwanger of the University of Chicago, who won the Heisman Trophy and was the first choice of the Philadelphia Eagles, and triple-threat Bill Shakespeare of Notre Dame, tapped by the Pittsburgh Pirates. The third selection, chosen by the Boston Redskins, did spend three years in the NFL. He was Riley Smith, a quarterback and linebacker from Alabama. Years later, Smith said that he had signed for $250 a game and a small bonus.

Eighty-one players were picked in the first NFL draft—nine by each team. Fewer than half signed contracts. Bell had terrible luck with the first draft. Not one of his nine choices agreed to play. But his Eagles did not come up entirely empty-handed because he traded the negotiating rights to Jay Berwanger to the Chicago Bears for lineman Art Buss, who *did* join the Eagles in 1937.

The player draft did not lift the Philadelphia Eagles very high in the Eastern Division standings over the next few years. They finished fourth or fifth in the five-team division every year until 1944, when they made Steve Van Buren, a speedy, punishing runner, the number-one draft pick. By that time, Bell was out of the picture, having sold the Eagles in 1941 to Alexis Thompson, a New York executive.

When the draft began in 1936, cynics said that team owners had another purpose besides equalizing team strengths—to hold down salaries by allowing draftees to negotiate with only one team. In his autobiography, George Halas admitted, "There is some truth in this argument. But time proved that by leveling the clubs, the draft system heightened the attractiveness of the sport. It created bigger audiences, which brought bigger revenue, which brought higher salaries for all players."

Not all former college players joined NFL rosters after 1935 through the draft. One who did not was Giants fullback Hank Soar. When the first draft was held in 1936, he was in his junior year at Providence College on a scholarship to play both football and baseball. That spring, he was told that Providence intended to upgrade its football schedule and would have spring practice. He wanted to play baseball in the spring, though, and when the athletic director insisted that he drop out of baseball for football practice, he dropped out of college instead.

Soar was working as a millwright that summer when the Boston Shamrocks of the new American Football League offered him $100 a game for two games a week. The new AFL had no connection with the AFL of 1926, but it was a well-regarded circuit made up of the Shamrocks, Cleveland Rams, New York Yankees, Pittsburgh Americans, Syracuse–Rochester Braves, and Brooklyn Tigers, who moved to Rochester when the Braves dropped out.

The Boston Shamrocks' home field was the baseball park of the old Boston Braves (now Atlanta Braves). They played on weekday nights as well as Sunday afternoons. Soar recalled:

> The brand of football wasn't quite as good as the NFL. The players were guys coming down from the NFL or younger guys going up. To me, it was a great stepping stone after college. Instead of going right into the National League, I had that stepping stone, and I was one of the stars of the league.
>
> The Shamrocks won the AFL championship, and after the season we went on a barnstorming tour south down to Miami with the New York Yankees. They had Ken Strong and the coach was Jack McBride, who had also been with the Giants.
>
> After the season, I was a free agent and I got offers from most of the NFL clubs. I chose the Giants. I didn't make a hell of a lot more money with them than when I was playing for the Shamrocks. They wanted to give me $125, but I got $200 a game. I wanted to play with the Giants. When I was a kid, I used to see them when they played the Providence Steam Roller in Providence.

The New York Giants' coach was a veteran tackle named Steve Owen, who had joined the team in 1926 and had been head coach since 1931. Owen preached tight defense and brought a new offensive formation called the A to football. The A-formation was a single wing with a twist; if the line was strong right, the backfield was strong left, and vice versa. It also had another peculiarity; center Mel Hein could snap the ball to any of three backs: a blocking back just a yard or two behind the line; the quarterback a couple of yards farther back and to the other side; or the fullback, who lined up in the normal tailback position. Hank Soar and Tuffy Leemans, a strong runner from George Washington University, alternated at fullback.

Owen and Soar developed a love–hate relationship during Soar's ten seasons with the Giants. Owen tended to be conservative, and Soar was a free spirit. Soar remembered:

> Yeah, he was conservative. He wouldn't take chances. I liked to play the game without thinking what you have to do, you just do it. Once he fined me fifty bucks for doing something he didn't like, but I haven't paid him yet.
>
> We had a feud going on, but it wasn't really a feud. When we were alone, we'd talk a lot. We lived in the same hotel, and we'd often discuss things about a game or the team.
>
> But yet, I'd get on the field and he'd fight me like hell. He used to get mad. I'd run the ball all the way down the field and get near the goal line, and he'd pull me out. He'd put Bull Karcis in and Bull would score, and I'd throw the helmet. He wouldn't pay attention. Oh, it was a great relationship we had. We gave a big party when he retired in 1953. Newspapermen were there, and they asked him, "Who was your favorite player in your coaching years?" And Steve said, "You're not going to believe this. It was Hank Soar." They said, "Why?" And he said, "Because he always came up with the ball. I said to Hank one time, 'You're either good or you're lucky!' And you know what he said to me? 'I'm both!' "

Soar had his best day as a professional player at a most opportune time—the NFL championship game of 1938 against the Green Bay Packers. It was a fiercely fought game before 48,000 fans in the Polo Grounds, the largest crowd ever to see an NFL title game up to that point. Arthur Daley, a *New York Times* sports columnist, gave some of the flavor:

> Perhaps there have been better football games since Rutgers and Princeton started the autumnal madness sixty-nine years ago, but no one in that huge crowd would admit it. This was a struggle of such magnificent stature that words seem such feeble tools for describing it. . . . What a frenzied battle this was! The tackling was fierce and the blocking positively vicious.

Victims of the carnage included Don Hutson, Green Bay's great end, who suffered a knee injury; Giants center Mel Hein, who got a concussion; and Giants guard Johnny Dell Isola, who suffered a back injury.

In the third quarter, with the Packers leading, 17 to 16, the Giants mounted a drive, culminating in a 20-yard pass from quarterback Ed Danowski to Hank Soar. Soar remembered:

> I was near the goal line, and when I came down with the ball, I had three or four Packers all around me. Clarke Hinkle grabbed me by one leg, but I pulled and pulled and jerked loose and went in. After that score, Ward Cuff kicked the point and Steve took me out of the game, and he said, "I want you to go back in again. You call the plays and don't call anybody's plays but your own. You carry the ball every goddamned time." Well, they hit me with everything except the stands, and that was because they couldn't move the stands. I carried the ball, and I was getting first down, first down, first down. It seemed like six years before the clock ran out.

There was no scoring in the fourth quarter. The final score was New York, 23; Green Bay, 17. Soar finished with twenty-one carries for 65 yards and three pass receptions for 41 yards. "I think that game was my biggest thrill as far as football is concerned," Soar said. A year later, the Green Bay Packers got sweet revenge, drubbing the Giants, 27 to 0, at Milwaukee to win the NFL title.

The 1930s was a period of stabilization for the NFL. The constant addition, subtraction, and shifting of franchises that characterized the league in the 1920s had stopped. After the league was split into two divisions in 1933, the only changes were the move of the Portsmouth Spartans to Detroit, the folding of the Cincinnati Reds–St. Louis Gunners franchise in 1934, the shift of the Boston Redskins to Washington, and the admittance of the Cleveland Rams in 1937. In 1936, all the NFL teams played the same number of games—twelve—for the first time.

The shift of the Portsmouth franchise to Detroit and the renaming of the team as the Lions left Green Bay as the only small city still represented in the NFL. The move was made necessary by the economic pinch caused by the Great Depression. Spartans star Earl (Dutch) Clark told writer Jerry Green, "Hell, we'd get 4,000 or 5,000 people out to watch practice and at game time we'd be lucky if we had 2,000."

The Portsmouth Spartans were bought for $15,000 by George A. (Dick) Richards, who owned radio stations in Detroit and California. Richards also paid off the $6,500 debt of the Spartans.

The new Detroit Lions started off in the NFL with a ten-game winning streak, including seven straight shutouts. The streak was no fluke because such fine backs as Dutch Clark, Ace Gutkowsky, Roy (Father) Lumpkin, Glenn Presnell, and Ernie Caddel and linemen like Ox Emerson and Frank Christiansen had made the shift from Portsmouth to Detroit. "They were great football players and persons," said Bob Emerick, a rookie tackle out of Miami of Ohio.

Emerick also had kind words for Potsy Clark, the coach who came to Detroit with the franchise. "He was a good leader and he could handle men," Emerick said. "You'd do anything for him."

The Lions paid the young tackle $100 a game, a good wage for a rookie, and were generous in other ways, according to Emerick. Unlike some clubs, the Lions furnished all equipment a player needed, except his shoes. "Dick Richards was a rich man," Emerick explained. "He was also forward looking and changed football a little bit." For one thing, Richards reached out to the auto executives in Detroit and placed some of them on his board, he said.

The Lions' 1934 winning streak went for naught. They lost their last three games, including two 3-point defeats by the Chicago Bears, the Western Division champions. One of the defeats, on Thanksgiving Day, was broadcast on a ninety-four-station radio network arranged by NBC at the request of Lions owner Dick Richards. The following year, the Lions won the NFL championship, drubbing the New York Giants, 26 to 7, in freezing rain at Detroit.

The early Lions may have had the first NFL scout, or so reported the *Detroit Times* in December 1934. The *Times* said that Jack O'Brien, a former coach at Minnesota, Oregon, and Western State Normal in Kalamazoo, Michigan, had been signed by Potsy Clark to scout rival teams in the 1935 season. Clark may not have had much confidence in O'Brien's reports, though, because he was said to have scouted the Giants himself in preparation for the title game.

The latter half of the 1930s was the heyday of strong minor leagues as well as stabilization of the NFL. Between 1936 and 1941, there were three AFLs—more or less distinct but having some of the same teams. The 1936 AFL (in which Hank Soar played for the Boston Shamrocks) had several former NFL stars, including Hall of Famers Ken Strong and Red Badgro. In 1937, the AFL's Cleveland Rams were absorbed by the NFL, but the AFL added what was probably an even stronger team. It was the Los Angeles Bulldogs, who won the league title with nine straight victories. The Bulldogs were the first West Coast professional team to host eastern rivals on a regular basis. They played their first seven games in the East and then stayed home to welcome the Easterners. The Bulldogs had by far the best home attendance in the league, with crowds of from 14,000 to 18,000, double what the AFL's eastern teams attracted. But the Bulldogs were so superior to the other league teams that interest dropped off and the league suspended operations after the season.

In 1939 another AFL was started with franchises primarily in the Midwest, but again with the Los Angeles Bulldogs as the West Coast representative. The Bulldogs won again, with a 7–1 record, edging the Cincinnati Bengals, who were 6–2. That was the Bulldogs' last year in the AFL because for 1940 a "major" minor league—the Pacific Coast Football League—was organized in the West, saving the Bulldogs the heavy expenses of eastern trips.

The various AFLs were not the only minor leagues in the 1930s. The Midwest Football League, later called the American Professional Football League, was organized in 1935. A year later, the South Atlantic Football League, later renamed the Dixie League, began play in Washington, D.C., and points south, mainly in Virginia. It continued until 1947, with time out during World War II.

One of the most significant minor leagues of the 1930s was the American Professional Football Association. The name was misleading, suggesting as it does a national organization, because nearly all the teams were within easy driving distance of New York City. Only the Providence Steam Roller, the NFL champions of 1928, were more than a three-hour drive from the Big Apple. Association teams drew quite well—3,000 to 10,000 a game—and received regular coverage in eastern newspapers. The most interesting thing about the American Association, though, is that two of its teams became the first farm clubs of NFL teams. In 1938 Tim Mara of the New York Giants bought a franchise for Jersey City, named it the Giants, and installed his son John as president and Bill Owen, a former Giant lineman and brother of Steve Owen, as coach. The team's star was former Giant Ken Strong, who had been blackballed by the NFL when he jumped to the AFL's New York Yankees in 1936 after a salary dispute with Mara. That AFL collapsed in 1937, and Tim Mara offered to return Strong to the NFL's good graces if he played for Jersey City. Strong agreed, and led the league in scoring and the Giants to the American Association championship.

The next year, George Halas bought the Newark Tornadoes franchise and renamed the team the Newark Bears. Former Chicago Bears Gene Ronzani and Joe Zeller were player-coaches and led Newark to the 1938 title in the American Association.

Although no one realized it at the time, a little-noticed event on October 22, 1939, foretold the future riches and popularity of professional football. It was the first televised broadcast of a pro game. It was so little noticed that many of the players did not even know it was being televised. Indeed, they may not have known that the technology to televise a football game existed.

The game was played at Brooklyn's Ebbets Field and matched Potsy Clark's Brooklyn Dodgers against Bert Bell's Philadelphia Eagles. It is likely that the 13,051 spectators at Ebbets Field outnumbered the television viewers. At the time, there were about 1,000 television sets in the New York area. The game was shown at the RCA Pavilion at the New York World's Fair in Flushing, Queens, but the audience there probably numbered in the hundreds, not thousands. NBC station W2XBS produced the broadcast, which was transmitted via an aerial atop the Empire State Building in Manhattan. The picture was, of course, black and white and full of the "snow" that bedeviled early television broadcasts. Television screens were tiny in 1939, ranging from 5 to 12 inches diagonally, so football players appeared to be miniature dolls gamboling in a snowstorm.

The announcer was Allen Walz, a former football star at New York University, who covered all sports for W2XBS. In 1975 he told writer Jim Campbell that October 22, 1939, was "a cloudy day and when the sun crept behind the stadium there wasn't enough light for the cameras. The picture would get darker and darker and eventually it would go completely blank and we'd revert to a radio broadcast." Walz himself had no television monitor at his broadcasting booth in the stadium's mezzanine, so he had to depend on the producer in a mobile unit outside the stadium for a report on what viewers were seeing. Two cameras were used, one alongside Walz on the mezzanine and the other at field level at the 50-yard line.

For the record, Brooklyn beat Philadelphia in the first televised game, 24 to 13. Three future Hall of Famers—tailback Ace Parker and tackle Bruiser Kinard of the Dodgers and end Bill Hewitt of the Eagles—took part. None seems to have known that the game was telecast. "I certainly wasn't aware of it," Kinard told Campbell in 1975. "That sure is interesting." NBC liked the results so well that it broadcast other Dodger games that season.

The Dodger–Eagles game was not the first sports event covered by television. The first was a baseball game between Columbia and Princeton on May 17, 1939, at Columbia's Baker Field in New York. That was followed by a heavyweight prizefight in June between former champion Max Baer and Lou Nova. In August, a tennis tournament in a New York suburb was shown on W2XBS, and the Cincinnati Reds and Brooklyn Dodgers appeared in the first televised professional baseball game, played at Ebbets Field. Before NBC aired its first pro football game, it had shown Fordham University playing Waynesburg College in the Bronx in the first televised football game. Why were all these sports events televised from New York? Because that's where the rudimentary broadcasting equipment was located.

From the beginning of sports television, it was apparent that football was a far better television spectacle than baseball and most other sports. Soon after the Fordham–Waynesburg telecast, Orrin E. Dunlap, Jr., of the *New York Times* wrote:

Science has scored a touchdown at the kickoff of football by television. So sharp are the pictures and so discerning the telephoto lens as it peers into the lineup that the televiewer sits in his parlor wondering why he should leave the comforts of home to watch a gridiron battle in a sea of mud on a chill autumnal afternoon.

With one all-seeing electric camera perched on the rim of the stadium for a birdseye view and the other for close-ups along the sideline, so amazing are the results that the majority of colleges in and around New York are shunning the idea of permitting a telecaravan to camp within the gates to toss the scenes over the fence to a nonpaying audience. Managers of athletics contend that it is not fair to those who buy tickets, and, furthermore, if the games are telecast successfully, ticket buyers will diminish. . . .

With the camera on a dolly at the 40-yard line, the coach himself has nothing on the televiewer in the armchair at home. Both are on the sidelines. When the players gallop directly in front of the camera the televiewer feels that he is plunging right through the line or sliding out of bounds with the ball runner.

Football by television invites audience participation. The spectator at the gridiron does not have that intimacy with the players; he knows the game is separate from him because he is sandwiched in the crowd; the gladiators are out on the field. But by television the contest is in the living room; the spectator is edged up close. His eye is right in the game. . . .

It would be some years before there would be many "televiewers" to share Dunlap's wonder, but he had seen the future of professional football.

8

A DEBACLE AND THE WARTIME BLUES

The year 1940 was a watershed for professional football for two reasons. First, millions of American sports fans were introduced to pro football by the first radio network broadcast of an NFL game. It was the astonishing 73 to 0 blowout of the Washington Redskins by the Chicago Bears in that year's championship game. The second reason, which is not unrelated to the first, is that the game heralded a revolution in offenses, not only in pro football but, by a trickle-down process, in colleges and high schools too.

Professional football had grown steadily in popularity during the 1930s. Late in the decade, attendance at NFL games was averaging more than 20,000. The annual College All-Star game, pitting the best of the graduating seniors against the previous season's NFL champion, became one of the summer's biggest sports attractions. The first one, in 1934, drew 79,432 fans to Chicago's Soldier Field.

The All-Star game was the creation of Arch Ward, the sports editor at the *Chicago Tribune*. He assembled a panel of sportswriters from thirty newspapers around the country to select the all-stars, who would spend two weeks in training in the Chicago area and then play the game against the reigning professional champions. Net proceeds went to charities. For the first few years, the All-Star game was competitive and popular. The first, with the Chicago Bears representing the NFL, was a scoreless tie. Of the first ten All-Star games, the pros won five, lost three, and tied two. When the last All-Star game was played in 1976, the score stood pros, 31; All-Stars, 9; ties, 2.

The growing dominance of the professional champions over the All-Stars mirrored the truth that was becoming plain: pro football players were more skillful and, on average, bigger than college players, and pro teams were too much for even the best college teams to handle. Ken Kavanaugh, a 6-foot, 3-inch, 205-pound end from Louisiana State who had been drafted by the Chicago Bears, played for the College All-Stars in 1940. He recalled his introduction to professionals:

> The first time I played against pros was in the All-Star game against the Green Bay Packers. They had Don Hutson and all those other stars.
>
> I was blocking on a fella named Baby Ray, a 6-foot-6, 240-pound tackle, and he just beat the living heck out of me. Later we became good friends, but in that game he'd knock me on the ground and sit on me like a wrestler. I felt like a fool out there on Soldier Field, and I tried to get away from him as much as I could. I hadn't run into anything like that.
>
> The pros were so much bigger and better. There was no comparison. You could score in college, and you'd think, we're doing all right, but in the pros they'd come right back at you, they'd score right after you. In that All-Star game, we scored first, and then they came right back and scored and scored and scored. They were just so much better than what you run into in college.
>
> Of course, in those days you didn't hear too much about the pros because you didn't have television. All they had was radio in those days, and you were lucky to get on radio.

Kavanaugh was a fast study, though, and he soon learned to handle himself against bigger men. He could run 100 yards in 9.9 seconds and threatened to go all the way with any pass he got his hands on. The Bears had a run-oriented offense in 1940, even though they had Sid Luckman, one of the era's best passers, at quarterback. Kavanaugh led the team's pass receivers with only twelve catches good for 276 yards and three touchdowns. The league leader that year was Don Looney of the Philadelphia Eagles, who caught fifty-eight passes for 707 yards and four touchdowns.

Ken Kavanaugh was one of five outstanding rookies who joined the Bears that year. The others were George McAfee, an explosive runner from Duke; tackles Ed Kolman of Temple and Les Artoe of California; and center-linebacker Clyde (Bulldog) Turner of little Hardin-Simmons College in Abilene, Texas. There may be more appropriate names for a professional football player than Bulldog Turner, but they do not come readily to mind. Turner chose his.

In 1936, when Turner was a sixteen-year-old high-school graduate in Sweetwater, Texas, Hardin-Simmons held tryouts for aspiring scholarship players, as did other colleges. Clyde Turner and his high-school teammate A. J. Roy went to the tryout at Hardin-Simmons. Worrying that if they didn't impress the coaches they might not get scholarships, Turner and Roy decided to imply that they were just having a bad day. Turner was to call, "Hey, Tiger, you're not acting as tough as you did back home," and Roy would yell, "Hey, Bulldog! Get in there and hit 'em like you did at home!"

In the event, both made the team and didn't need the deception, but Roy told their Hardin-Simmons teammates about the idea, and the nickname Bulldog stuck to Clyde Turner. He reflected on it in 1994 at his home near Gatesville, Texas:

> The name Bulldog has never hurt me. It's embarrassing now, as old as I am. Even the telephone company suggested I put Bulldog with my name in the book because people would call down here to Gatesville for information and they don't even know my name is Clyde. I've got teammates and classmates I went to school with for four years who don't know my name is Clyde. The telephone company asked me if I'd list my name as Clyde Bulldog Turner for their benefit.

Bulldog Turner came to the Bears by a roundabout route that led to a change of ownership of the Detroit Lions. He had earned Little All-American honors at Hardin-Simmons in his senior year and won high praise for his play in the post-season East–West game and the College All-Star game. So Lions owner Dick Richards ordered coach Gus Henderson to take Turner in the first round of the draft of college players in the spring of 1940. He also gave Turner some cash and told him to tell other teams that he did not plan to play pro football.

Henderson disobeyed, selecting instead a quarterback from the University of Southern California, where he had previously coached. The Chicago Bears tapped Turner as their first choice. Richards promptly fired Henderson, who then told NFL officials about Richards's payments to Turner. Carl Storck, who became NFL president after Joe Carr's death in 1939, fined Richards $5,000. Annoyed, Richards, who owned radio stations in Detroit and California, sold the Lions to Fred Mandel, a department-store owner in Chicago. The sale price was announced as $200,000. That was $180,000 more than Richards had paid for the franchise in 1934—an indication of pro football's growing acceptance as a viable business.

Bulldog Turner proved to be worth the trouble it took for the Bears to get him. He was 6 feet, 1 inch tall and 232 pounds of muscle. Turner was also speedy and quick to react to an opponent's moves, and he enjoyed a Hall of Fame career with the Bears from 1940 to 1952. Turner gets at least one vote as the greatest football player of all time. It comes from his Bears teammate, quarterback and kicker Bob Snyder, who had played for a year with the Pittsburgh Americans of the AFL and for two years with the Cleveland Rams (now the St. Louis Rams) before joining the Bears in 1939. Said Snyder:

> The best passer I ever played against—the best passer who ever lived, in my opinion—was Samuel Adrian Baugh of the Redskins. The best running back I ever played against was Cliff Battles. The *strongest* running back I ever played against was Bronko Nagurski, and I also played with

him. But I think the best football player I ever played with or saw—this is going to sound strange because he did not play a glamorous position—was Bulldog Turner.

He was just an outstanding football player. He was a great blocker, a good pass defender, everything. I used to do the punting for the Bears and I never had to move my hands *that* far to take the snap. He could have played almost any position. He couldn't have been a scatback, but he could have been a fullback, a guard, a tackle, and he was probably the best football player at his position I've ever seen. I don't know of any weakness he had. He was a complete leader, a good team leader. He never was injured, and of course, like the rest of us, he played both ways, linebacker and offensive center.

Snyder recalled that the military draft was instituted in October 1940 as the United States began preparing for the possibility of being drawn into World War II. "Bulldog could not sign up for the draft because he was not twenty-one years of age," Snyder said. "We had a lot of fun over that. We bought him baby bottles and nipples." Turner *was* young but not that young when he reported to the Bears. "They thought I was twenty," he said. "I think the problem was my writing. My 'March 10, 1919,' looked like 'November 10, 1919,' so everybody called my birth date November 10 when it's actually March 10. It worries my sister to death that they've got that wrong. Anyway, I was twenty-one when I first went up." He was also married and a father, and at the time the Selective Service board in his home county in Texas was not drafting married men. (In 1944, during World War II, Turner was drafted and served for a year in the Army Air Corps.)

Bulldog Turner was one of five Chicago Bears players in the 1940 championship game who were later elected to the Pro Football Hall of Fame. The others were quarterback Sid Luckman, guard Danny Fortmann, halfback George McAfee, and tackle Joe Stydahar. Bears coach George Halas is also a Hall of Famer. But their victims in the championship debacle also had several future Hall of Famers: quarterback Sammy Baugh, tackle Turk Edwards, and end Wayne Millner. Redskins coach Ray Flaherty also earned Hall of Fame honors as an end and as a coach.

Clearly, the Redskins were no pushovers. In fact, they had a better regular season record—9–2—than the Bears, who were 8–3. One of the Bears' losses, just two weeks before the championship game, was to the Redskins on a disputed play. The Redskins led, 7 to 3, when a pass thrown by Sid Luckman bounced off the chest of Bill Osmanski. The Bears claimed heatedly that defensive back Frankie Filchock had interfered with Osmanski.

Afterward, George Preston Marshall, the Redskins' owner, made one of the most ill-advised statements in sports history: "The Bears are a bunch of crybabies. They can't take defeat. They are a first-half club. They are quitters. They are the world's greatest crybabies."

George Halas may never have taken Psychology 101 (the discipline was in its infancy during his college years at the University of Illinois just before World War I), but he knew what to make of Marshall's comment. For the next two weeks, Halas made sure his players didn't forget, and neither did the press. For the first time, national attention was focused on the NFL's title game.

At game time in Washington's Griffith Stadium, 36,034 spectators were on hand. So were 150 sportswriters—no doubt a record number for a pro football game up to that time. Ticket scalpers did a land-office business; eight were arrested on the spot. In the broadcast booth, Red Barber was ready to describe the game to fans all over the country over the radio waves of the Mutual Network. Pro football was big-time at last.

Like many Super Bowls of later generations, the game was an anticlimactic mismatch. Arthur J. Daley of the *New York Times* summed it up in the lead paragraph of his report: "The weather was perfect. So were the Bears." On the second play from scrimmage, Bill Osmanski ran 68 yards for a touchdown, aided by a crushing block by end George Wilson that knocked two Redskins defenders out of the play.

The Redskins threatened to match that touchdown almost immediately, driving downfield to the Bears' 26-yard line. From there, Skins tailback Sammy Baugh spotted end Charlie Malone all alone at the 5-yard line and threw to him. Malone may have been blinded by the lowering sun; in any case, the ball bounced off his chest. From that point, the Redskins' fortunes went downhill in a hurry.

At the end of the first quarter, the score was 21 to 0, and Ken Kavanaugh added to the Skins' misery in the second period by snatching a pass from Sid Luckman out of the hands of two Redskins for another touchdown. It got worse. Three of the Bears' eleven touchdowns were the result of intercepted passes. (One of the interceptions was by center-linebacker Bulldog Turner, who ran it 30 yards for the eighth touchdown.)

By the fourth quarter, nine footballs had been kicked into the stands on points-after-touchdown kicks and kept by fans. The supply of new footballs was getting low. Turner remembered:

> The next time we scored, Bob Snyder came running in to kick the extra point. I remember that he had forgotten his headgear and he was scratching his head. He says, "Coach Halas said for you to make a bad pass from center, so we can't kick the extra point and lose another football." And I said, "You tell Mr. Halas to go to hell. I'm going to put it right in the holder's hands and if he doesn't want it he can drop it." I did, I put it right

in his hands, and he dropped it like a hot potato. . . . I never made a bad pass in my life and I wasn't going to.

After the last three touchdowns, the Bears either ran or passed for the extra point. By that time, the Redskins fans were understandably restless. When the Skins' public-address announcer began a pitch for 1941 season tickets, the stadium shook with boos.

When the game mercifully ended, with the Bears on top by a shocking 73 to 0, Redskins owner George Preston Marshall was uncharacteristically gracious. "We were awful, but they were tremendous," he declared. "So far as Chicago having piled it on—well, that's the way it should be in this league. I don't blame the Bears for all that scoring. If they could have made more, all the more credit to them." Redskins coach Ray Flaherty was equally magnanimous. "The Bears were a great ball club today," He said. "They didn't make a mistake. We did lots of times, and that was that."

More than fifty years after the game, Bears end Ken Kavanaugh said, "We were a very good team but we weren't 73 points better than the Redskins. But I think we'd beat them by 40 points going away every day. We had a *good* football team."

The 1940 championship game was a milestone in another way besides being the most one-sided title game ever played. It was the last time a pro football player played without a helmet. Dick Plasman, a 6-foot, 3-inch, 210-pound end from Vanderbilt, was bareheaded for that game. Helmets were made mandatory by the NFL in 1943, but they were in universal use by then anyway.

When the 1940 NFL title game was played, the Chicago Bears were the only professional team using the T-formation. Few college teams had the T, but one of them was Stanford, which had enjoyed an undefeated season and beat Nebraska in the Rose Bowl. The Stanford coach was Clark Shaughnessy, who had coached at the University of Chicago until 1939, when it dropped football as an intercollegiate sport. Shaughnessy was a believer in the T-formation before it became fashionable.

Within a couple of years after the Bears' demolition of the Redskins in the championship game, the T-formation was the offense of choice by almost all teams, not just in the pros but in colleges and high schools too. At the end of the 1940s, the Pittsburgh Steelers were the only NFL team still lining up in the single wing.

George Halas had used the T-formation almost exclusively ever since he organized the Decatur Staleys in 1919. Occasionally he dabbled with the single and double wing, but he was a true believer in the T. During the 1920s, while other NFL teams were lining up in the single or double wing or the Notre Dame box, Halas was considered a moss-back for sticking with the T.

Halas's original T-formation was not designed for wide-open action. The line was bunched, with only a foot or so between the center, guards, and tackles and about 2 feet between the tackles and ends. The backfield lined up as backfields had done in the 1890s, with the quarterback a yard or so behind the center, the fullback 4 or 5 yards behind the quarterback, and the halfbacks on either side of the fullback. The center passed the ball between his legs to the quarterback, who pivoted and lateraled or handed the ball to another back—or maybe, on third and long, tried a forward pass. But the original T was designed for power football.

In 1930 George Halas and his partner, Dutch Sternaman, agreed to stop coaching. They had suffered through a ninth-place finish in the NFL in 1929 and were constantly bickering. (Two years later, Sternaman sold his interest in the Bears to Halas and left football.)

Halas's choice for the new Bears coach was an imaginative man named Ralph Jones, who had been his freshman football coach at Illinois. Jones was then the athletic director at Lake Forest Academy, a secondary school in a Chicago suburb. One of his sterling qualifications, in Halas's view, was that he was a strong proponent of the T-formation.

Jones promised Halas a championship within three years. Perhaps he was aware that among the Bears rookies that year were fullback Bronko Nagurski and quarterback Carl Brumbaugh, a talented passer from the University of Florida. Among the veterans was Red Grange, now twenty-seven years old, no longer the open-field threat he had been in 1925 but still a competent runner and pass receiver. The ingredients were there for Ralph Jones's vision of an explosive T-formation attack.

The key was to put one of the backfield men in motion laterally behind the line before the ball was snapped. Red Grange became the first man in motion. He had a lot of opportunities to make trouble for the defense. He might take a long lateral from the quarterback, go downfield for a long forward pass, sprint over the middle for a short pass, or turn sharply and block the defensive end for another back on an end run.

Jones placed the quarterback behind and in direct contact with the center, as is common today. The quarterback took a handoff from the center, who found himself for the first time able to look ahead at the opposing linemen instead of having to look back between his straddled legs to center the ball.

The other linemen had new jobs too. The guards and tackles were lined up about a yard apart instead of a foot apart, and the ends were 2 yards from the tackles. Blocking assignments now called for deflecting but not necessarily flattening a defender. The idea was to render him hors de combat for a couple of seconds, just long enough for the runner to slip through the hole.

The overall purpose of the T-formation with man in motion was to emphasize speed and deception rather than power. As Halas put it, *"Football became a game of brains.* Instead of knocking men down, Jones tried to entice the defense into doing something helpful for us. Best of all, the public found our brand of football exciting."

Ralph Jones left the Bears after keeping his promise of an NFL championship within three years. His last game was the victory over the Portsmouth Spartans for the 1932 NFL title in Chicago Stadium. George Halas, now sole owner of the Bears, resumed coaching them. He continued to refine the T-formation with man in motion, adding counter plays, spreads, and swing passes to the basic mix. In 1937 he got help from Clark Shaughnessy, then the coach at the University of Chicago and another innovator of football strategy.

By 1940, Ken Kavanaugh's rookie year, the Bear offense was dazzling in its complexity. Halas expected every player to master it. Kavanaugh remembered:

> We had 2,300 plays in the playbook. I counted them up when I was a rookie. Now that's counting a play in which a guard pulls one way and a separate play that is basically the same except that the guard pulls the other way.
>
> Halas would never let you make a play up. Once I and Scooter McLean, a halfback, were inventing pass patterns that weren't in the playbook, and we'd score with them. George called me into the office and asked what we were doing. I said, "I'm going down and doing this and Scooter is doing that." George says, "Where is it in the playbook?" I said, "It's not in the playbook." He says, "Don't you know you're not supposed to call any plays that aren't in the playbook?" I said, "I know, but it works; it was good for a touchdown." He asked me to draw it up for him. I did, and he finally put it in the book.

T-formation quarterbacks had to be excellent ball handlers, since they got the ball on every play except punts, as well as good passers. They no longer were blocking backs. Most were former tailbacks in the single or double wing. A prime example was Sid Luckman, the Bears' quarterback from 1939 to 1950. A 6-foot, 195-pound tailback, he had earned All-American honors at Columbia University in 1938, but was not sure that he was good enough to play with the pros. Halas thought differently and talked him into giving it a try. Halas's judgment proved to be gilt-edged, as Luckman forged a Hall of Fame career with the Bears.

It wasn't all easy. "It was a very difficult transition from playing tailback at Columbia to quarterback for the Bears," Luckman told Richard Whittingham for his book *What a Game They Played*. "The signal-calling was diametrically opposite. The spinning was very difficult because you had to be so precise and so quick. . . . We had counter-plays and double-counters and fakes. It was very hard for me to adjust, to get my hand under center, and to get back and set up."

Luckman's counterpart for the Redskins in the 73 to 0 debacle, Sammy Baugh, also had trouble learning the skills of T-formation quarterbacking. Like Bulldog Turner, Baugh had played his first organized football game for Sweetwater High School in Texas, which must be the smallest secondary school in the country with two alumni in the Pro Football Hall of Fame.

Baugh was an All-American at Texas Christian University when he became the first draft choice of the Redskins in 1937. In high school, in college, and in his first seven years as a pro, he had been single wing tailback. "I hated the T when we went to it in 1944, but my body loved it," Baugh said. "I probably could have lasted a year or two more as a single-wing tailback, my body was so beat up, but the T gave me nine more seasons."

Baugh had a very strong arm and quickly earned the nickname Slingin' Sammy because his throws arrived as if by slingshot. He was also amazingly accurate, and his contemporaries judge him to be the best passer of all time. He trails only Ken Anderson of the Cincinnati Bengals on the all-time list of passers with the best completion percentage in one season. Baugh completed 70.3 percent of his passes in 1945; Anderson's completion percentage was 70.6 thirty-seven years later. Baugh was the Redskins' punter and led the league four times for the average distance of his kicks; in 1940 his average was 51.3 yards, which is still a record.

While Sammy Baugh threw bullets on a football field, Sid Luckman's passes were less spectacular but got the job done. One of his receivers, Ken Kavanaugh, recalled: "He didn't throw a real long ball, but every ball he threw was so catchable and it was soft. He threw on target. And he was a good leader and a smart player."

Bulldog Turner, who centered for Luckman over most of his career, said that Baugh was probably the better passer:

> Luckman was a great passer, too, but Sammy was in a class of his own as a passer. He could really get rid of that ball. It had to be talent.
>
> Sid had a tremendous record and would score points, but it seemed like his pass was often behind the receiver but he would catch it. But it had to be a talent because Sid made it, Sunday after Sunday.

With the two chief practitioners of the T-formation—the Chicago Bears and Stanford University—winning big in the 1940 season, everybody wanted to learn the T. George Halas was happy to provide missionaries. At the request of Army coach Red Blaik, Sid Luckman was dispatched to West Point to show the Army staff how to play the T-formation with man in motion. In the spring of 1942, Bob Snyder, the Bears' backup quarterback, put the T in at Notre Dame and Creighton University and helped Clark Shaughnessy install it at the University of Maryland. Shaughnessy himself introduced Sammy Baugh and the Redskins to the T's intricacies in 1944.

By that year, more than 50 percent of college teams had converted to the T-formation. So had most pro teams. Henceforth, the old single-wing formula of "three yards and a cloud of dust" as the ideal offensive play would go the way of the rugby ball in pro football.

Flushed with the notoriety generated by the 73 to 0 championship game of 1940, the NFL sought to solidify its position on the national sports scene. Early in 1941, the team owners appointed Elmer Layden, one of the fabled Four Horsemen of Notre Dame, as commissioner of professional football. Layden, who had been football coach and athletic director at his alma mater, was given a five-year contract for $20,000 a year.

Carl Storck of Dayton, Ohio, who had been serving as NFL president since Joe Carr's death in 1939, had not been consulted about the appointment. "It's all news to me," he told the Associated Press. Storck soon resigned the presidency.

There was a flurry of protests among a minority of owners, not because they opposed Layden but because they felt that George Halas, one of the owners assigned to interview candidates for commissioner, had acted precipitously in announcing Layden's appointment. E. P. Bruch, president of the Cleveland Rams, said the dissension "gives a perfect illustration of why the National League needs a commissioner."

The commissioner's duties were not spelled out in detail, but the owners said that he would be the "czar" of professional football, the counterpart of baseball's commissioner, Kennesaw Mountain Landis. This did not sit well with the existing minor leagues. William D. Griffith, president of the minor AFL, said,

> As far as we're concerned Layden is just an employee of the National Football League. Not a single official of the American League was approached concerning the idea of a football commissioner. Officials of the Pacific Coast League and many other minor leagues were not contacted. . . . But now the officials of the National League name a "czar." He means nothing to us.

The NFL sought to change pro football's image from a working stiff's sport to high-class entertainment. In August 1941, Elmer Layden called a meeting of team publicity men at the league's Chicago office to offer advice:

- In keeping National League publicity on a high, dignified plane, club publicity men are charged with the responsibility of preventing coaches and players from indorsing [*sic*] or lending their name to advertisements for liquor, cigarets [*sic*] and laxatives.
- Commercials over the public address systems in National Football League parks are highly undesirable and shall be eliminated where it can be done without violation of contracts already signed.
- Publicity men are instructed by the commissioner to forbid the taking of any pictures [of players] in dirty, tattered or misfit [*sic*] uniforms and it is especially emphasized that all players must wear stockings in publicity pictures.

The 1941 pre-season games brought the NFL's first experiments with unlimited substitution, which within a decade would change the game profoundly by ending the time-honored practice of playing "both ways"—that is, on both offense and defense. The intercollegiate Football Rules Committee led the way. The committee approved unlimited substitution for 1941, primarily with the idea that injuries would be reduced if there were fewer exhausted players on the field.

The new rule was used by the pros for the first time in games with College All-Star teams in August. Bob Snyder of the champion Chicago Bears remembered that in their game against the College All-Stars for *Chicago Tribune* charities that summer, four men could be substituted at one time. "That was how it started in the pros," he said.

In the East, relaxed rules on substitutions were also used for the first time by the New York Giants in their annual pre-season game against the Eastern College All-Stars. Professional rules then said that a player who was taken out of the game could not return in the same quarter, and it had long been Giants coach Steve Owen's practice to use four backfield men in the first and third quarters and four others in the second and fourth. With the unlimited substitution rule, he designated one backfield as offense and one as defense. The *New York Times* reported that "Hank Soar, Dom Principe, Nello Falaschi and Ward Cuff, the defensive quartet, entered the game at least a dozen times." The *Times* said that the frequent substitutions were an "irritating distraction," and "as a result the contest was decidedly lacking in continuity and dragged out half an hour beyond the normal course of a football game." It would be another two years before the NFL adopted the unlimited substitution rule for league games.

The Chicago Bears continued their dominance, losing only to the Green Bay Packers in the regular season and beating them in a playoff for the Western Division title. They then whipped the New York Giants, the Eastern Division titleholders, 37 to 9, for the NFL championship. The Bears' T-formation with man in motion continued to fascinate (and convert) coaches. Greasy Neale installed it in the Philadelphia Eagles' offense, and the Eagles' game against the

Bears—the first pitting two T-formation pro teams against each other since before the days of Pop Warner—drew a large audience of college and high-school coaches. The Bears licked the rookie-studded Eagles, 49 to 14.

These results may have fascinated the growing number of fervent NFL fans, but they faded into insignificance in the shadow of World War II, which had been raging in Europe for two years. The United States was plunged into the war on Sunday, December 7, 1941, when the Japanese Navy attacked the U.S. fleet at Pearl Harbor in Hawaii. It was, of course, a game day in the NFL. The first bombs fell at Pearl Harbor at 7:55 A.M. Hawaii time—just before 1:00 P.M. along the East Coast. Communication of news was not instantaneous, as it is now, and most NFL games were in progress when fans learned of the attack. During the game, announcements were made that all soldiers, sailors, and Marines were to report to their bases immediately.

The war against the Axis powers—Germany, Italy, and Japan— lasted for nearly four years and profoundly affected American society, including the little world of professional football. Before the war ended in final victory after the dropping of the atomic bomb on two Japanese cities in August 1945, a total of 638 active NFL players had gone into the armed forces. Sixty-nine had been decorated, and twenty-one had been killed in action or died while training.

Two weeks after the attack on Pearl Harbor, the NFL got a taste of problems in the offing at the league's championship game. Just over 13,300 fans turned out at Chicago's Wrigley Field. There were about 32,000 empty seats as the Bears bludgeoned the Giants, 37 to 9. Evidently, Chicago fans had other things on their minds than the Bears' chances to win a second straight NFL title.

By the spring of 1942, the manpower shortage was becoming apparent as players enlisted in or were drafted into the armed forces. A league survey in May found that 112 of the 346 players—32 percent— on the league's ten teams in 1941 were already in the military services. "Naturally, we're proud of that record," said Commissioner Elmer Layden, "and I believe it's additional proof of the worthwhileness of football. Action on the playing field has fitted these boys with something special."

Complicating pro football's manpower problem was the fact that few college seniors could look forward to playing immediately, since most would be taken by the military soon after graduation. But, Layden said, "we're going ahead and planning for conduct of our regular schedule. But everything we decide today may have to be abandoned tomorrow. While we believe professional football has a definite place in the recreational program of a nation at war, nothing connected with it should or will be permitted to hinder the war effort."

The NFL did its bit for war-relief agencies. In 1942 the league gave $680,000, the largest contribution by any single sports organization. Army Emergency Relief got $463,000, and the Navy Relief Fund received $51,000. The remainder, $165,000, was distributed among the Red Cross; the USO, which helped to entertain service personnel in cities; and the United Seaman's Fund. The biggest single contribution came from the pre-season College All-Star game, which attracted 101,000 spectators and produced $154,000 for the army and navy relief funds.

Jimmy Conzelman, the veteran coach of the Chicago Cardinals, issued a combative defense of football as good preparation for war in a May 1942 statement for the radio:

> Football coaches have always been apologists for their profession. For years we've been on the defensive against attacks from reformers who regard us as muscle-bound mentalities exploiting kids for an easy living. Football has been under fire because it involves body contact and it teaches violence. It was considered useless, even dangerous.
>
> But that's all over now. The bleeding hearts haven't the courtesy to apologize to us, but they're coming around and asking our help in the national emergency. Why?
>
> Why, because the college commencement classes this month find the customary challenge of life a pale prelude to the demands of a world at war. Instead of job seekers, or home makers, the graduates suddenly have become defenders of a familiar way of life, of an ideology, a religion and of a nation. They have been taught to build. Now they must learn to destroy.
>
> It may seem reprehensible to inculcate a will to destroy in these amiable young men; but war is reprehensible—and its basic motive is to destroy. The transition will not be an easy one. Democracy makes us a pacific people. The young man must be toughened not only physically but mentally. He must become accustomed to violence. Football is the No. 1 medium for attuning a man to body contact and violent physical shock. It teaches that after all there isn't anything so terrifying about a punch in the puss.

Like millions of other Americans, professional football players were profoundly affected by the war. Many lost one, two, or three years of their careers in sports. One of them was Vince Banonis, an All-American center-linebacker from the University of Detroit. His senior season there was 1942, and he was selected for the North–South All-Star game for seniors at Montgomery, Alabama. "I was down there when the news came that I had been drafted by Chicago," he remembered. "I thought it was the Bears, but it was the raggedy-ass Cardinals. They were at the bottom of the barrel then." (After the war, they won the NFL championship.)

Banonis played the 1942 season with the Cardinals and then joined the navy. Jimmy Conzelman, who was then the coach of the Cardinals and had been a commander in the navy during World War I, used his influence to get Banonis into officers training school. After receiving his commission, Banonis was given navy assignments in Chicago, at Marquette University, and at Iowa Pre-Flight School, which boasted one of the strongest football teams in the services. "We were the national service champs in 1943, and I made service All-American," Banonis remembered. "The only game we lost was to Notre Dame, 14 to 13, in South Bend. I had gotten a lot of college scholarship offers, but I never got one from Notre Dame, and that was the school I had always wanted to go to. So in the Navy, I finally got to Notre Dame! It was a great experience."

The NFL was hurting for players in 1943 and 1944. In 1944 it got so bad that the Chicago Cardinals and Pittsburgh Steelers merged their rosters and played as the Card-Pitts, usually pronounced "Carpets." They didn't win a single game, dropping ten straight. Banonis remembered:

> I was stationed with the Navy at Wildwood, New Jersey. One day I got a call that the Cardinals–Pittsburgh Steelers needed some help. So I played two or three games for them when they were in New York or Philadelphia. Then I decided I wouldn't play anymore, but they kept calling me about their game against the Bears in Chicago. The Saturday before that game, I left Wildwood, New Jersey, and hitchhiked to Philadelphia. I couldn't get a flight to Chicago right away; I had to wait till midnight. I flew to Chicago and got a cot in a big exhibition room at the Palmer House to sleep on. Sunday morning I got up and went to church, and then I played the whole game against the Bears. I got hurt in the first ten minutes, and I was pooped at the end, not having had any training.
>
> After the game, I got on a plane for Philly that evening. A guy picked me up and drove me back to Wildwood, and I got there in time for duty at 6:00 A.M. Monday.

Vince Banonis's experience was not unusual. Hank Soar managed to get back to New York for Giant games while he was stationed in Massachusetts and Pennsylvania in 1944. "Jack Mara didn't like it because I wasn't there working out all week long," Soar recalled. "I said, 'I don't like it either but what the hell can I do about it? I'm in the Army.' " The following season, Soar couldn't commute to New York for games because he was a special services officer at a base in Greenland, conducting sports and other recreational activities for servicemen in transit to and from Europe.

Bulldog Turner missed most of the 1945 season with the Bears, but he didn't miss much football. He was drafted in 1944 and played the 1945 season with the Second Air Corps team in Colorado Springs.

"We didn't even have a base. We stayed in a college there. I didn't have any duties besides playing football." Turner recalled:

> I played two games with the Bears that season. One of my teammates out there in Colorado Springs with the Second Air Corps was a pilot. He had to get so many hours in the air every month to collect his check. I'd get a three-day pass, and he'd check out a plane and we'd fly to Chicago, and I'd play with the Bears and then I'd drive back. Nobody in Colorado Springs knew I'd been gone but me and the pilot, Tom Fears.
>
> One day he and I flew into Chicago on Saturday, but the Bears weren't playing there the next day. They were going to play in Detroit. So we went out late partying, because I knew some people in Chicago. We got up the next morning to fly to Detroit. Tom was going to take a little nap and he set the plane on automatic pilot. He told me what to do. He said, "Keep that horizon right there in that spot on the instrument," and he went to sleep. I'm rassling that thing! I'm just pushing with all my might to keep that horizon where it's supposed to be. When he woke up, I said, "Man, I can't hold this thing anymore." He reached down and touched a little wheel that tilted the plane to where it was supposed to be.
>
> We got into Detroit. The Bears had a uniform ready for me, but it didn't have a belt. So I wore my regular army belt with my football uniform.

Not every NFL player who went into the military played football with service teams. One who did not was Ken Kavanaugh, who joined the Army Air Corps in 1942 after his second season as an end with the Chicago Bears. "Believe me, I knew nothing about an airplane," Kavanaugh said. "I didn't know a rudder from an aileron, but I said to myself: There's no way I'm ever going to dig a foxhole: I'll get killed before I ever get the thing dug, so I'm going to try flying."

After getting his wings, he piloted bombers on antisubmarine patrol in the Atlantic Ocean and the Caribbean Sea. In 1944 Kavanaugh was trained to fly B-24 and B-18 bombers and was sent to England. From bases there, he flew twenty-five missions over Germany. "I never lost a man," he said thankfully. "The airplane was shot to hell. The engines were out all the time, and there were holes in it everywhere, but we didn't even earn a Purple Heart. We were just flat-assed lucky."

Kavanaugh was discharged shortly after the war ended, at about the time the Chicago Bears were starting the exhibition games for the 1945 season. He reported to the Bears in Bethlehem, Pennsylvania, the day before a game against the Philadelphia Eagles. "George Halas made me play, and I scored three times," Kavanaugh said, laughing.

Another player who got his football baptism by fire almost immediately after his military discharge was Ed Frutig, an end with the Green Bay Packers. Frutig had played the 1941 season with the Packers after graduating from the University of Michigan and playing on a team that starred Tom Harmon and Forrest Evashevski. He joined the navy in January 1942, just weeks after the Packers lost a playoff to the Chicago Bears for the Western Division championship.

Frutig learned to pilot dive bombers and fighter planes and became a flight instructor. He also played service football at the navy base in Corpus Christi, Texas. "They called the team the Comets, and they played in the Southwest College Conference," Frutig remembers. "We called them the Comical Comets because we didn't practice too much." It was his last football for the duration. Frutig was discharged from the navy in September 1945. He recalled:

> I contacted Curly Lambeau of the Packers and joined them in Washington for the next to last exhibition game before the regular season. The next week we played Detroit.
> He had his team all set by then, but I think he wanted to see what kind of shape I was in. He put me in the game and called a long pass play—the kind that Don Hutson was awfully good at, and I couldn't get under it. I was in terrible shape.
> After we got back to Green Bay, he called me in and said, "You've been traded to Detroit."

The Pacific Coast Football League, one of the top minor leagues during the heyday of the minors from the mid-1930s to 1950, continued to operate during the war. Like the NFL, it suffered from a dearth of players. But some of the Coast League teams, including the San Diego Bombers, benefited from the talent they could call on at the numerous military installations in southern California. On the Bombers' roster in 1944 and 1945 was Bruce Thyberg of Whittier College, aka Bob Dove, an end from Notre Dame.

Bob Dove had earned All-American honors in 1942 and 1943, was named lineman of the year by the Touchdown Club in Washington, and played in the East–West All-Star game. At the urging of Notre Dame coach Frank Leahy, he and other graduating football players joined the Marines. After boot camp and officers training school, he was posted to the Headquarters Company of the Fifth Marine Division on the West Coast. He also joined the El Toro Marines team in Santa Ana, California, one of the strongest service teams during the war. Dove remembered:

> We played both college teams and service teams like the Fleet City Bluejackets and Iowa Preflight on Saturdays. Then on Sunday, Wee Willie Wilkin, the Redskins tackle, Crazy Legs Hirsch, who starred for Los Angeles after the war, a kid named Pat Leahy and I would ride to San Diego, and under assumed names we would play for the Bombers.
> Now, of course, in the Marine Corps the navy was our boss, and they

didn't want us playing outside ball. They didn't care if we got killed or got our leg broken playing football in the Marine Corps, but they didn't want us doing it on Sunday. So we played under assumed names. I was Bruce Thyberg.

The El Toro Marines practiced every day in season, as did the other top service teams. The San Diego Bombers did not practice much in 1944, Dove said, but in his second season with them, the Bombers were required to come to the team office on Tuesday to collect their checks. They also had to attend a two-and-a-half-hour practice session.

In the off-season, Dove was given other duties in the training battalion, teaching pilots about night fighting and weapons. He was later assigned as a replacement in a unit that had been shot up in the South Pacific, but the war ended before he was sent overseas.

To deal with the dearth of quality players, the NFL cut its team player limit from thirty-three to twenty-five in 1943 and voted to permit unlimited substitutions. Until 1943, a player could enter a game only once in each quarter, except that in the fourth quarter, two players on each team could be brought in twice. Colleges had been using the unlimited substitution rule for a couple of years. (But many colleges, especially smaller ones, had dropped football for the duration of the war due to the small number of physically fit male students on campus.)

NFL coaches were not happy with the unlimited substitution rule and hoped that it would not become permanent. Their argument was that if such stars as Sammy Baugh of the Redskins, and Don Hutson and Cecil Isbell of the Green Bay Packers, were allowed to rest, they would score easily when they reentered a game against tired opponents.

Some retired players rejoined their old teams during the war. One was Mel Hein, the former All-Pro center for the New York Giants, who had retired to coach at Union College in Schenectady, New York, in 1943. Although Union dropped football for the rest of that season, Hein stayed on as an associate professor of physical education. When the Giants were playing at home during the next three seasons, he took a train to New York on Friday evening, practiced with the Giants on Saturday, and played the game on Sunday. With that regimen, Hein completed a fifteen-year career as a two-way center and linebacker for the Giants. Ken Strong also came back to the Giants at the age of thirty-eight to help out.

The Chicago Bears induced Bronko Nagurski to leave retirement on his farm in Minnesota and return to the Bears for the 1943 season. By then, the Bears had lost their coach to the military; George Halas, a navy veteran of World War I, reenlisted and at war's end was in the South Pacific as a lieutenant commander. But he continued to keep in touch with his assistant coaches, Heartley (Hunk) Anderson and Luke Johnsos, even at that far remove.

The Bears won the NFL championship again in 1943 by whipping the Redskins, 41 to 21, with Sid Luckman throwing five touchdown passes. Nineteen of the twenty-eight Bears on the championship squad were gone the next season as the manpower situation grew more desperate. Johnsos and Anderson sought help everywhere. "We held tryouts and signed up anybody who could run around the field twice," Johnsos recalled. "We had players forty, fifty years old. We had a very poor ball club."

Luckman had joined the Merchant Marine but was able to get to most Bear games in 1943 and 1944. Halas feared that Luckman's sea duties might make it impossible for him to play football, so he sought quarterbacking insurance. Thirty-year-old Bob Snyder, the former Bears quarterback, who had spent the 1942 season teaching the T-formation to various college teams, said he got a phone call from Halas before the 1943 season:

> He was in Norman, Oklahoma, with the navy then, and he says, "Snyder, how about coming back with the Bears?" I said, "There's no way, George, I'm up to about 240 pounds—about 50 pounds over my playing weight— and I'm full of beer. I haven't run, haven't done anything."
>
> He said, "I'll tell you why you have to come back. Sid is in the Merchant Marine, and I can't be sure he can play. We don't have a T quarterback; we'll have to go to a single wing." And I said, "George, I don't care if you go to a short punt formation. I'm not coming back." He said, "Well, work out a little." Now this is June.
>
> I came home after playing golf one day, and my wife, Eleanor, said, "Coach Halas wants you to call. I really think you ought to think this over." That son of a gun—he called my wife and got her to work on me a little bit.
>
> So I called George and told him there is no way. He said, "I'll tell you what I'm going to do. I'll have somebody come down from the Bears office and bring you a contract, and you can fill in any number you want."
>
> Well, I figured there was something wrong with him; he had been out in the sun too long or something because he doesn't give money away. But anyway, as it turned out, I said okay and he paid me $350 a game.
>
> George was desperate. As it turned out, the Merchant Marine allowed Sid to play on weekends. Anyway, I got to the Bears training camp on a Thursday, and on Friday we got on the train to go to Baltimore to play the Redskins—an exhibition game. It was 102 degrees. I went over to Hunk Anderson, the head coach, and I said, "Let me tell you something. I'm out of shape, and I haven't run in two years." He said, "All you have to do is kick off." So I kicked off and came over to the bench and sat down. I was enjoying the game, and then that damn Luckman got hurt, and I went in and played the whole ball game.
>
> I pretty near died! But I played the whole season.

The war years saw some shifting of franchises. The Cleveland Rams suspended for the year in 1943, and the Philadelphia Eagles and Pittsburgh Steelers combined rosters and divided their home games between their home cities. The "Steagles" divorced in 1944, with the Eagles assuming their former identity and Pittsburgh joining with the Chicago Cardinals for the 1944 season.

Like Bob Snyder, Bill Hewitt found that he could command a lot more money during the war years than he did from 1932 to 1939 with the Chicago Bears and Philadelphia Eagles. Hewitt, a 5-foot, 9-inch, 190-pound end from the University of Michigan, never earned more than $250 a game during a career that led to posthumous election to the Pro Football Hall of Fame in 1971. (He was killed in an automobile accident in 1947.) But when Bert Bell pleaded successfully for Hewitt to come out of his three-year retirement in 1943 and join the Steagles, he offered $400 a game, a princely salary at the time, especially for a lineman.

The 1944 season, the nadir of the NFL's war years, was a terrible time for recruiting football players. Greasy Neale, coach of the Philadelphia Eagles, despaired of their prospects. In September, Eagles general manager Harry Thayer said that Neale had cut his own salary from $12,000 to $3,000 because the team would be poor: "Neale tore up his contract and said he wouldn't accept more than $3,000. He said he couldn't produce an improved team with the material on hand because good college players are unobtainable these days."

Neale was wrong. Star rookies were rare but not unobtainable. The Eagles signed Steve Van Buren, a powerful runner out of Louisiana State University, that season, and Van Buren became the chief building block of the Eagles' postwar NFL champions. In his rookie year, Van Buren, who could run 100 yards in 9.8 seconds and was shifty in an open field, led the NFL in punt-return yardage and averaged 5.6 yards a carry from scrimmage. Neale found himself finishing second to the Eastern Division champion New York Giants with a 7–1–2 record—far better than the Eagles had ever done before.

The 1944 season was a time of optimism for the American people. The forces of the United States and its allies had landed in Europe in June and were pressing toward German territory during the football season. In the Pacific war, the United States took back the Philippines from Japan and bombed Japanese cities. It was clearly just a matter of time before the war would be over.

By the time the 1945 season rolled around, it was. Players began to trickle back to their teams. The team player limit went back to thirty-three. The fans returned too. In 1942 total attendance at NFL games had dropped below 900,000 and remained low throughout the war years. In 1945 the ten NFL teams played to a record total of 1,918,631 spectators—an average of 28,636 for sixty-eight games, including exhibitions. During the war, playing the national anthem had become a ceremonial prelude to NFL games. Commissioner Layden announced that the anthem would continue to be played. "It should be as much a part of every game as the kickoff," he said. "We must not drop it simply because the war is over. We should never forget what it stands for."

The Cleveland Rams had returned to action in 1944 and won the 1945 title, beating the Washington Redskins with the help of an archaic rule. The Redskins' Sammy Baugh fired a pass from his end zone that struck the goal posts, which were still on the goal line. It was a safety worth 2 points for Cleveland under the existing rules, and Cleveland went on to win by 1 point, 15 to 14.

It was the end of an era. Better times—much better times—were coming.

9
THE POSTWAR WAR

I n a prescient column in *Newsweek* in October 1945, sports columnist John Lardner foretold football's future. "Pro football has growing pains," he wrote. "The end of the war may be the event which will build the sport into national proportions both geographically and commercially, just as the end of the last war gave pro players their original impetus and made them begin to think of organization and respectability." Major college football was still the game of choice for most football fans, but Lardner predicted a coming change. He pointed out that the college game had grown big because it had cultivated millions of ticket buyers who had no interest in the colleges as educational institutions:

> New York night clubs, to name one area of synthetic college spirit, are packed on the night of the Army–Notre Dame game with snake-dancers and weeping patriots who have a hazy idea that the Notre Dame campus lies near Quogue, Long Island. It seems easy on paper to transfer this huge and strictly game-minded national audience from the support of college pro teams to the support of true pro teams.

Lardner concluded, "If colleges persist with high-pressure football, they will logically become the minor leagues of football, and boys who attend them to play football will leave as soon as possible—just because they are the minor leagues."

The *Newsweek* columnist was writing at a time when the first serious challenge to the supremacy of the NFL was being mounted. The challenge came from a new league called the All-America Football Conference (AAFC), which planned to begin sanctioning games in the 1946 season. (Another circuit, called the United States Football League, had been proposed in the spring of 1944. It was to have had ten teams, mostly in northeastern and midwestern cities, plus a franchise in Honolulu, but it never got off the ground.)

The AAFC was the brainchild of Arch Ward, the *Chicago Tribune* sports editor who had also conceived the College All-Star game. He enlisted the support of several well-heeled men to back the AAFC teams, none of whom had an extensive background in football. Three of them—Anthony J. Morabito, who had a lumbering empire in San Francisco; James F. Breuil, an oil man; and Arthur B. (Mickey) Mc-Bride, who owned a taxi fleet in Cleveland—had previously applied for NFL franchises. All had been turned down.

The other wealthy owners were John L. Keeshin, a trucking magnate in Chicago; Daniel R. Topping of New York, co-owner of the baseball Yankees; William D. Cox, former owner of the Philadelphia Phillies baseball team; and Benjamin F. Lindheimer, who had race-track interests in Los Angeles. Lindheimer headed a syndicate that included actor Don Ameche and Louis B. Mayer, head of MGM. The only shoestring operator in the AAFC was Harvey Hester, owner of the Miami Seahawks.

The AAFC presented direct challenges to NFL teams in three cities: New York, Chicago, and Los Angeles. The NFL's New York Giants would be competing with the AAFC's New York Yankees and Brooklyn Dodgers. In Chicago, the AAFC's Rockets would try to attract Bears and Cardinals fans, and in Los Angeles the AAFC's Dons would face off against the transplanted Cleveland Rams, the 1945 champions. Rams owner Dan Reeves had been trying vainly to take his team to Los Angeles for years. George Preston Marshall of the Washington Redskins fought the idea until Reeves said that either he would take the Rams to Los Angeles or he would sell them. That did it; a month after the Rams beat the Redskins in freezing weather in Cleveland for the 1945 NFL title, they were on their way west. The Pacific Coast Football League, which continued to operate during the war, was still in business in 1946, but the coming of the Rams and the establishment of two AAFC teams, the Los Angeles Dons and the San Francisco 49ers, brought the first major league sports teams to the West Coast.

The AAFC leaders did their best to reach an agreement with the NFL to respect each other's player contracts and territorial rights. In April 1945, John Keeshin, owner of the AAFC's Chicago team, and Paul Brown, coach of the prospective team in Cleveland, met with NFL commissioner Elmer Layden to seek an accommodation. They got nowhere. After the meeting Layden said, "Let them get a football and play a game, and then maybe we'll have something to talk about."

Shortly after that, Jimmy Crowley, Layden's fellow rider among Notre Dame's Four Horsemen, was named commissioner and president of the AAFC. He had words of warning for the NFL: "We originally resolved not to tamper with National League players, but since the NFL snubbed us we see no reason why we can't hire their players." By that time, the AAFC claimed to have more than 150 players under contract for its eight teams, including four former NFL stalwarts. (One whole NFL franchise jumped to the new league. Daniel Topping, co-owner of the New York Yankees baseball team and of Yankee Stadium, had the NFL's Brooklyn franchise and wanted to play in his own stadium. But New York Giants owner Tim Mara, who had territorial rights in New York City, refused to allow it. So Topping took his franchise and went to the AAFC, calling his team the New York Yankees and playing at the stadium.)

There is nothing like a player war between two leagues to raise salaries. Take, for example, the experience of Marine First Lieutenant Bob Dove, the Notre Dame end who had played for the El Toro Marines service team and, under an alias, for the San Diego Bombers of the Pacific Coast Football League. Dove remembered:

> Dick Hanley, the old Northwestern coach who coached the El Toro Marines, called me in before the end of the war and said, "The war is going to end soon, and I'm the new coach of the Chicago Rockets of the All-America Football Conference."
>
> "Well," I said, "I belong to the Washington Redskins." They had drafted me in about the third round. Before I was discharged in the spring of 1946, George Preston Marshall visited me at Santa Ana. He asked me when I was getting out, and he offered me $1,800 for the 1946 season.
>
> Anyway, Dick Hanley pointed to a big map of the South Pacific behind him. "Now see here," he said. "Do you know what this island is? Tarawa. Here's Iwo Jima. See this island? It's got a number on it—Number Seven. See these islands up here? They don't have a name or a number, Bob. If you don't sign this contract with me, your ass is going to be on those islands and they may never find you again."
>
> So I signed with the Chicago Rockets after a little back-and-forth with the Redskins. The Rockets gave me $5,250 for the first year, a three-year no-release contract with automatic raises of $500 each year, and guaranteed me a job on the side in Chicago. I worked for Fruehauf Trailer Company there for five years.

Dove had a strange season as a first-year pro in 1946. The Chicago Rockets finished last in the AAFC's West Division, but they had a respectable record of 5–6–3. Bob Hoernschemeyer, a rookie tailback from Indiana, and another rookie, end Elroy (Crazy Legs) Hirsch, Dove's teammate on the El Toro Marines, sparked the Rockets' offense. Dove said that the team drew fairly good crowds to Soldier Field, but the Rockets did not reach the level of popularity of the NFL's Chicago Bears and Chicago Cardinals. "I remember that for our first game, against the Browns, they didn't have enough ticket takers at Soldier Field and they delayed the game a half hour to get the people in," Dove said.

Coach Dick Hanley clashed with owner Jack Keeshin after the Rockets got off to a so-so start in their first three games. "Keeshin wasn't satisfied, and he and Dick started going head to head," Bob Dove said. "Keeshin said, 'Gentlemen, it's like a marriage situation. Dick Hanley and I don't get along, and he's no longer coaching this team.' "

Keeshin named a coaching committee of three to take over the reins: Bob Dove, a twenty-five-year-old-rookie; Ned Mathews, a halfback and veteran of four pro seasons; and Willie Wilkin, a tackle who had started with the Washington Redskins in 1938. "They called the team the Coachless Wonders," Dove laughed. "The league didn't like it because when all three of us were in the game, there was no coach on the bench. So after five games, Keeshin brought in Pat Boland from Minnesota to coach the last six games."

Many returning NFL stars were offered big raises to jump to the AAFC. Chicago Bears quarterback Sid Luckman said before the season, "They have been hounding me for several weeks, and their offers have been fabulous." A couple of his teammates succumbed to the lure. One was Charlie O'Rourke, a Boston College All-American halfback who had backed up Luckman in 1942. During the war, he quarterbacked the Fleet City navy team in California. O'Rourke recalled:

> With the Bears in 1942 I had a contract for five years at $5,000 a year. After the war I called George Halas; I wanted to talk with him about going back with the Bears, but somehow we never did get together. Lee Artoe, a tackle who had been with the Bears too, had jumped to the Los Angeles Dons of the AAFC, and he called me up and asked me to play with the Dons. So I had to call Halas again and tell him I was going to play with the Dons.
>
> He said, "No, I've got you on a five-year contract." And I said, "Well, did you read the small print of the contract? At the bottom it says if this man goes into the service his contract is null and void. George, that seems as though I'm a free agent." With that, I told him I was going to sign with the Dons. They offered me $10,000.

Some players were leery of the new league and declined attractive offers to jump. One was Ken Kavanaugh, the Bears' pass-catching end, who was also approached by Lee (Jelly) Artoe to go to Los Angeles. He remembered:

> Jelly was a good friend of mine—in fact, he was my roommate on the Bears—when he went with the LA Dons. I think I was making $8,000 with the Bears, and they offered me $20,000 to go with the Dons. I said, "No, I don't want to do that, I'll stay with the Bears because they were a solid outfit."
>
> I just didn't want to jump. I guess I wasn't a rebel or anything like that. But I did tell George Halas what I was offered, and he did raise my salary up to $12,000 or $14,000. So the AAFC did result in a salary jump for me.

Another player who had a similar experience was Chicago Cardinals quarterback Ray Mallouf. He was the son of Lebanese immigrants and had grown up in the rural village of Sayre, Oklahoma (population 2,000), where his father was a bootmaker. Like many other football players in America's outback during the 1930s, Mallouf had never heard of pro football during his youth. He was a junior at Southern Methodist University in Dallas before he learned that it was possible to make a living playing football.

He was drafted by the Cardinals after his graduation in 1941 and played that season for a salary of $3,500. Mallouf spent the next three years in the navy, serving primarily as an instructor in physical education and academic programs for the navy's aviation cadets. When the war ended in August 1945, Mallouf tried to get out of the navy in time to play with the Cardinals that season. He remembered:

> But there was a captain out in California who wanted to have a football team, and they shipped me and some other players out to Oakland so they could have a team at a station out there. About a dozen players who had pro experience had to play out there before being discharged. After the season, they let us all go home.
>
> I had several letters from teams in the AAFC, but I didn't get any offers because I had already signed with the Cardinals. I told them I wasn't interested. Since I knew most of the boys on the Cardinals, I wanted to go back with them. The Cardinals offered me about $10,000. So my salary was almost tripled after the war.

The AAFC brought into professional football a coach who arguably had greater influence on the sport than any other before or since. He was Paul Brown, an autocratic disciplinarian whose devotion to the game and the teams he coached has rarely been approached, much less surpassed.

Brown was born in 1909 and grew up in Massillon, Ohio, one of the hotbeds of pro football in the early years of the century. His father was a railroad dispatcher. Naturally, football was *the* sport at Massillon's Washington High School, and, just as naturally, Brown wanted to play despite his small size. (He weighed only 140 pounds.) He did, as the Massillon Tiger quarterback and at Miami University of Ohio after he had been rejected as too small by Ohio State. Inevitably, perhaps, Brown became a coach and teacher after graduation.

Brown began developing and refining the methods that would bring important changes to pro football while he coached his alma mater's teams at Washington High School. Over a nine-year span, his teams compiled a cumulative record of eighty victories, eight defeats, and two ties. In his final season at Massillon in 1940, Ohio State had suffered a disaster in its last game, absorbing a 40 to 0 whipping at the hands of Michigan. That was too much for Ohio State's fervent alumni and boosters throughout the state, and the Buckeyes' head coach, Francis Schmidt, was fired.

Ohio's high-school coaches' association immediately began pressing Ohio State to name Brown as coach of the Buckeyes. Ostensibly, the coaches wanted him to strengthen Ohio State's football, but there was a suspicion that they also wanted to get the invincible Brown out of their circle. In any event, Brown became Ohio State's football coach in 1941. The following year, his Buckeyes won the Big Ten title and were acclaimed as national champions. Their only loss in a 9–1 season was to Northwestern, whose tailback, Otto Graham, would join Brown as quarterback for the Cleveland Browns after World War II.

Brown was commissioned in the navy after the 1943 season and spent the following two years coaching the strong team at the Great Lakes Naval Training Center near Chicago. He was still in the navy at Great Lakes when he was approached with the idea of coaching in the proposed AAFC. Brown was reluctant because, he said, the coaching posts at Washington High School and Ohio State were the only jobs he ever wanted. But when Ohio State's athletic director seemed lukewarm about inviting him to return, Brown, a proud man, began looking with favor on professional football.

He showed his negotiating mettle at once. When he signed to coach and be general manager of the Cleveland team in February 1945, the terms of his contract were probably unprecedented for a coach who was not also the team's principal owner, as the Bears' George Halas was. Brown's salary was set at $25,000 a year. He was given a 5 percent share of the ownership and a monthly retainer of $1,500 for his remaining months in the navy. Most important to Brown, he was also given complete control of the team, with freedom to sign players and coaches.

Brown made it plain to the principal owner, Arthur (Mickey) McBride, that he had little interest in the financial picture. All he cared about was a winning team. McBride never winced at such loose talk about money, perhaps because he had a lot of it. McBride owned Cleveland's taxi fleet and had large real-estate holdings in Florida, as well as a sports wire syndicate.

The team was named the Browns in a contest for fans. Possibly fans from the Massillon–Canton area, sixty miles south of Cleveland, stuffed the ballot boxes on behalf of their favorite son. (The first choice had been Panthers, until McBride learned that it had been the name of an unsuccessful semipro team in Cleveland years earlier.)

Paul Brown was still in the navy when the Browns began signing players, but he kept a close eye on the process. In fact, he chose the men he wanted and had his assistant, John Brickels, an old friend and fellow coach in Ohio, and Creighton Miller, a former Notre Dame player, do the actual signing. Brown was partial to his players from Ohio State and Great Lakes. Some signees, such as Otto Graham of Northwestern, had starred on opposing teams. Brown also accepted those who came highly recommended by people whose opinion he valued. Because McBride had deep pockets, the Cleveland Browns were able to offer players who were still in the armed forces what amounted to a bonus; each was given from $200 to $250 a month during his remaining time in the service.

One of them was guard Lindell (Lin) Houston, who has the unique distinction of having played under Paul Brown at all three levels—high school, college, and professional. Houston's family had moved to Massillon from southern Illinois in January 1937 when he was a sophomore in high school. "I had never even seen a football game," he said. "I was a farm kid. Our school in Illinois wasn't big enough to have football."

Brown was already well known in Ohio football. He was also the basketball coach at Massillon, and Houston played on his basketball team, which was the runner-up in the state tournament in the 1935/1936 season. Brown invited the 6-foot, 190-pound youngster to come out for spring football.

That fall, Houston played in the first football game he had ever seen. He made first team guard, a remarkable achievement for an athlete in his first year in a high-powered high-school program. In his second year of football and his final year of high school, Houston made the All-Ohio high-school team and had forty-two college scholarship offers. At Paul Brown's suggestion, he went to the University of Michigan. Houston dropped out after a few weeks because he did not believe that Michigan was fulfilling the terms of his scholarship. He wound up at Ohio State.

He had already played for two years for the Buckeyes when Brown became the coach at Ohio State. Houston was on the national championship squad in 1942. In January 1943, he joined the army. He was assigned to the field artillery, but he spent the 1943 football season playing for the team at Fort Bragg, North Carolina. As soon as the season was over, his unit was sent to the South Pacific. "I was there for over a year," Houston said. "We were in on the retaking of New Guinea and the Philippines. In the field artillery, you're back a ways, but still, we were in the middle of it."

Houston, a staff sergeant, got his first contract with the Browns while he was overseas. "It was for the 1946 season," he remembered. "It was a good contract. My salary was to be $6,000, with a $2,000 bonus. But there was no guarantee. I had to make the team, but I knew I could do that."

Lou Groza, who earned the nickname "The Toe" for his place-kicking prowess, was another player signed by the Browns while fighting in the war. Groza was born and raised in Martins Ferry, Ohio, a steel town on the Ohio River, and played on state championship football and basketball teams in high school. He was a tackle but showed early talent for place kicking. Groza recalled:

> I began kicking before I went to high school. I had an older brother who kicked field goals for the high school, and he showed me how. I used to practice in the street, trying to place kick over the telephone wires. I developed a natural ability for it.
>
> No, I wasn't a soccer player. Soccer was unheard of in those days in Martins Ferry.

Groza was one of the last "straight-ahead" kickers, who approached the ball in a direct line to the goal posts and hit it with the toe rather than with the instep, as today's soccer-style kickers do. He was also one of the last kickers who was not a specialist. Groza was a Hall of Fame tackle as well as a kicker for most of his nineteen-year career with the Browns.

Groza was attending Ohio State on a football scholarship and had played with the freshman team when the Enlisted Reserve Corps, which he had joined, was called into army service. He went to the Pacific with the Ninety-sixth Division and took part in the battles for Leyte and Okinawa, two of the most bitterly fought struggles of the war against Japan. Master Sergeant Lou Groza was a surgical technician in a medical battalion. "We took heavy casualties on Okinawa," he said. "I didn't get wounded, though. I was lucky."

Groza's unit was to take part in the invasion of Japan, which was scheduled for November 1945, but the war ended in August. He was discharged in February 1946 and returned to Ohio State to finish his freshman year before reporting to the Browns' training camp. Groza remembered his arrival in training camp:

> Now I had never played college football except for three freshman games at Ohio State. I showed up at training camp and I said, to myself, "Oh, boy, what did I get myself into?" For tackles the Browns had Jim Daniel, who was an All-American at Ohio State and played with the Chicago Bears before the war, and Lou Rymkus, who had played with the Washington Redskins, and Ernie Blandin, an All-American tackle at Tulane, and Chet Adams, a pro with the old Cleveland Rams before the war.
>
> Paul Brown knew about me because he was the varsity coach while I was on the freshman team at Ohio State. In my first year in 1946, I was mostly a kicker for the Browns. In 1947 I became the starting left tackle.

Another charter member of the Cleveland Browns who had been in the thick of the fighting during World War II was end Dante Lavelli. An army sergeant with the Twenty-eighth Division, Lavelli fought in the Battle of the Bulge, the desperate fight in Belgium in December

1944 in which American troops repulsed the last major offensive of the German army. "I was shot in the foot, but I had my boots on and it wasn't too serious," Lavelli remembered.

Lavelli had been a star end in high school in the village of Hudson, Ohio, twenty-five miles south of Cleveland, and had gone to Ohio State in 1941 on a football scholarship. (He also played basketball and baseball for the Buckeyes. An excellent hitter in baseball, he had a trial with the Detroit Tigers. Later he had to make a choice of sports because the Tigers didn't want him to play football and Paul Brown didn't want him to play baseball. He chose football and had a Hall of Fame career.)

At Ohio State, Lavelli played with Brown's national champions of 1942 before going into the army in the spring of 1943. He was back home in December 1945 and preparing to go to baseball spring training when he was visited by an emissary from the Cleveland Browns, who offered him $5,000 for the 1946 season. He signed.

So did a lot of others—so many, in fact, that they could not all be accommodated under the thirty-three-man limit for squads in the AAFC in 1946. Paul Brown kept them available (and off the rosters of rivals) by asking Mickey McBride to get them jobs in Cleveland so that they would be free to practice with the Browns but would not count on the roster. Every afternoon while the regulars were at practice, a fleet of McBride's Yellow Cabs would arrive from every direction and disgorge the nonroster players. Thus was born the "taxi squad" in pro football.

The AAFC did very well in the player war with the NFL. Of the sixty players on the College All-Star team in 1946, forty-four opted to play in the AAFC. About 100 men who had played in the NFL jumped to the new league, but the owners and coaches of the older league continued to pooh-pooh the upstart circuit for most of its four-year life.

The AAFC debuted with a splash. Its first league game pitted the Miami Seahawks against the Browns in Cleveland. The largest crowd ever to attend a regular-season league game—60,135 fans—turned out at Municipal Stadium. The gathering was the product of vigorous promotion in newspapers and on radio and a well-publicized battery of pretty women who took phone orders for tickets. The Browns noted proudly that the crowd was only about 12,000 fewer people than had appeared at all four home games of the departed NFL champion Rams in 1945.

The game, however, was a paradigm of one of the AAFC's major problems—too much Cleveland Browns, not enough opposition. The Browns won, 44 to 0, without breaking much of a sweat, even though it was shirtsleeve weather. The Seahawks were so bad that the sportswriters had more praise for a group of thirty comely baton twirlers who entertained at halftime than for the game. Dan Taylor of the *Cleveland Press* reported:

> To say that George (Red) Bird's Musical Majorettes made a distinct hit with the fans is putting it mildly.
> After the gaily-clad, high-stepping, precision-marching young ladies treated the assemblage to a snappy 30-minute show between the halves, they drew an ovation that was louder and longer than any offered during the night to the athletes.

Paul Brown had used mainly the single-wing formation in Massillon and at Ohio State. At Great Lakes and Cleveland, his teams used the T-formation. His personnel fit in perfectly. In Otto Graham he had the ideal T quarterback, a superb athlete who had earned All-American honors in both football and basketball at Northwestern. Graham was 6 feet, 1 inch tall and weighed 196 pounds. He had a very strong arm and pinpoint accuracy as a passer. In Marion Motley, Brown had the ideal fullback. Motley, a powerful, 6-foot, 2-inch, 235-pound pile-driving runner and excellent blocker, went back a long way with Brown. He had starred at Canton McKinley High School in Ohio for three years while Brown was at archrival Washington High School in Massillon and had played for him at Great Lakes during the war. Motley was one of two black players on the Browns—the other was guard Bill Willis—who integrated the AAFC. Like Graham, Motley, Groza, and Lavelli, Willis earned a place in the Pro Football Hall of Fame.

So did Paul Brown himself. His achievements with the Browns and later as founder of the Cincinnati Bengals included the following:

- His Cleveland Browns won all four championships in the AAFC from 1946 to 1949, as well as seven NFL conference titles and three league championships from 1950 to 1962.
- He was the first to hire full-time, year-round assistant coaches.
- He was the first to give players intelligence and psychological tests to judge their ability to learn and improve.
- He introduced playbooks and classroom instruction to pro football.
- He was the first to test players' foot speed in the 40-yard dash.
- He was the first to use messenger guards to send in plays to the quarterback (but not in his first three years with the Browns because unlimited substitution was not permitted until 1949).
- He was the first to use game films to grade players.
- He was one of the first to station assistants high up in the stadium for a bird's-eye view of the action. The spotters had a telephone to the bench to suggest plays and defensive alignments.

Brown is often credited with inventing the face mask, and he did in fact devise and patent a double protective bar for helmets after Browns quarterback Otto Graham was smashed in the face. But face masks were already being used during the 1930s, though the helmets in those days were so floppy that it was hard to attach a bar to them. Even earlier, in 1928, Bucknell halfback Eddie Halicki, who later played with the Frankford Yellow Jackets and Minneapolis Red Jackets in the NFL, wore a mask to protect his broken nose. It was basically a leather extension of his helmet that covered his nose and cheeks like the mask of Zorro. It was not until 1939 that the first hard-shell helmet was developed and another decade after that before it was perfected enough to support today's bird-cage masks.

Paul Brown was not an imaginative innovator of offensive and defensive formations in the tradition of Pop Warner, Amos Alonzo Stagg, and Clark Shaughnessy. His forte was precise execution of the fundamentals of blocking and tackling and an insistence on striving for perfection. However, Brown did claim to have had a part in the origin of the now-familiar draw play. In his autobiography, Brown wrote:

> During a 1946 game Motley and Graham collided trying to run a trap play on a muddy field. The collision created a broken play, and Otto, in desperation, seeing the linemen charging in on him, just handed the ball to Marion as they stood next to each other. The opposing linemen simply ran past Motley, and he took off for a big gain. We didn't think much of it at the time, but looking at the game films, Otto said, "I think that could become a play," so we developed the blocking assignments and the techniques which went with it. At first we called it a pick, but since that word was also part of the passing terminology, I changed the name to draw, because we wanted our offensive linemen to visualize it as drawing in the pass rushers.

Brown had the respect, though not necessarily the love, of his players since he wanted perfection and unstinting effort. Lou Groza said:

> I say he professionalized pro football coaching. Before him, the assistant coaches were part-time. He had a full-time staff and he assigned different responsibilities to them, and they worked year round. They had contacts with college coaches around the country, and he developed a scouting system for drafting players.
>
> He used movies to teach new offensive and defensive plays, and he had films showing the effect of plays against various defenses.
>
> He believed that in football the solid foundation was blocking and tackling.

Brown was a strict disciplinarian and brooked no flouting of his rules. Dante Lavelli remembered:

> He was so far ahead of other coaches. He knew every man's assignment on every play. We had to learn them too and write them in longhand. The backfield men had to be able to draw out the pass patterns for three people. You just didn't have it in your playbook; you had it up here, in your head, because you had to write it ten times.
>
> In training camp we had a test every Sunday. One year we had a

rookie named Stan Heath, who had played at the University of Nevada. He was all-everything, and people said he was going to replace Otto Graham.

He came into training camp, and on Sunday four or five days later he had to take the test about the plays we'd learned. So he came down to this room and is there for an hour, hour and a half. He's faking it, see, just drawing on the paper. We had about forty-five guys on the squad at that time, and when there's three or four left in the room, he figured he'd better turn his paper in and not be the last one.

He never had a play written down. Paul Brown was furious. He runs up to the third floor to the guy's room and says, "Get in your car and don't come back!" He sent him right home and never gave him a second chance.

Brown had rules for players' conduct off the field too. In his autobiography he wrote:

I always stressed to our players . . . that they should be good examples for the kids who saw them away from the football field. That's why I had rules against smoking in public, swearing or bad language and required coats and ties on the road. I wanted our players to show class. College players had a good reputation, but the public perception of the professional football player back then was of a big, dumb guy with a potbelly and a cheap cigar. That kind of person disgusted me, and I never wanted anyone associating our players with that image, so I always tried to make our pro teams collegelike.

The Cleveland Browns were not alone in having a strict code of behavior. The 1946 Washington Redskins, for example, were told:

You will be expected to conduct yourself in such a manner as to always be a credit to the game, and to your club. . . . Violation of publicly accepted and traditional training rules for athletes—rowdiness, boisterousness, and ungentlemanly conduct of any and every sort—will not be tolerated.

In hotel lobbies, dining rooms and other public rooms, in dining cars and restaurants, and at all public functions where the team appears as a unit, shirts, ties and coats are to be worn, unless otherwise instructed.

Night clubs, bars, cocktail lounges and gambling spots are definitely out of bounds.

The AAFC began play in 1946 with eight franchises in two divisions: East and West. In the East, Topping's New York Yankees took the honors, with a 10–3–1 record. The Brooklyn Dodgers, Buffalo Bisons, and Miami Seahawks were far back, with just three victories each. In the West, the Cleveland Browns were equally dominant, their 12–2 record leading the San Francisco 49ers (9–5), Los Angeles Dons (7–5–2), and Chicago Rockets (5–6–3). The Browns won the first AAFC championship by beating the Yankees, 14 to 9, before 41,000 fans at Cleveland.

In the sense that all franchises finished the season and completed their schedules, the AAFC's debut was a success. But financial trouble had appeared before the league was a week old. The hapless Miami Seahawks, who were drubbed by the Cleveland Browns in the new league's first game, left Cleveland without paying their hotel and restaurant bills. At Paul Brown's behest, the Browns paid them. But the Seahawks were a season-long financial as well as professional disaster. They drew slim crowds for home games, and the league ended up paying the players' salaries and taking back the franchise at the end of the season. The franchise was reborn in 1947 as the Baltimore Colts.

Meanwhile, the NFL continued to look down its collective nose at the AAFC. The player war continued unabated for the four years of the AAFC's existence. In January 1946, even before the AAFC had played its first game, Elmer Layden, commissioner of the NFL, was ousted because the owners appeared to blame him for the escalation of players' salaries. He was succeeded by Bert Bell, co-owner of the Pittsburgh Steelers, a wise and tolerant leader but no wonder worker. Over the next four years, the AAFC made no progress in its efforts to establish friendly relations with the older league.

Bert Bell had not completed his first year in the commissioner's seat before he was faced with the first betting scandal in NFL history. The story broke on the morning of December 15, 1946, just hours before the New York Giants were to meet the Chicago Bears at the Polo Grounds for the NFL championship. Frankie Filchock, the Giants' tailback and star passer, and Merle Mapes, who was to start at fullback for New York because Bill Paschal, the regular, was injured, were said to have been offered bribes by a small-time gambler to make sure the Bears won by at least ten points. Neither Filchock nor Mapes accepted the bribe offers of $2,500 each, plus a $1,000 bet for themselves. But neither had reported the bribe offer to the Giants' management or the police. Filchock, in fact, did not admit then that he had even received a bribe offer. Commissioner Bell barred Mapes from the title game but permitted Filchock to play because he denied having been approached, while Mapes did not. Filchock suffered a broken nose in the first quarter, but he played for fifty minutes and threw two touchdown passes to account for 12 of the Giants' points in their 24 to 14 loss to the Bears. He was intercepted six times in his twenty-eight tosses, but this was not a suspicious occurrence because Filchock was noted for having his passes picked off by opponents.

Nothing about the attempted bribery appeared in the press before the game, but there was a buzz on the streets in New York because of the point spread favoring the Bears. During the regular season, the Giants had beaten the Bears, 14 to 0, but for the title game the spread favored the Bears by at least 10 points; some said 14 points. The Giants players spent three or four days before the game at a camp at Bear Mountain, New York. Veteran fullback Hank Soar remembered:

> They took us up to Bear Mountain on Wednesday, and I said, what the hell are we doing up here? They've never done this before. They said they were trying to keep us away from the people who were bothering us for tickets and stuff; you don't want to be bothered like that before a game. I thought, that's bullshit. I know there's something wrong here. First thing Sunday morning, somebody called and said, "Did you hear what's going on? Filchock and Mapes are in the soup. Some guy says they want to sell the game."

It was an upsetting experience, according to Giants center Lou DeFilippo. "We were shaken to the roots just to hear about it," he said. "There was a big to-do, and we didn't know what the hell was going on. The whole team was shaken up."

The fix attempt was made by a twenty-eight-year-old self-styled big-time bettor named Alvin J. Paris. The police reported that he had wined and dined Filchock and Mapes several times before the title game. A week before the game he offered the bribes, which were turned down. Paris was subsequently convicted on two counts of bribery and served nine months in jail. At Paris's trial, Filchock admitted that he had lied when he claimed not to have received a bribe offer. He said he didn't think it was necessary to inform his team or the police about the offer. "I just forgot all about it after saying no to Paris's proposition. I wouldn't even think of doing anything dishonest in football."

Commissioner Bell suspended both Mapes and Filchock indefinitely after the title game. The suspension of Filchock was lifted in 1950 and that of Mapes in 1954. Filchock played for the Baltimore Colts in 1950 and finished his playing career in Canada. Mapes never again played professional football. Filchock returned to American gridirons in 1960 and spent two years as the first coach of the Denver Broncos in the new AFL.

The Mapes–Filchock affair was not the first report of gambling by NFL players. Two years before the bribe attempt was made in New York, there had been rumors of gambling in Washington. The *Washington Times-Herald* reported that Commissioner Elmer Layden was investigating the possibility that Redskins players were consorting with gamblers and perhaps betting on games. Layden said he did not find the "slightest bit" of evidence of collusion between gamblers and anyone connected with professional football. "The penalty for betting is expulsion from the league, and it will be enforced swiftly and vigorously," he promised.

Redskins owner George Preston Marshall asked District of Columbia police chief Edward J. Kelly to investigate the rumors. Kelly said that his men could find no evidence that any Redskins had been "frequenting gambling houses or liquor bars." Marshall offered $5,000 to anyone with proof that any Redskin player had been betting on games. There were no takers. The rumors died out without serious effect on the fans' perception of professional football as an honest sport.

The AAFC enjoyed its best year in 1947. Attendance dropped off by 200,000 from the inaugural season, but most franchises remained stable. The Cleveland Browns continued to dominate the AAFC, but even their ticket sales were down. The Browns won the league championship by defeating the New York Yankees again, 14 to 3. The war between the leagues and a postwar dip in the economy contributed to an attendance drop in the NFL too. Its teams sold 300,000 fewer tickets than the 1.5 million of the 1946 season.

New York Giants owner Tim Mara accused the AAFC of inflating its attendance figures even as they dropped. The figures are "absolutely false," Mara told New York sportswriters. "The All-America Conference has lost so much money [that] it is the biggest flop in American sports promotions." Mara saw no end to the battle between the leagues. "The day would never come when the National League and the All-American Conference would get together on common ground," he said.

The attendance slide continued in 1948. Ticket sales at AAFC games dropped off by 7 percent from 1947. All AAFC teams except the Cleveland Browns were said to be losing money. Still, the fight between the leagues to sign promising rookies continued unabated.

Dan Edwards, an outstanding pass receiver who was graduating that year from the University of Georgia, was among the beneficiaries of the bidding battle. He had been drafted by the Brooklyn Dodgers of the AAFC and number one by the Pittsburgh Steelers of the NFL. "The Dodgers offer was $500 better—$8,500," he remembered.

Naturally, Edwards took the Dodgers' offer. Branch Rickey, president of baseball's Brooklyn Dodgers, had taken over football's Dodgers in the hope of matching his success in the diamond sport. Edwards recalled:

> That franchise was a total wreck! After being with an organization like coach Wally Butts had at the University of Georgia—to fall off into a deal like that! I couldn't understand it. We weren't getting very big crowds, but they did pay our salaries.
>
> By the end of the year, it got to be a joke. All the players could recognize the trouble we were in. We were lucky to get paid.

At the end of the season, Branch Rickey dropped out of football and turned his Dodgers back to the AAFC. The franchise was merged with the New York Yankees. The Dodgers' players were distributed to other teams in the conference. For the 1949 season, Edwards was assigned to the Chicago team of the AAFC. Now called the Hornets, Chicago had its fourth set of owners since the AAFC began play in 1946. It was a case of going from the frying pan into the fire for Dan Edwards.

The AAFC's Chicago franchise had been a drag on the conference from the beginning, being unable to compete for fans against the Bears and Cardinals. "We played in Soldier Field," Edwards said, "and it looked like just a few buzzards up in the stands. The Hornets folded after that season. It looked like everything I got a hold of would collapse."

Even as the AAFC staggered toward oblivion, its teams continued to battle the NFL for players. (The AAFC also offered to battle the NFL on the field. In 1947 the AAFC's new commissioner, Jonas H. Ingram, an admiral who had commanded the Atlantic Fleet during the war, issued a challenge for the NFL's title winner to meet the AAFC's best for the "world championship." The NFL ignored him.)

Agents had not yet appeared to help players negotiate contracts, but Mario (Yo-Yo) Gianelli, a strong 265-pound guard from Boston College, had help when he agreed to sign with the Philadelphia Eagles for the 1948 season. His "agent" was Boston College coach Denny Myers.

Gianelli had played at Boston College for two years before he joined the army in March 1943. He was in service for three years and was in the second wave that hit the beach for the bloody invasion of Okinawa, one of the stepping stones in the conquest of Japan, on April 1, 1945. When he returned to Boston College after the war, he joined a select group of linemen. It included future Pro Hall of Fame tackles Art Donovan and Ernie Stautner; Ed King, a tackle who played with Buffalo and Baltimore in the pros and was later governor of Massachusetts; and John Kissell, a tackle who starred at Buffalo and Cleveland.

While he was still on Okinawa in 1945, Gianelli was drafted by the Boston Yanks of the NFL. They sent him a contract for $2,500 for twelve games, an offer he declined indignantly. After his discharge, he returned to Boston College and played there in 1946 and 1947. In 1946, the Cleveland Browns approached him with an offer of $3,500. "Geez, that was a lot of money right after the war," Gianelli said, "but I didn't sign with the Browns either."

Boston College coach Denny Myers urged Gianelli to delay signing with anybody until he had talked with his friend, coach Greasy Neale of the Philadelphia Eagles. He said he would ask Neale to get NFL draft rights to Gianelli. "So that's what happened," Gianelli said.

"The Eagles got draft rights to me, and I signed with them right after the 1947 season for $6,000. That was pretty good money. I think the highest-paid guy in the league that year was Charlie Trippi of the Cardinals. Steve Van Buren, our great halfback, was getting $18,500. Tommy Thompson— he was my roommate—he was getting $14,500, and he was the quarter- back!"

The Eagles were looking for big, strong linemen like Gianelli be- cause they had lost the 1947 NFL championship game to the Chicago Cardinals, who had exploited the Eagles' defensive alignment. There was no middle linebacker in the Eagles' defense, and the Cardinals' "dream backfield" of Charlie Trippi, Paul Christman, Pat Harder, and Elmer Angsman had rushed for 282 yards on quick openers.

Gianelli did well in training camp after reporting late because he had played in the College All-Star game in Chicago. He got his baptism in the NFL at a preseason exhibition game in Indianapolis against the Chicago Bears. Gianelli remembered:

> It had to be about 92 degrees. It was *so* hot. In the locker room, Greasy Neale was calling out the starting lineup and he calls my name. I had done well in two scrimmages, but I didn't even know the plays yet. I said, "Coach, I don't know any plays." He said, "Bucko Kilroy will tell you what to do." Bucko was playing the other guard.
>
> Now in those days, if you had a man in front of you, especially for pass blocking, you'd take him. Or sometimes you'd pull and get the end. It all depended on how the line was set.
>
> Now who do I get in front of me but Bulldog Turner—the great Bulldog Turner. I had read about him. He was the only guy who had a nose guard then. I said to myself, "I'll *hit* this guy, because if you showed him you were scared, you're done!" So I hit him a good one, and he says, "What are you, a wise guy? You a fresh guy?"
>
> On the next play he grabbed me by the shirt and turned me, and the Bears back went for about 15 yards. "Aha!" he says, "You'll learn," he says.

Gianelli, who was already twenty-seven years old in his rookie year because of his army service, was a stalwart on the Eagles' NFL cham- pionship teams of 1948 and 1949 and continued to play with them through 1951. He was then traded to the Green Bay Packers after he had knee surgery in 1951. The Packers refused to guarantee to pay him if he got hurt, so Gianelli retired and went to work for a liquor distrib- utor in Massachusetts. "But I had four great years with the Eagles," he said. "They were the greatest people."

By the end of the 1948 season, the AAFC was on the ropes and the NFL wasn't in much better shape. In the AAFC, only the Cleveland Browns and San Francisco 49ers were solid franchises, though the Buf- falo Bills (originally Bisons) were coming on strong. Ben Lindheimer, owner of the Los Angeles Dons, was helping to prop up the Chicago Hornets and was also giving financial transfusions to other weak clubs, even while his own team was losing money. Even the Cleveland

Browns were affected; their crowds had dwindled from an average of 50,000 in 1946 to 20,000.

In the NFL, attendance was down by 250,000. Ted Collins, owner of the Boston Yanks, moved his franchise to New York. The team became the New York Bulldogs and played at the Polo Grounds when the Giants were away in the vain hope of improving attendance. Out in Wisconsin, the Green Bay Packers survived the threat of bankruptcy by collecting $170,000 in a statewide appeal. The Packers had suffered as much as anyone in the bidding war for players.

It was clear to all that a merger would be required if pro football was to survive and prosper. Just before Christmas in 1948, delegations from the AAFC and the NFL met in Philadelphia. It was the first recognition the older league had ever given the AAFC, but it did not lead to peace. Many owners in the NFL were said to favor bringing in the Cleveland Browns and San Francisco 49ers, but George Preston Marshall of the Washington Redskins opposed it, and the AAFC wanted more of its teams included in a merger.

Even as the two leagues were tottering, they still bid high for players. John Panelli, Notre Dame's star fullback and linebacker who had played on two teams that claimed national college championships, was able to pit team against team after his graduation in 1949. Unlike Mario Gianelli, Panelli was his own agent in contract negotiations. He was in law school at Notre Dame that summer. He remembered:

> I had been drafted by the Lions number one in 1949. I had also been drafted by the New York Yankees of the AAFC. I had wanted to play in New York at Yankee Stadium because that's only twenty-six miles from Morristown, New Jersey, where my family home was. But I also wanted a good contract, and fortunately for me, I was able to do that because I had the two offers, which upped the ante a little.
>
> I had an exceptional senior year at Notre Dame, averaging 7.5 yards per carry. I wasn't a consensus All-American, but I made some All-American teams. I had a pretty good bargaining position.
>
> Red Strader, the coach of the Yankees, came to South Bend while I was in law school. Bo McMillin, the coach of the Lions, visited me the same day. One of them was in an office and the other in a hotel room across the street, and I'd go back and forth between them.
>
> I told Strader that I would sign for $30,000 for two years. He said he'd have to make some calls. I went to McMillin and said, "Here's what I got offered across the way—$30,000—$15,000 a year for two years, and a $1,500 signing bonus for each year, that's another $3,000." He says, "Well, I think we can handle that."
>
> So I went back to Strader and told the truth about what I was offered by the Lions, and he says, "John, I don't think I can guarantee that." So I shook his hand and went back to Bo and agreed to sign with the Lions.

John Panelli had been a linebacker as well as a fullback at Notre Dame. "I thought I could go both ways in the pros too," he said. "A lot of us did in those days." But he had injured his left knee while playing at Morristown High School and aggravated the injury at Notre Dame. Cartilage was taken out of the knee in his senior year, so by the time he arrived in the pros, his mobility had decreased. "I couldn't be a running back anymore, and when platooning came in 1949 I played mostly on defense." Panelli had two years with the Lions and three years with the Chicago Cardinals.

Panelli's first year as a professional—1949—was the last of the AAFC. The conference was down to seven teams. The division system was scrapped. The teams played a round-robin schedule, and at the end there was a playoff involving the first four finishers: the Cleveland Browns, San Francisco 49ers, New York Yankees, and Buffalo Bills. As usual, the Browns won the title, though they had to survive a stiff challenge from San Francisco. The Browns got the shock of their lives when they visited Kezar Stadium during the regular season and came away with a 56 to 28 licking. But they still managed to finish on top, beating the 49ers back home in the final playoff game, 21 to 7, before a disappointing gathering of 22,500.

In a way, the game was anticlimactic because two days before, the AAFC had effectively ceased to be. The NFL agreed to take in the Cleveland Browns, San Francisco 49ers, and lowly Baltimore Colts, who had finished last in 1949. The remaining four AAFC clubs—the New York Yankees, Buffalo Bills, Chicago Hornets, and Los Angeles Dons—were consigned to the scrap heap. Their players were put into a special pool for an NFL draft.

James F. Brueil, the Buffalo owner, tried hard to get the Bills into the NFL, but he was rebuffed. The Bills had developed a solid base of fans in Buffalo and had improved so much on the field that in their final year they tied the mighty Browns twice and extended them to the limit in the playoffs before losing, 31 to 21.

Buffalo was a great town for a pro football team, said Chet Mutryn, who was the Bills' ace running back for all four years of their first incarnation. Mutryn, a 5-foot, 9-inch, 185-pound bundle of elusiveness and football smarts, had been a Little All-American at Xavier University in Cincinnati. He had spent two years in the navy during the war after graduating in 1943. Mutryn had been drafted by the Philadelphia Eagles, but after the war he elected to join the new Buffalo franchise. His coach at Xavier, Clem Crowe, was on the Bills' coaching staff, and besides, the Bills offered him $10,000—well above the going rate for rookies in the NFL.

Mutryn made the AAFC's all-league time for three straight years. He remembered:

I enjoyed playing in Buffalo a great deal. I thought the people were tops as far as accepting us goes. They supported the team well. We didn't have the 50,000 or 60,000 attendance like they have nowadays, but we would draw 30,000, 32,000 at War Memorial Stadium. The crowds didn't drop off the way they did in some cities. In the last years of the AAFC, the Browns and the 49ers were doing the best financially, and the Bills were just about breaking even, I think.

The players were local heroes there. I guess I was out once or twice a week speaking at some lodge or church event, something like that.

The Bills would be reincarnated in 1960 with the birth of the AFL. Until then, though, Buffalo's fervent fans could only enjoy pro football from afar, like those in most of the country.

The post–World War II years were the last gasp of the minor leagues as an important part of professional football. The biggest of the minors—the Pacific Coast Football League (PCFL)—had, as already noted, continued to operate during the war. It was able to survive chiefly because so many capable players were stationed at armed forces bases on the West Coast.

After the war, the PCFL expanded to include Honolulu, Sacramento, Salt Lake City, and Tacoma. The Hawaiian Warriors, who had three players from the University of Hawaii, were the best team in the league after the war. They played all games at home in Honolulu. The visiting teams would stay for two weeks and play games on consecutive weekends. Crowds as large as 26,000 would appear at Honolulu Stadium for games against such strong teams as the Los Angeles Bulldogs.

The PCFL was rocked by a gambling scandal in 1947 when several Hawaiian Warriors admitted to having bet on their own team. Four were barred from pro football for life, and eleven others were suspended by the league. Police found that the players had put $6,700 into a pool and bet it through bookies on themselves to beat the Los Angeles Bulldogs by at least fourteen points and to have a seven-point lead by halftime. The Warriors won all right, but by a margin of only 7 to 6— not nearly enough to cover the spread. So not only did the players disgrace themselves, but they lost their money.

PCFL commissioner J. Rufus Klawans said, "The players involved have been guilty of bringing disrepute upon the game of professional football and have all admitted their guilt." Some of the players said they didn't think they had done anything wrong, since they bet on their own team to win.

The PCFL was effectively doomed when the NFL and the AAFC planted franchises in Los Angeles and San Francisco in 1946. The league stumbled on, though, for three seasons before succumbing in 1948.

The American Professional Football Association, the "major" minor league in the East, which had suspended operations during the war, resumed in 1946. It was reborn with a new name—the American Football League. Its teams were the Jersey City Giants, Long Island Indians, Newark [N.J.] Bombers, Paterson [N.J.] Panthers, Akron Bears, Scranton [Pa.] Miners, Bethlehem [Pa.] Bulldogs, and Wilmington Clippers. Six of the eight teams had working agreements with clubs in the NFL, which made them basically farm clubs of the major teams. The AFL had several shifts of franchises before the league died in the 1950 season. Only two teams—the Richmond [Va.] Rebels and the Erie [Pa.] Vets—were able to play their complete schedules in the final season.

The Rebels had jumped to the AFL from the Dixie League in 1947. The Dixie was the third of the three "major" minor leagues in the postwar era. The Dixie League had been formed in 1936, suspended in 1942 for the duration of the war, and resumed operations for the 1946 season. Its teams were the Charlotte [N.C.] Clippers, who had a working agreement with the Detroit Lions; Richmond Rebels (Pittsburgh Steelers); Norfolk [Va.] Shamrocks (Washington Redskins); Portsmouth [Va.] Pirates; Greensboro [N.C.] Patriots (Chicago Cardinals); and Newport News [Va.] Builders.

The Dixie League had only that one relatively serene year after World War II. It died with the defection of the Richmond Rebels to the AFL in 1947.

10

BLACK PLAYERS AND BLACKBALLS

The first year of the war between the leagues—1946—was notable for another reason besides the birth of the AAFC. It was also the year when the apparent gentlemen's agreement barring black players from professional football at the top level (though not in the minor leagues) came to an end. Black players performed in the NFL for the first time since 1933, and the new AAFC opened its ranks enough to allow a couple of black stars to slip through.

The twelve-year lily-white period in the NFL is an aberration. A handful of African-Americans had been on NFL rosters ever since its founding in 1920, and a few blacks had been on professional teams since the early years of the century. Why were they excluded after 1933?

The question can't be answered with certainty. Myron Cope put it to George Halas while he was interviewing football pioneers for *The Game That Was*. Halas, one of the founding fathers of the NFL, who was still active as the Chicago Bears owner when Cope interviewed him in the late 1960s, was as qualified a man to answer the question as could have been found at the time. Cope reported:

> In the 1930s pro football became exclusively white. Judging from available evidence, no purge had taken place. Indeed, Chicago Bears owner George Halas was startled when I suggested to him that there may have been one. There had been no ban on black ballplayers, he said—"In no way, shape, or form."
>
> Why then, had the blacks vanished? "I don't know!" Halas exclaimed. "Probably it was due to the fact that no great black players were in colleges then. That could be the reason. But I've never given this a thought until you mentioned it. At no time has it ever been brought up. Isn't that strange?"

Strange, yes, and also disingenuous. Halas could not have missed the brouhaha that exploded on sports pages in 1939 when Kenny Wash-

ington, a black halfback at UCLA who had led the nation's college players in gaining 1,370 total yards, was relegated to the second-team
All-Americans. Washington was probably the best of that year's graduating seniors and almost surely would have been a first-round NFL
draft choice had he been white. But he wasn't drafted at all.

Sam Balter, a sports broadcaster on NBC, protested vigorously,
according to historian Thomas G. Smith:

> In an "open letter" over the airwaves he asked NFL owners why "nobody
> chose the leading collegiate ground gainer of the 1939 season." Those
> who had seen him play agreed that he was "not only the best football
> player on the Pacific Coast this season, but the best of the last ten years
> and perhaps the best in all that slope's glorious football history—a player
> who has reduced to absurdity all the All-American teams selected this
> year because they did not include him—and all know why." NFL scouts,
> he continued, all ranked Washington the best player in the nation but
> "none of you chose him."

New York *Daily News* sports columnist Jimmy Powers also exco-
riated the NFL owners. Responding to fears that there might be trouble
among the players or the fans if a black player took the field in the NFL
that season, Powers pointed out that Washington had played in the
College All-Star game without incident: "He played on the same field
with boys who are going to be scattered throughout the league. And he
played against the champion Packers. There wasn't a bit of trouble
anywhere."

Washington said later that after the All-Star game, Halas asked
him to stick around Chicago while he tried to figure out how to get the
black star into the NFL. This seems unlikely because if, as owners
maintained, the league had no color line, there could be no problem
about signing Washington. Nothing came of the prospect; Washington
said he stayed in Chicago for a week, with no word from Halas, and
then went home. In his autobiography, Halas made no mention of trying to sign the black halfback.

Washington later played for several seasons in the minor PCFL. In
1946 he was one of the first blacks to cross the color line in the NFL
when he joined the Los Angeles Rams.

Football was not alone in discriminating against black players.
Both the major and minor baseball leagues had been all-white enterprises since the late nineteenth century, though baseball's magnates,
like their counterparts in football, denied the existence of a color line.
So did the owners and managers in the struggling professional basketball leagues of the time.

These sports were in society's mainstream in their attitudes and
practices concerning race. African-Americans suffered crippling dis-

crimination in nearly every facet of life. In the southern states, segregation of the races was pervasive. White and black children went to separate—and very unequal—schools. Black people rode in separate cars on trains and in the back on buses. In the Deep South, most public accommodations—hospitals, playgrounds, restaurants, swimming pools, and parks—were off-limits to blacks or divided by race. In many cities, blacks and whites could not play together or compete in sports. In the North, there were fewer legal restrictions, but African-Americans were second-class citizens there too.

So the color line in professional sports was not unique. But because sports were often viewed as democratic bastions in which he is best who plays best, some rationale had to be offered if a color line was to be drawn. In major league baseball, which had not admitted a black man to a team since 1884, five justifications were given. They can be summarized thus:

- One-third of all big leaguers were Southerners who would not take the field with a black player.
- Black players could not travel with a big-league club because hotels and restaurants would not accommodate them.
- The clubs trained in the South, where blacks and whites were forbidden by law to play together.
- Fans might riot in the stands if there were trouble on the field between white and black players.
- Blacks were not good enough to play in the big leagues anyway.

The same or similar evasions were offered in football, and there was one more. It was the concern that because football is a contact sport, with plenty of violent hitting, there was a very good chance that a black player would be deliberately and seriously injured in a game against whites. That was not an unreasonable concern, and there is plenty of testimony from black pros that they tended to absorb a lot more blows, both before and after the whistle, than their white colleagues.

Fritz Pollard, an All-American halfback from Brown University who was the first black star in the NFL, said, "The white players were always trying to hurt me, and I had to be able to protect myself if I was going to stay in the game." John M. Carroll, Pollard's most recent biographer, wrote:

> Pollard responded to the threat in a typically restrained but direct manner. When players roughed him up or called him foul names, he recalled, "I'd pay them no mind, but I would notice who the player was, and the first opportunity that presented itself I'd kick them right in the guts or hit my knee up against their knee, knocking it out of joint. And then I'd let them know, quietly, why I did it."

Pearce Johnson, who was in the front office of the Providence Steam Roller during Pollard's prime, said that the NFL's attitude toward black players then was "bad, very bad." Johnson added: "It was always, 'Get that nigger!' No matter where you went on away games, it was the same thing: 'Get that nigger! Get that nigger!' Pollard got drilled badly. . . . He was a marked man, no question."

Despite such violence, Pollard thought the owners' fears of gang attacks on black players were overblown. "I played twenty years with white teams and against them, and was never hurt so I had to quit the game. . . . So they can't say that's the reason they're keeping us out of the game." Pollard had long since retired as a player when he made that remark; he was objecting to the color line that was drawn after 1933.

Some football men blamed George Preston Marshall, owner of the Redskins, for the color bar. He came into the professional ranks in 1932 as part owner of the Boston Redskins. A native of West Virginia, Marshall was soon an influential figure in the league's affairs. In 1937 he moved the team to Washington, a distinctly southern city in its racial customs. It was the first NFL franchise south of the Mason–Dixon line. Historian Thomas G. Smith speculated that "to avoid offending Marshall and southern players and fans, NFL owners may have tacitly agreed to shun black athletes. Marshall himself once publicly avowed that he would never employ minority athletes. Indeed, the Redskins were the last NFL team to desegregate, holding out until 1962."

In retrospect, perhaps it is less surprising that there was a color line after 1933 than that there wasn't one before that. Professional baseball, after all, had been a segregated sport ever since 1898, when the last black players appeared in the minor leagues. Why wasn't pro football too?

The question is as hard to answer with certainty as that of why a color bar was effectively imposed in 1934. We can guess that it might be because pro football in its infancy and adolescence was far less structured than major and minor league baseball, and therefore it would have been difficult to conspire to keep all black players out. Scheduling was haphazard, and the home team never knew who would appear on the field for any opponent. It would have been hard to ban a black player who took his place on the field at kickoff time with thousand of fans in the stands. In organized baseball, though, the league office had a copy of the contract of every player and could control who could play and who could not.

Another factor may have been familiarity. A large majority of the white players had played against a few blacks in their college days, if not in high school. And nearly all the pioneering black players whose background is known had played football in predominantly white colleges and universities. None came from the historically black colleges until 1947, when Ezzret Anderson, an end from Kentucky State, and center John Brown from North Carolina College joined the Los Angeles Dons of the AAFC and halfback Elmore Harris of Morgan State played for the Brooklyn Dodgers in the NFL.

The first black professional football player appeared in the Ohio League in the early years of the twentieth century. He was a 6-foot, 200-pound halfback named Charles W. Follis, who starred for the Shelby, Ohio, team from 1902 to 1906. Follis was born in Cloverdale, Virginia, in 1879 but grew up in Wooster, Ohio. He helped to organize the first football team at Wooster High School in 1899, according to Milt Roberts, who has researched Follis's career. After starring for the high-school team and graduating in 1900, Follis entered the College of Wooster in the spring term of 1901. He was a power-hitting catcher on the college's baseball team that spring and again in 1902.

He did not play football for the college, however, instead choosing to perform for the Wooster Athletic Association, an amateur team. The Wooster Athletic Association met the Shelby Athletic Association, which claimed the championship of the Ohio League, twice that season. Follis evidently impressed the Shelby management because he was asked to play for their team in 1902. It is not clear that he was paid to play that year, but he might be described as at least a semipro because he was given a job in a hardware store with working hours that permitted him to practice football.

Dubbed the "Black Cyclone from Wooster," Follis soon was recognized as one of the stars of the Ohio League. Among his admirers was Branch Rickey, a teammate in Shelby, who was primarily responsible for the integration of organized baseball more than forty years later. Rickey was then a student at Ohio Wesleyan University and often played for pay at Shelby. In 1903, according to Roberts, Rickey was player-coach of Wesleyan's second team, which played the Shelby Athletic Association and was shredded by Follis, with runs totaling 150 yards. Afterward, Rickey described Follis as a "wonder."

In 1904 Follis was clearly a professional player because the *Shelby Daily Globe* announced that he had signed a contract. He led Shelby to an 8–1–1 season that year. The only loss was to Massillon, which claimed the Ohio League championship. Follis played pro football for two years after that, retiring in 1906 because of lingering injuries. His days in sports were not finished, though. He continued to play baseball, reaching the black professional ranks in Cleveland. Follis died of pneumonia in 1909 at the age of thirty-one.

The second black pro was probably Robert W. Marshall, an end for the University of Minnesota, who in 1905 and 1906 was chosen by Walter Camp as a second-team All-American. In the pre-NFL era, Marshall played for the Minneapolis Marines and Rock Island Independents. When the NFL was organized in 1920, he was with Rock Island. Marshall, who was called both Bobby and Rube, was on the NFL's Duluth roster in 1925 when he was forty-five years old. Marshall was 6 feet, 2 inches, weighed 195 pounds, and was obviously an iron man in those days of two-way football.

Not much is known about the next black pioneer, Charles (Doc) Baker. He is believed to have grown up in an orphanage in Akron, Ohio, during the last years of the nineteenth century. From 1906 to 1908 and again in 1911, he was a halfback for the Akron Indians, one of the strong teams in the Ohio League. His nickname came from the fact that his workaday occupation was physician's aide. Baker must have been a good ball carrier and a durable player. In an article in the PFRA's 1985 *Annual* historian Joe Horrigan quoted the *Canton Repository* as reporting that in an Akron–Canton game in 1911, Baker "was in every play both on offense and defense and seemed impervious to injury. On several occasions he was thrown hard, with several others on top of him. But he always came up smiling. His plunges through and outside of tackle were the best ground-gainers for the Akron team."

Henry McDonald, a speedy halfback for the Rochester [N.Y.] Jeffersons, was the fourth black player in professional football. He was a native of Haiti, but was adopted as a child by an American importer and grew up in Rochester and the nearby town of Canandaigua. He was a star in football and baseball and was the first black graduate of East High School in Rochester. McDonald had a pro career lasting from 1911 to 1920, mostly with the Rochester Jeffersons, the best-known team in western New York State. He also performed for the Oxford [N.Y.] Pros, the All-Lancasters, and the All-Buffalos.

McDonald apparently suffered little abuse on the field. The only untoward incident he recalled for an interviewer when he was an old man happened in Canton, Ohio. McDonald was with a Syracuse team that played Jim Thorpe's Bulldogs in 1917. Canton end Earle (Greasy) Neale, a West Virginia native and later a much respected coach of the Philadelphia Eagles, is alleged to have thrown the 145-pound McDonald out of bounds and told him, "Black is black and white is white where I come from, and the two don't mix." McDonald, who had boxed some, was ready to meet violence with violence, but Thorpe stepped between him and Neale. "We're here to play football," Thorpe told the combatants. "I never had any trouble after that," McDonald said. "Thorpe's word was law on that field."

Two years earlier, the Canton Bulldogs had signed a black tackle for a single big game. He was Gideon (Charlie) Smith, a graduate of both Hampton Institute, a historically black college in Virginia, and Michigan Agricultural College, now Michigan State. Canton manager

Jack Cusack signed him as insurance for the crucial game with the Massillon Tigers that would decide the 1915 Ohio League title. Smith, who did not get into the game until the fourth quarter, saved it for Canton. The Bulldogs were leading, 6 to 0, when Smith recovered the "fumble" in the end zone when the trolley-car conductor kicked it out of the arms of a Massillon ball carrier as he crossed the goal line. Smith never again played pro football, but he became a footnote in the annals of the sport with that one play.

The next black pioneer in professional football is easily the greatest star among them and the most important figure—black or white—from the early years who has not been elected to the Pro Football Hall of Fame. He is Frederick Douglas (Fritz) Pollard, a man of many talents, interests, and accomplishments.

Pollard was the first black All-American who played a backfield position. (The first at any position was Harvard's center, William Henry Lewis, in 1892.) Pollard was accorded the honor by Walter Camp in 1916 for his exploits at Brown University. He and Bobby Marshall integrated the NFL when it began as the APFA in 1920. He was the first black coach in the league, as well as the first black to play quarterback. (His usual position was halfback or tailback in the single-wing formation.) Pollard organized and coached the first all-black professional football team, the Chicago Black Hawks.

His life was full off the field as well as on. During the 1920s, he established the first all-black investment securities company, according to his biographer, John M. Carroll. Pollard was also the publisher of the first black tabloid newspaper in New York City, and he had a hand in producing movies for African-Americans. He also became an important booking agent for black entertainers and had a role in getting them into nightclubs where black actors and singers previously had been barred.

Pollard was born in Chicago in 1894 and grew up in a racially mixed neighborhood on the North Side. During his childhood and youth, there was an influx of southern black workers into Chicago's South Side and a subsequent rise of racial tensions in the city. But Pollard and his family seem not to have been affected. One of his best childhood friends was a white boy named Charles (Chick) Evans, later a winner of the U.S. Open golf championship.

Pollard played baseball and football and swam with white playmates. He attended Lane Technical High School, where he starred on the football team, played baseball, was a member of the track team, and was a trombonist in the band. At his graduation in 1912, Fritz Pollard had reached his full size of 5 feet, 8 inches and 155 pounds.

He was an indifferent student but, wanting to continue his athletic career, tried to enroll in several colleges. He did matriculate in a couple and practiced with their football teams. He also played semipro football for one season after leaving Lane Tech. But it was not until the fall of 1915 that he became a fully accredited student and football player at Brown University in Providence, Rhode Island. He became Brown's most valuable player almost immediately.

Pollard was not only a swift and shifty running back but also an excellent defender. In naming the Brown halfback to his All-America team in 1916, Camp wrote that Pollard was "the most elusive back of the year or of any year." In addition, Camp said that Pollard "is hard and resilient as an india-rubber ball; but often his offensive work, on account of its very brilliancy, obscured his really sterling defense."

Pollard dropped out of Brown after the United States entered World War I and served as a physical director for black troops in the army. His final assignment in the army was in the Student Army Training Corps (SATC) program at Lincoln University near Philadelphia. He became head football coach at Lincoln, one of the oldest black colleges in the country. After the war ended in November 1918, Pollard stayed on at Lincoln to coach.

During the 1919 season, he coached the Lincoln Lions and played a few games with the professional Union Athletic Association team of Phoenixville, Pennsylvania. Late in the season, he was offered $200 by the co-owner and coach of the Akron Indians to play with them in an important game at Akron against the Massillon Tigers. Pollard agreed, and after coaching Lincoln to victory over Virginia Union in Baltimore on a Saturday, he traveled overnight by train to Akron for the Sunday contest.

His presence was not enough to bring victory to the Indians, but Pollard accounted for their only score in a 13 to 6 loss. He was sensational in running back punts and made several long gains from scrimmage, the *Akron Beacon Journal* reported. The Massillon Tigers piled on Pollard at every opportunity, the newspaper said, "but Fritz would always come up smiling."

By the end of the season, Pollard said later, he was paid $500 a game by the Akron Indians. If that is true, he undoubtedly would have been the highest-paid player in pro football, earning more than even Jim Thorpe. Later in his career, he said he got $1,500 for big games, which seems most unlikely. Pollard spent the next seven seasons in big-time pro football during the infancy of the NFL. In addition to Akron, he played for and coached the Milwaukee Badgers, Hammond Pros, and Providence Steam Roller, all members of the NFL during the 1920s. In 1923 and 1924, while he was on the roster of the Hammond Pros, Pollard spent most autumn Sunday afternoons in Pennsylvania's coal region playing for the Gilberton Catamounts. In those years, coal-town teams in eastern Pennsylvania were competing on equal financial terms with the NFL teams. Coal-town salaries were around $200 a game. Many big stars appeared in the uniforms of Pottsville, Shenandoah, Gilberton, Coaldale, and Wilkes-Barre.

In 1926 Pollard was back in Akron. He was thirty-two years old and clearly past his prime as a runner, and he was given his unconditional release in October. But he was not finished.

In his waning days as a player, he returned to the coal region. The teams there were not as powerful as they had been. The Pottsville Maroons were in the NFL, and the Anthracite League had expired. Shenandoah, Coaldale, and Gilberton had joined the Eastern Pro Football League, which also had teams in Newark, New Jersey, and Bethlehem and Lancaster, Pennsylvania. Pollard finished his playing career with the Catamounts, playing his final football game against the Pottsville Maroons, third-place finishers in the NFL, in a blizzard at Pottsville's field.

In 1928, back home in Chicago, Pollard formed the first all-black pro football team, the Chicago Black Hawks. The team played white teams in the area, but did not draw very well. For the next three seasons, the Black Hawks played most games on the road, many of them in California. The team disbanded while playing on the West Coast in 1932.

Three years later, Pollard became coach of the Brown Bombers, a black pro team in New York City. The Bombers played white semiprofessional and professional teams around New York, but could not entice the NFL's New York Giants and Brooklyn Dodgers to take them on. After leaving the Bombers, Pollard was engaged in the ultimately successful effort to open professional football at the top level to players of all colors. He died in 1986 at the age of ninety-two.

In the NFL's inaugural season in 1920, Fritz Pollard and Rube Marshall of the Rock Island Independents were the only blacks in the league. In 1921 they were joined by two others: Paul Robeson, an All-American end from Rutgers who was with Pollard on the Akron Pros; and Jay Mayo (Inky) Williams, an end for the Hammond Pros who had been Pollard's teammate at Brown University in 1916.

Like Pollard, Robeson, a 6-foot, 1-inch end at Rutgers, had earned a place on one of Walter Camp's All-America teams. Camp selected him in 1918, saying, "The game of college football will never know a greater end." Unlike Pollard, Robeson was an outstanding student and was named to Phi Beta Kappa. He was attending the Columbia University Law School in New York City in 1921 when he began traveling to the Midwest on weekends to earn money by playing football for the Akron Pros. Not surprisingly, Robeson was a star performer at both end and tackle for the Pros.

The next year, he joined Pollard on the Milwaukee Badgers, a new

NFL franchise that Pollard helped to organize and coached. Robeson's biographer, Martin Bauml Duberman, wrote that the star end had enjoyed football in college but was not happy as a professional. During his two-year pro career, he was already gaining fame as a singer and actor. Long after he left football in 1922, Robeson was renowned as a concert and opera singer and actor on the stage and in the movies.

Inky Williams, a 5-foot, 11-inch, 165-pound end, enjoyed a six-year career in the NFL. He started with Hammond in 1921 and also played for Canton and Dayton before finishing up in 1926 with the last-place Hammond Pros. Among his teammates at Hammond were two other black players. One was Sol Butler, a well-known sprinter and football star from Dubuque College. The 5-foot, 8-inch, 184-pound Butler, who played all backfield positions, first played professionally in 1923 with the Rock Island Independents. Later he was with Canton and Akron before finishing up with Hammond in 1926. The other was Dick Hudson, who did not play college football but started in the pros with the Minneapolis Marines in 1923. A 180-pound fullback, Hudson also ended his football years with the Hammond Pros in 1926.

Several other black players were in the NFL for a season or two during the 1920s. Fullback John Shelbourne of Dartmouth was with the Hammond Pros in 1922 and then became a high-school teacher in Evansville, Indiana. James Turner, a wingback from Northwestern, was with the Milwaukee Badgers in 1923. Guard Hal Bradley, who did not attend college, was a guard for the Chicago Cardinals in 1928.

The black player who had the longest career in the NFL's pioneer days was Fred (Duke) Slater, an All-American tackle from the University of Iowa who joined the Rock Island Independents in 1922 and moved to the Milwaukee Badgers the same year. He then spent three seasons in Rock Island. In 1924 he was benched when Rock Island visited Kansas City because the Blues refused to play with a black man. While with the Chicago Cardinals from 1926 until his last season in 1931, Slater was an attorney in Chicago. He later became a municipal judge.

Another African-American in the league in 1930 and 1931 was David Myers, a 5-foot, 11-inch, 185-pound guard and wingback from New York University. He was with the Staten Island Stapletons briefly in 1930 and with the Brooklyn Dodgers the next year.

As the Great Depression deepened in the early 1930s, the NFL and its member teams began retrenching. Twenty-two-man squads became the norm as the owners sought to cut expenses. Among the casualties were the last black players in the NFL for a dozen years.

In 1932 there was only one, a dazzling tailback named Joe Lillard, who played with the hapless Chicago Cardinals. Lillard was an all-around athlete who excelled at baseball and basketball as well as football. He had grown up in Mason City, Iowa, and played college football at Oregon. Two games had been played in Oregon's 1930 season when Lillard was suspended, allegedly for having played pro baseball the previous summer with the traveling all-black Gilkerson Giants. Lillard claimed that he had only driven the team bus, but he was ousted anyway.

During 1931 Lillard played semipro football with black teams in Chicago and on the West Coast. He caught the eye of the Chicago Cardinals and was invited to join the then lowly Cards. He quickly became a star as the team's best running back, punt returner, and kicker. After the Cards beat the Boston Braves for one of only two victories they enjoyed that year in the NFL, the *Boston Globe* reported: "Lillard is not only the ace of the Cardinal backfield but he is one of the greatest all-around players that has ever displayed his wares on any gridiron in this section of the country."

He was not, however, sufficiently team oriented, in the opinion of Cardinals coach Jack Chevigny. Lillard missed practices, did not exert himself in blocking assignments, and flouted team rules. He was suspended with two games remaining on the Cardinals schedule, and he immediately began playing with an all-black basketball team, the Savoy Big Five, in Chicago. The following spring, he was on the roster of the Chicago American Giants, one of the strongest teams in Negro Leagues baseball.

For the 1933 football season, the Chicago Cardinals had a new coach, Paul Schissler, who agreed to take a chance on the temperamental Lillard. The black star responded well, again leading the Cardinals' woeful offense with his running and kicking. The Cardinals finished in the Western Division cellar with only one victory. Lillard was not invited back for the 1934 season.

Historian Thomas G. Smith has written:

> In 1935 Coach Schissler conceded that an unwritten rule barred blacks from the game for their own protection. Lillard, he said, had been a victim of racism. "He was a fine fellow, not as rugged as most in the pro game, but very clever," he explained. "But he was a marked man, and I don't mean that just the southern boys took it out on him either; after a while whole teams, northern and southern alike, would give Joe the works, and I'd have to take him out." Lillard's presence, the coach continued, made the Cardinals a "marked team" and the "rest of the league took it out on us! We had to let him go, for our own sake, and for his, too."

In Lillard's second and last season in the NFL—1933—the Pittsburgh Pirates had the only other black player in the league. He was Ray Kemp, a tackle from Duquesne University in Pittsburgh. After graduating in 1931, Kemp joined Art Rooney's semipro team in Pittsburgh, the J. P. Rooneys, and later played with another semipro aggregation, the Erie [Pa.] Pros. When Rooney got an NFL franchise in 1933, Kemp was on the roster. Pirates coach Jap Douds, who also played in the backfield, released Kemp after only two games, but he was recalled for the last three on the Pirates' schedule. Kemp was not offered a contract for 1934. He became a professor of sociology and the football coach at Tennessee Agriculture University in Nashville.

The exclusion of black players from the NFL after 1933—whether deliberate or not—meant that African-Americans who wanted to continue playing after their college years had to look to the minor leagues. Two of the minors—the American Professional Football Association and the Pacific Coast Football League—were hospitable to blacks.

The APFA, which operated from 1936 to 1941, when it was forced to suspend play due to World War II and the consequent dearth of players, was composed of teams in the New York metropolitan area. In the association's first year—1936—Clarence Lee, an end from historically black Howard University, played for the Mount Vernon [N.Y.] Cardinals. He returned to the Cardinals for two games in 1937 and was joined in the league by two other black players. One was halfback George Burgin, a backfield star from Western Reserve University, who performed for both the Brooklyn Bushwicks and the Newark Tornadoes. The other was a 185-pound halfback from the University of Iowa named Ozzie Simmons, who played for the Paterson Panthers.

Simmons was one of the most celebrated stars in the Big Ten during his college career. Thomas G. Smith wrote that in Simmons's first varsity game, he ran back a kickoff for a touchdown, gained 166 yards from scrimmage, and ran back seven punts for 124 yards in a game against Northwestern. As a junior, he had five touchdown runs of 50 yards or more and was named to the Associated Press All-America second team. He was ignored in the NFL's draft after his senior season and settled for two years in the minor APFA.

Lillard, who had played for a couple of seasons with the all-black Brown Bombers after being dropped by the Chicago Cardinals, came into the APFA in 1938 as a halfback for the Clifton [N.J.] Wessingtons. He played for two more seasons in the APFA with the Union City [N.J.] Reds, the Brooklyn Eagles, and a traveling team called the New York Yankees, which had no connection with the earlier or later Yankees in the AFL and the AAFC. In 1941 Lillard was joined on the Yankees by Hugh Walker, an end and backfield man from Hampton Institute.

Even more receptive to black players than the APFA was the PCFL, which began play in 1940, ran through the World War II years, and died of box-office anemia after both the NFL and the AAFC invaded its turf in 1946. The PCFL nurtured the two players who integrated the

NFL as members of the Los Angeles Rams: Kenny Washington and Woody Strode, both former UCLA stars.

Bob Gill, author of a year-by-year review of the PCFL titled *Best in the West*, had this to say about the league's receptiveness to black players:

> In the course of its nine-year history, the PCFL employed at least two dozen blacks—and the number may have been significantly higher. Blacks were common enough on the coast that newspapers felt no obligation to trumpet the fact that a particular player was "the Clippers' dusky pass-catching star," or to use similarly descriptive phrases. Thus most players who can be identified as black were in the league for several years, while in that time their color may have been mentioned in no more than a single article. At this date, there's no way to tell how many one-season players may have been black. As for their ability, Kenny Washington was, of course, the best player of any color in the PCFL; but really he was just the tip of an impressive iceberg. Mel Reid was clearly good enough to play regularly in the NFL; so was Ezzrett Anderson, an end who played four seasons on the coast. And so, likely, were several others who never had the chance to prove it.

Washington and Strode, the first black players to be signed by a big-league football team after 1933, and Jackie Robinson, the pioneer in organized baseball, were teammates on the UCLA football team in 1939. It was by pure coincidence, not design. Robinson was chosen to be the trailblazer in baseball by Branch Rickey, Charles Follis's teammate at Shelby, Ohio, in the early years of the century. Rickey was president of the Brooklyn Dodgers (now the Los Angeles Dodgers) in October 1945 when he signed Robinson to play for the Dodgers' top farm club, the Montreal Royals, in the International League in 1946. Robinson's signing was the culmination of a lengthy search by Rickey's organization.

Washington and Strode, however, were forced on the Los Angeles Rams. Both were quality football players, and Washington was much more than that. But it is unlikely that they would have been picked by the Rams in 1945 when they represented Cleveland and won the NFL title.

Washington had been UCLA's first All-American and was a local hero. When the Rams decided to move to Los Angeles, they needed a place to play. The obvious choice was the huge Coliseum, which was owned by the county. When Rams owner Dan Reeves and general manager Chili Walsh approached the county commission about a lease, they were asked whether they would give Washington a tryout. The inference was clear: no Washington tryout, no Coliseum. Washington was formally signed on March 21, 1946. Strode was signed later, in part so that Washington would have a roommate on the road and in part because Strode was a proven talent at end for UCLA, the Hollywood Bears of the PCFL, and the army's March Field Flyers.

Washington was born in Los Angeles, the son of Edgar (Blue) Washington, a versatile athlete who had played baseball in the segregated Negro Leagues. He became an excellent baseball player himself and had a better college career at that sport than Jackie Robinson did. As UCLA's tailback in football, he developed into one of the best backs ever produced on the West Coast. In his senior year—1939—UCLA was undefeated, and Washington set a UCLA career record with 3,206 yards in total offense. Robinson—an elusive, scatback type of runner—was a wingback on that team, and Strode was at end. Washington, who was 6 feet, 1½ inches tall and 190 pounds, was not as fast as Robinson, but he was a powerful runner with a great sense of where both teammates and opponents were on the field and how best to use his blockers. He was also a fine passer and could throw a football 60 yards with accuracy.

Robinson offered this assessment of Washington many years later in *Gridiron* magazine: "To start off, let me say that Kenny Washington was the greatest football player I have ever seen. He had everything needed for greatness—size, speed, and tremendous strength. Kenny was probably the greatest long passer ever."

Ignored in the NFL draft of 1940 despite his impressive statistics, Washington joined the Hollywood Bears of the PCFL in 1940. So did Strode. In 1941 Robinson graduated from UCLA and played with the Los Angeles Bulldogs of the PCFL. After that season, Robinson went into the army and served until 1945. After being discharged, he joined the Kansas City Monarchs of the Negro American League, his stepping stone to organized baseball and enduring fame as the first black player in the major leagues in modern times.

Like many running backs, Washington was plagued with leg injuries, but he led the PCFL in scoring in 1945, the year before he was signed by the Rams. Because of his gimpy legs, he was no longer the scintillating tailback of his days at UCLA, and he did not achieve the superstar status that might have been expected if he had started in the NFL in 1940. Dick Hyland of the *Los Angeles Times* called Washington a greater back than Ernie Nevers of Stanford and the Duluth Eskimos, Red Grange, and Tommy Harmon, the Michigan tailback who was with the Rams in 1946. He continued:

> Had Kenny Washington been signed by a National League team in 1940, he would undoubtedly have been, with one year's experience, one of the greatest professional backs and a drawing card from one end of the league to the other.
>
> But that was six years ago. In the meantime, Washington has become a beaten-up ball player who is neither so strong nor so quick in his

reactions as he was before the war. He has a trick leg which kept him out of games on many occasions last season and he has lost just enough of his speed to enable tacklers who would have missed him or run into his murderous straight arm when he was at his best to handle him with punishing tackles which in turn help cut down his speed, strength, and effectiveness.

Even so, Washington had three good seasons with the Rams before retiring in 1948. His best year was 1947, when he ran sixty times for 444 yards—an average of 7.4 yards a carry. His best effort was a 92-yard run against the Chicago Cardinals in a 27 to 7 victory over the eventual NFL champions.

Like the other pioneering black players in the NFL, Washington had to endure extra punishment. Bob Snyder, the Rams' head coach in 1947, said that Washington and Strode were well accepted by their teammates, but had to watch out for themselves on the field:

> The only bad incident I remember concerning Kenny happened in Green Bay in our second ball game that year. The Packers had a big tackle who was from Tennessee or one of the other southern schools. Right before halftime I saw this big tackle hit Kenny right in the jaw with an elbow. And I saw Kenny start to draw back and then talk to him.
>
> When we were coming off the field, I said to Tommy Harmon, "What happened out there?" And he said, "That guy called Kenny a black bastard. Kenny started at him and then he got his composure, and he said, 'Listen, that was a pretty good shot.' And then he said, 'I want to tell you something, you white trash. If you want to wait till the game is over, meet me under the stadium and I'll knock your goddamn block off.' "
>
> Well, our other players heard about that, and I think if we had an election he would have been elected captain.

Strode did not get much playing time with the Rams. He was cut from the team after the exhibition season in 1947 and ended his playing days in the Canadian Football League. He also wrestled professionally and became a well-known movie actor.

Kenny Washington and Woody Strode must be credited with being the first players to cross the color line in big-time pro football. Both were signed by the Los Angeles Rams early in 1946. But the other two black players on major league rosters that season, Marion Motley and Bill Willis of the new Cleveland Browns in the AAFC, had a far greater impact. They played for a much stronger and more successful team than Washington and Strode did and also lasted much longer. Motley was in the league for nine years and Willis for eight, and both are now in the Pro Football Hall of Fame.

In his autobiography, Cleveland Browns coach Paul Brown said that he had made up his mind to sign Motley, a bruising fullback, and Willis, a cat-quick guard, for the Browns even before Branch Rickey signed Jackie Robinson for baseball's Brooklyn Dodgers' Montreal farm team in October 1945. Brown said that in order to minimize the intense attention that he knew both men would attract as black pioneers in pro football, he decided to wait until the new Browns were in training camp before bringing them in.

Both Motley and Willis were well known to Brown. Motley had played for Canton McKinley High School, archrival of Brown's Washington High School team, and he had also been the fullback for his Great Lake Naval Training Center team. Willis had been a member of Brown's national champions at Ohio State in 1942.

Willis had a name in football because he made All-American at Ohio State before graduating in 1944. Motley did not because he had played at the University of Nevada at Reno—not a collegiate powerhouse—before the war. He was back home in Canton working in a mill when Brown invited him to the Browns' camp.

Willis almost slipped away. He had been coaching at Kentucky State in 1945 and had accepted an offer to play football in Canada in 1946, though he had not yet signed a contract, when Brown got in touch with him. Both Willis and Motley accepted Brown's invitation and quickly earned starting positions. Motley was a punishing runner between the tackles. He became adept at traps and draw plays and was the AAFC's all-time rushing leader, with 3,024 yards. Motley was also an excellent blocker and a devastating linebacker.

Willis was 6 feet, 2 inches tall and 206 pounds, and so quick off the ball on defense that he often disrupted the center's handoff to the quarterback. Brown wrote that in Cleveland's first game in the AAFC, the Miami Seahawks' quarterback never once got a smooth exchange with the center because Willis was on him instantly.

Neither Motley nor Willis had any trouble being accepted by the white players on the Browns. Paul Brown had used black players in Massillon and at Ohio State and had a well-earned reputation for fairness. He was also an authoritarian who insisted that rookies introduce themselves and shake hands with Motley and Willis, so there was no question that the black players were a vital part of the team. In Willis's words, "Paul treated every man alike."

The two black players were, as they expected, targets of racial epithets and physical abuse from their opponents. In the early years of the AAFC, opponents would make it a point to plant their cleats on Motley's hands after a play. That practice was ended by referee Tommy Hughitt, who had been player-coach of the Buffalo All Americans in the early 1920s. Motley told Myron Cope:

> When he caught a guy stepping on us, he wouldn't tell him nothing. He'd just pick up the ball and start walking off fifteen yards. They'd ask him

why, and then he'd say, "For stepping on that man." The other referees saw what this ref was doing, and they looked around and saw that we were bringing in the crowds as well as the white guys, so they started to protect us.

Of course, the opposing players called us nigger and all kind of names like that. That went on for about two or three years, until they found out that Willis and I was ballplayers. Then they stopped that shit. They found out that while they were calling us names, I was running by 'em and Willis was knocking the shit out of them. So they stopped calling us names and started trying to catch up with us.

Motley and Willis were the targets of Jim Crow laws once during their first season. Laws were in effect in Miami prohibiting whites and blacks from competing in sports, so when the Browns went south to meet the hapless Seahawks for the second time, Motley and Brown stayed home. James E. Doyle, sports columnist at the *Cleveland Plain Dealer*, commented acidly,

> It seems that a majority of the law-makers down in Florida don't know yet that the Civil War is over, wherefore Marion Motley and Bill Willis aren't leaving for Miami today with the rest of the Cleveland Browns. . . . Those cracker solons may get the war news by pony express or some such before next fall, but by that time Miami will have been given a boot out of the All-America Football Conference. Should have been a quick kick.

Marion Motley, Bill Willis, Kenny Washington, and Woody Strode had nowhere near the impact of Jackie Robinson on the psyches of either blacks or whites. One reason, no doubt, was that major league baseball was far more popular than pro football in the late 1940s, though the gap was beginning to close. More important, though, was the fact that Robinson was *the* trailblazer.

Some football men argue that Motley, Willis, Washington, and Strode should be accorded greater honors because they reached their sport's major leagues before Robinson joined the Brooklyn Dodgers in 1947. Quite true, but irrelevant. There was never any doubt that Robinson was being groomed for the majors during his 1946 season in Montreal. Only if he failed on the field or failed to maintain his composure in the spotlight of national attention would he not join the big-league club. That's why his season with the Montreal Royals was covered with more interest in the black press than were the flourishing black baseball leagues. The baseball season was winding down after a triumphant year by Robinson and the Royals, who won the International League pennant and the Little World Series with the American Association champions, before sports fans turned their attention to football and the black pioneers on pro gridirons. Perhaps the fans had used up their quota of emotional involvement with Robinson and had none left for the gridders.

The pace of integration after the 1946 debuts of Motley, Willis, Washington, and Strode was not breathtaking. No NFL team other than the Rams had a black player until 1948, when the Detroit Lions signed halfback Melvin Groomes from Indiana and end Bob Mann from Michigan and the New York Giants took Emlen Tunnell, a halfback from the University of Iowa, who had a Hall of Fame career as an outstanding defensive back.

The AAFC was somewhat more receptive to black players. In 1947 the Cleveland Browns added a third black, punter and end Horace Gillom of Nevada, to their roster. The Brooklyn Dodgers, Chicago Rockets, New York Yankees, and San Francisco 49ers all had at least one black player on their rosters that year. The prize was Claude (Buddy) Young, a 5-foot, 5-inch, 170-pound speedster from Illinois, who joined the New York Yankees.

Young, a native of Chicago, entered the University of Illinois during the war and almost made the Illini forget Red Grange. On the first play in his first varsity game in 1944, he ran 64 yards for a touchdown against Iowa. The next time he got the ball, he scored on a 30-yard run. Young had the ability to accelerate to full speed in just a step or two. He finished his first season at Illinois with thirteen touchdowns and a rushing average of 8.9 yards a carry. He earned a place on several All-American teams. Young was also a star sprinter on the track team, winning national championships in the 100- and 220-yard dashes. He tied the world's record for the 45- and 60-yard dashes.

Young was drafted into the military in January 1945 and assigned to the navy. He starred for the Fleet City [Ca.] Bluejackets in 1945. After the war, he returned to the University of Illinois and played the 1946 season there. He helped the Illini beat UCLA in the 1947 Rose Bowl.

He signed with the New York Yankees of the AAFC and joined tailback Spec Sanders in the backfield to lead the Yanks to the East Division title with an 11–2–1 record. Young continued to be a dangerous runner and a good pass receiver, but he never played on another team that won a title in a career ending in 1953 with the Baltimore Colts (now the Indianapolis Colts). Historian Bob Carroll reports that when Young was with the Yankees and first played in Baltimore, "racists came to the stadium in blackface. Yet, when he played for Baltimore in 1953, fans voted him the most popular Colt."

The experience of Wally Triplett, a halfback from Penn State who played for four seasons with the Detroit Lions and Chicago Cardinals, was perhaps typical of black players in the post–World War II period when the color bar in professional sports was coming down. The son of a postal worker, Triplett was born in 1926 and grew up in an integrated neighborhood in La Mott, a village on the northern fringe of Philadelphia. He played football, baseball, and basketball on integrated teams at Cheltenham High School in Pennsylvania and matriculated at Penn State in June 1945, right after graduation. (Before graduating, he had received a recruiting letter from the University of Miami asking about his interest in playing there. "They didn't know I was black, of course," Triplett said. "They must have sent letters to all-state or all-scholastic players. So I sent them a stinging letter, and the athletic director replied that in time they might have integrated football, but now they weren't prepared for it.")

Even at a northern institution like Penn State, there was some segregation of black athletes in 1945. "The tradition had been that there were a couple of homes that turned themselves into boarding houses for black athletes," Triplett said. "Ours was called Lincoln Hall. I don't know why because, as I tried to explain to them, Abe Lincoln wasn't for integration." In his junior year, he moved into the dormitory for football players.

Many of Triplett's teammates at Penn State were veterans of the military services, an experience that broadened the outlook of many men who had gone to war with ingrained prejudices against blacks and other minorities. Triplett gave an example:

> The veterans came back as older and wiser men. They were more under-standing. In 1946 the University of Miami was on our schedule. Miami was to be our last game, and we were going to play them in the Orange Bowl.
>
> Miami made it known that when you played in Miami you couldn't bring your colored players. That was the custom. The tradition was that when northern schools went south to play, they left their black players home.
>
> Well, we had a team meeting, and it surprised the heck out of me. The coaches said, well, we ought to play, and the players said, no, we play together, we'll stay together. The captains spoke—one was from western Pennsylvania and one from New York—they were veterans, and they said, this stuff has got to stop. I was proud of them. So the team voted. It wasn't unanimous, but after the captains spoke, guys raised their hands slowly. It was one of the high points of my life.

In reporting on the cancellation of the Miami game, Penn State's student newspaper, the *Daily Collegian*, made no mention of the team's vote. It reported that Carl Schott, dean of the School of Physical Education and Athletics, said that Penn State and Miami had agreed to cancel:

> We recently advised the University of Miami that the two colored boys [Wally Triplett and end Dennie Hoggard] are regular members of the

Penn State football squad, and that it is the policy of the college to compete only under circumstances which will permit the playing of any or
all members of its athletic teams. The officials of the Miami school ad-
vised us that it would be difficult for them to carry out the arrangements
for the game under these circumstances.

Penn State was not alone in refusing to play southern teams if
black players could not play. The year after the Miami–Penn State cancellation, Ohio Wesleyan, which had a black player, called off a trip to
Winter Garden, Florida, to play Rollins College despite the intercession
of Branch Rickey. The Brooklyn Dodgers' president, an alumnus of
Ohio Wesleyan, made a fruitless attempt to convince Rollins authorities that it was feasible to play the game despite the Florida state law
barring interracial competition. The Rollins trustees issued a statement
saying that the college

> has no objections whatsoever to playing a game in which a Negro partic-
> ipates. However, a football game is a community affair, and after con-
> sultation with leading members of our community, both white and
> colored, officials of Rollins College have decided that in the best interests
> of racial relations, they are unwilling to take action which might interfere
> with the good progress now being made in Florida, and especially in our
> community.

Triplett starred in the Penn State backfield through the 1948 season. He was chosen by the Detroit Lions in the nineteenth round of the
1949 NFL draft and has the distinction of being the first black draftee
to play in the NFL. The pioneers who preceded him had not been
drafted. (George Taliaferro, a halfback from Indiana, was selected by
the Chicago Bears in an earlier round of the 1949 draft, but he signed
with the Los Angeles Dons of the AAFC.)

Triplett played for two years with the Detroit Lions and two with
the Chicago Cardinals as halfback and safety. In his last year with the
Cardinals, he was primarily a kickoff returner. Triplett retired at
twenty-seven. He remembered:

> I got a knee injury in a kickoff return once. That starts you thinking; you
> can get hurt in this game. I'd never really gotten hurt before. Oh, I had
> teeth knocked out in my first year in a game with Green Bay.
>   When that kind of thing happened, I was sure it was racial. Bo
> McMillin, the Lions' coach, said, "Wally, you've got to swing back." Once
> we were playing in Chicago, and a Bear player was vicious. The play
> called for a swing pass to me. I went out toward the flat, and it looked
> like I was going to block the end. When I went by him, the next thing I
> felt—pow!—I could feel my face cave in. It spun me around, and I hit the
> ground on my hands and knees, trying to stop the world from turning

over. Bo says, "Wally, Wally, you've got to go wider, you can't go that close."

Despite such ordeals, Wally Triplett recalled his years as a pro with pleasure. "I enjoyed it," he said. "I had a lot of fun, and it opened doors for me. It helped me later when I went into teaching and in my insurance business."

11

THE TELEVISION ERA BEGINS

There are three reasons that 1950 was a watershed year for the NFL. First, professional football was finally at peace after four years of interleague warfare with the AAFC. Second, the league made permanent the experimental rule permitting unlimited substitution. The NFL had tinkered with variations of the substitution rule during World War II and in 1949 had set a one-year trial for unlimited substitution. Making that rule permanent in 1950 led to the now universal practice of having separate teams for offense and defense and the development of such specialists as place kickers and punters. Finally, 1950 marked the beginning of pro football as *the* television sport. For the first time, an NFL team—the Los Angeles Rams—permitted the televising of all games, both home and away. (It turned out to be a mistake, since ticket sales dropped off precipitously, but it heralded the future of pro football.)

The strongest of the AAFC's surviving teams, the Cleveland Browns, was placed in the NFL's Eastern Division, which was renamed the American Conference. The other two AAFC refugees—the San Francisco 49ers and the Baltimore Colts—were put into the Western Division, now called the National Conference.

Displaying an exquisite dramatic sense, NFL commissioner Bert Bell arranged for the 1950 season opener to pit the NFL champion Philadelphia Eagles against the Cleveland Browns, winners of all four AAFC titles. The game was scheduled for Philadelphia's Shibe Park, home of the baseball Athletics. Demand for tickets was so brisk that Bell moved the game to the larger Municipal Stadium and changed the time from Sunday afternoon to Saturday night.

The Eagles had won two straight NFL championships, and their coach, Greasy Neale, touted them as the "best team ever put together. Who is there to beat us?" Neale asked. Little did he know.

Meanwhile, the Cleveland Browns were looking forward to playing the NFL champions with something approaching religious fervor. They and the other AAFC teams had endured four years of put-downs from the NFL. Only the year before, George Preston Marshall, owner of the Washington Redskins, had said of the AAFC, "The worst team in our league could beat the best team in theirs."

Such published sneers were invariably clipped and posted on the Browns' locker room bulletin board by Paul Brown. Browns quarterback Otto Graham said, "For four years Coach Brown never said a word. He just kept putting the stuff on the bulletin board. We were so fired up we would have played them anywhere, anytime."

The NFL got its come-uppance when the Browns buried the Eagles by a score of 35 to 10. Graham passed for three touchdowns and more than 300 yards. The Eagles were held to total gains of 118 yards by the relentless Browns defense, led by guard Bill Willis, who rolled over All-Pro Eagles center Chuck Bednarik on the first two plays of the game, and by linebacker Marion Motley. The game attracted 71,237 fans, most of them Eagles rooters who had trouble believing what they saw.

Throughout the season, the Cleveland Browns proved that their debut in the NFL was no fluke. They finished the regular season with a record of 10–2. The losses were to the New York Giants by scores of 6 to 0 and 17 to 13. The Giants had long been known for stout defenses. To deal with the Browns' potent passing attack, with Otto Graham pitching and Dante Lavelli, Mac Speedie, and Dub Jones catching, Giants coach Steve Owen introduced the 4–3 "umbrella" defense in which the ends frequently dropped back as linebackers and pass defenders. By the end of the 1950s, the 4–3 alignment of linemen and linebackers was the preferred defense in the NFL.

Like the Browns, the Giants had a 10–2 record for the 1950 season. In the playoff for the American Conference title, the Browns nipped the Giants, 8 to 3, in a defensive battle. It was a 3 to 3 tie with less than a minute to go when Lou Groza kicked his second field goal. The Browns added a safety just before time ran out.

The NFL's National Conference also enjoyed a tight race, with both the Los Angeles Rams and the Chicago Bears recording 9–3 won–lost records in the regular season. The Rams, who had the highest scoring average in NFL history (38.8 points a game), won the playoff in Los Angeles, 24 to 14. In the NFL championship game, played in Cleveland on Christmas Eve, the Browns capped their first season in the NFL by edging the Rams in an exciting game. The Browns' Otto Graham and the Rams' Bob Waterfield engaged in a passing duel that had the Rams ahead by 28 to 27, with only twenty-eight seconds left and the Browns in possession on the Los Angeles 11-yard line. Place kicker Lou Groza calmly split the uprights from the 16-yard line, giving the Browns the first of their three NFL championships during Paul Brown's tenure.

The two other teams from the AAFC fared much less well than the Browns in 1950. The San Francisco 49ers lost their first five games en route to a 3–9 record. The Baltimore Colts managed only one victory (over the Green Bay Packers) while losing eleven games, many by lop-sided scores. Colts owner Abraham Watner turned his franchise back to the league after the season.

The unlimited substitution rule had been coming by fits and starts for several years before it arrived for good in 1950. Like many other foot-ball innovations, the idea of unlimited substitution began in the college game.

It was first introduced in 1941. The rules committee of the National Collegiate Athletic Association (NCAA) theorized that if there were no limits on substituting players, more men would be able to play, injuries would be less frequent because players would not become exhausted, and the smaller colleges would be able to make the best use of whatever football talent was available.

The reality was somewhat different. More players did take the field as teams developed separate units for offense and defense, and since the players specialized, they tended to become more skilled at their positions than the old two-way players. But contrary to expectations, injuries increased, presumably because players had little chance to warm up before reentering a game after a spell on the sidelines. Two-platoon football was, of course, also more expensive because nearly twice as many players had to be equipped and more coaches were needed for instruction. More than fifty colleges gave up football, mostly for economic reasons, during World War II and in the postwar period.

In 1953 the NCAA reversed itself on the substitution rule. In a move that caught most coaches by surprise, the rules committee barred free substitutions. A new rule said that a player who came out of the game in the first and third quarters could not return until the next period. In the second and fourth periods, he could go back in during the final four minutes. College coaches were divided on the change. Ivy Williamson, whose Wisconsin Badgers had lost the Rose Bowl game that year, com-plained that "football won't be the same without the two-platoon sys-tem. It made for a better game." Speaking for the opposite view, Tuss McLaughry of Dartmouth said, "The two-platoon system was like having a team of hitters and a team of fielders in baseball. Now we'll go back to playing the game as it was played for seventy-five years—the way it ought to be played."

The NFL apparently never considered following suit. By 1953, when the colleges adopted the change, most professional players were members of an offensive or a defensive team and rarely played with the other unit. Such specialists as kickers and punters, however, were still in the future. In the NFL champion Cleveland Browns, for example, kicker Lou Groza was an offensive tackle, and punter Horace Gillom was a two-way player as an end.

Without doubt, two-platoon football raised the skill level required for pro football. It also extended the careers of some players because they no longer had to take a beating on both offense and defense. Vince Banonis, star center for the Chicago Cardinals and Detroit Lions after World War II, remembered:

> I retired after the 1953 season, but I didn't miss a play on offense that year. Of course, by that time, my legs were too far gone for defense; I was strictly on offense. On defense you've got to have range to cover guys man-for-man, guys like Elroy Hirsch and Boss Pritchard from the old Philadelphia Eagles.
>
> By the time I retired, there weren't many two-way players left. They were falling by the wayside. Today's players are all specialists. Do you realize that today people can go through a whole season and not make a block or a tackle? They're all specialists. They're fresher today, whereas when I started in 1942 we played forty or fifty minutes every game.

The last two-way player on a regular basis was center-linebacker Chuck Bednarik of the Philadelphia Eagles. He played both ways in the Eagles' victory over the Green Bay Packers in the 1960 NFL championship game. In fact, the thirty-five-year-old Bednarik was one of the game's heroes, stopping Packer fullback Jim Taylor near the goal line in the waning seconds to preserve the Eagles' 17 to 13 win.

Men who played during the early years of platooning generally agree that free substitution brought specialization and perhaps a higher level of skill as a result. But they are virtually unanimous in their disdain for the soccer-style kicking specialists who do nothing but kick off and boot field goals and extra points. Typical of the critics is Don Doll, a defensive back for the Detroit Lions, Washington Redskins, and Los Angeles Rams in the early 1950s, and later a college and pro coach:

> They're a pet peeve of mine. I think a player should *play*—be a *player*. I know I'm fighting a losing battle on that. At Southern Cal, we had a guy who came out of the band to kick field goals and extra points. I think there's some resentment among players now, although they love a kicker when he kicks the winning field goal.
>
> I would like to see the rules changed to make the uprights narrower to make field goals tougher. Or have two sets of uprights; if the ball went through the wide set they'd get two points, and if through the narrow set, three points.

I've never accepted the ease of kicking field goals these days, even though I used to coach kickers in the pros. I loved Tom Skladany, who was with the Lions around 1980, because he would tackle the ball carrier on his own kickoffs. He was as good a tackler as I had when I was coaching secondaries.

I liked these little guys who kick soccer-style, but there must be another game for them—soccer, maybe, or something.

The 1950s was a golden age for the NFL. Average attendance at games went from 25,353 in 1950 to 40,106 in 1960. (In 1960 interest in pro football was even higher than the figure indicates because a new AFL—the seventh or eighth bearing that name—began play that year, and its teams averaged 16,539 fans a game. This latest, and last, AFL lasted through the 1969 season and bequeathed to the NFL the Buffalo Bills (in their second incarnation), the Cincinnati Bengals, Denver Broncos, Houston Oilers, Kansas City Chiefs, Miami Dolphins, New England Patriots, New York Jets, Oakland Raiders, and San Diego Chargers.

While pro football was prospering during the 1950s, some other sports were hurting. Attendance slumped for both major league and minor league baseball. College football was losing favor, too, and even the movies were no longer the big draws they had been before and immediately after World War II.

One of the reasons was changing patterns of living. World War II veterans were marrying and setting off a baby boom of unprededented proportions. There had been little home building during the Great Depression because of skimpy incomes or during the war because of a dearth of building materials, so there was a great need for new housing. The Veterans Administration helped to meet the need by subsidizing interest on home mortgages for veterans.

Automobile sales also went way up, to satisfy the demand for greater mobility than had been possible during the war. Many young families wanted to live in the suburbs rather than stay in cities, so population dropped in many big cities while a ring of suburbs grew up around them.

The young suburbanites were inclined to find their leisure-time pursuits in the suburbs rather than in the cities they had fled. It was usually easier and more pleasant to go bowling, attend church, or go hunting or fishing in their own neighborhoods than to go to a stadium, concert hall, or museum in the big city. For many young marrieds, their homes were the first piece of real estate anyone in their families had ever owned, and they took pride in keeping them spick and span—which, as anyone who has battled crabgrass knows, takes a lot of time.

There was another reason why football was the only team sport that enjoyed growth during the 1950s: television.

Very little progress had been made on television's technology since

1939, when the first sports events were televised in New York City. Few television sets had been manufactured during World War II, partly because some of the components were needed for radar installations and other electronic applications and partly because the nation had more pressing matters than entertainment to consider. By 1946, when production resumed, 5,000 sets were manufactured, bringing the total for the whole country to 12,000. Most were in New York City, with a few in Chicago, Philadelphia, and Schenectady, New York, which had a television-broadcasting station too.

For the next several years, production skyrocketed. By 1950, nearly 4 million sets were in operation, reaching 30 million viewers—one-fifth of the nation's population. Set owners were watching five hours a day on average. Comedian Milton Berle was already a star, and boxing and wrestling flourished on the tube. Wrestling, which had become a staged morality play rather than an athletic contest, was joined by the roller derby as an exercise in showmanship. In the roller derby, teams of male and female skaters sped around a steeply banked track, body-checking and fist-fighting all the way. For a time, it was the rage of all saloons.

Boxing was the biggest prime-time sports attraction around 1950. Fights were broadcast on television nearly every night of the week. Fans could see such excellent fighters as Sugar Ray Robinson, Ezzard Charles, Tony Zale, and Rocky Graziano on the small screen for free in those days before cable television and pay-per-view.

Pro football and major league baseball never were shown during the prime evening hours, but these sports were cautiously testing the waters of television. As early as 1947, Chicago Bears owner George Halas agreed to have station WBKB televise all six home games of the Bears for a fee of $4,500. Chicago had only about 7,000 television sets, and Halas put aside his concern about empty seats in the stadium in the hope that the new medium would spur interest in the Bears. Apparently it did; attendance rose and the Bears' receipts almost doubled in 1947.

A year later, many more television sets were installed in the Chicago area, and Halas was less enthusiastic about giving fans the chance to see Bears' games for free. Only the Bears' final game, against the crosstown Cardinals, was on television. The broadcast was sponsored by Pabst Brewing Company, which paid $5,000 for the rights. By 1949, Clevelanders who owned television sets could tune in to Browns' games. A utility company that sponsored radio broadcasts of Browns' games over many stations in Ohio picked up the $5,000 tab for the television rights.

Pro football's owners had good reason to fear television's effect on the box office. In 1948 the NCAA had commissioned a study of the effects of televising football games on the sale of tickets. The survey covered colleges primarily in the Boston–New York–Philadelphia corridor and found that television apparently had caused decreased attendance at the games, though not much. But the most disquieting finding was that 80 percent of the fans said they preferred watching the games on television to attending in person.

Despite such concerns, Daniel F. Reeves, owner of the Los Angeles Rams, agreed to allow the televising of all Rams games in 1950. The result was a qualified disaster. The Rams had drawn 205,000 fans in 1949 while winning the NFL's Western Division title (and while competing for fans with the AAFC's Los Angeles Dons). In 1950, with no competition from another pro football team, attendance dropped by nearly half to 110,000 (at a time when only 42 percent of the homes in Los Angeles had television sets). The box-office disaster was qualified by the fact that Reeves had taken the precaution of putting in the contract with Admiral, a television-set-manufacturing company that sponsored the broadcasts, a provision that Admiral would reimburse the Rams for any drop in ticket sales compared with the 1949 season. Admiral paid $307,000 to make up for the fact that Angelenos stayed home in droves to watch the Rams on television. Reeves did not make the same mistake in 1951, when he permitted the televising of only away games. Home attendance jumped to 234,000.

The first network telecasts of pro football appeared in 1951. The Chicago Bears set up their own network of stations in ten cities: Minneapolis; Rock Island, Illinois; Omaha, Nebraska; Indianapolis and Bloomington, Indiana; Columbus, Cincinnati, and Dayton, Ohio; Louisville, Kentucky; and Nashville, Tennessee. The stations sold local advertising to pay line costs for the Bears "network," but the club lost $1,750 for the year. However, the loss was made up by profits from the Bears' *Quarterback Show*, a Tuesday night telecast of highlights from the team's game the previous Sunday.

NBC and CBS, the big names in the broadcast business, showed no interest in pro football, but the Dumont Network did. At the time, it was a fairly extensive network, and in 1951 it showed five regular-season games, as well as the championship contest in which the Los Angeles Rams turned the tables on the Cleveland Browns, 24 to 17. Dumont paid $95,000 for the rights to the title game each year until the network folded in 1955. (Only nine years later, the CBS network paid $1.8 million for the championship contest.)

By this time, most NFL teams were following the practice of allowing the televising of their away games back to the home city, but forbidding it for home games. After the 1951 season, Commissioner Bert Bell got the owners to cede to him the power to decide the league's policies on television. But the Department of Justice filed suit in federal district court in Philadelphia charging that the NFL and its twelve member teams were violating antitrust laws by restricting television coverage of games. Judge Allan K. Grimm denied the league's motion to dismiss the suit, saying that the case was of "great importance to the public." The judge's ruling reflected the gradually growing interest in pro football.

New York Giants president John V. Mara, son of Tim Mara, the club's founder, submitted a brief to the court in support of the NFL's contention that banning telecasts of home games was necessary for the league's economic health. Sales of reserved seats, he said, had declined steadily as television sets proliferated in the metropolitan area. Mara wrote that when the Giants began televising their games in 1946, 91.5 percent of the reserved seats at the Polo Grounds had been sold in advance. In 1947 advance sales had dropped to 87.5 percent; in 1948 to 86 percent; in 1949 to 73 percent; and in 1950, to 62.5 percent. No percentage was given for the 1951 season. Mara conceded that

> these figures do not necessarily constitute a complete indictment of television as the sole factor affecting the economics of our business. However, it had to be recognized that television was more than a straw in the wind—that it was a new, powerful and growing factor capable of great influence on the attendance of the public at football games.

Judge Grimm finally ruled in November 1953 that the NFL could continue to restrict television broadcasts of games in the home areas of its teams, but it could not stop radio broadcasts or television broadcasts of games that would not affect attendance at any NFL game. As a result of his ruling, the NFL could forbid the televising of any of its games within seventy-five miles of a game in progress, but could not interfere with telecasts outside that limit. In short, if the Chicago Bears were playing the New York Giants in New York, the league could black out the New York area to all telecasts of any of its games while the game was in progress. It could not forbid the televising of games in a team's home territory when the team was playing elsewhere. The NFL's owners had hoped for more control over the league's television policy, and there was some talk of appealing Judge Grimm's ruling to a higher court, but it fizzled out.

Commissioner Bert Bell told the press, "Throughout the trial we expressed continuously our desire to learn to live with television. That's what we will try to do in this situation." Actually, Bell was pleased with Grimm's decision because it did not forbid home-game blackouts even though it did crimp his power to control broadcasts of all league teams.

By the mid-1950s, the big networks were starting to pay attention to pro football. Important advertisers were interested because the football audience was made up primarily of a choice target, eighteen- to forty-nine-year-old men. In 1954 nearly 37 percent of all homes that had television sets turned on on Sunday afternoons were tuned to an NFL game. By that time, pro football was being broadcast to many localities far from NFL cities. By 1956, CBS was telecasting regular-season games (and paid over $1 million for the rights), while NBC had taken over broadcast rights to the championship game.

The television screen was still black and white, and only two or three cameras were used for football games. Such enhancements as slow motion, color, and instant replay were futuristic dreams, but television and pro football were growing and thriving together. Benjamin G. Rader, who has studied how television has affected sports, wrote of the symbiotic relationship of television and football:

> Television created millions of new fans for pro football. It helped the novice to understand and appreciate the intricacies of the sport. As one fan put it: "You watched a game on television and, suddenly, the wool was stripped from your eyes. What had appeared to be an incomprehensible tangle of milling bodies from the grandstand made sense. [Television] created a nation of instant experts in no time."

Several pro football teams besides the Chicago Bears developed their own network of television stations. The New York Giants had one stretching north from the Big Apple, the Cleveland Browns network blanketed Ohio and points north and east, and the Washington Redskins attempted to become the South's favorite football team with telecasts to stations in North Carolina and Georgia.

While football's owners were searching for a middle ground between giving away their product and harnessing television's undoubted power to cultivate new fans, baseball's magnates were suffering from a nearly terminal case of greed. Phil Patton has noted that television nearly killed minor league baseball. During the late 1940s, he wrote, nearly 400 major league games were broadcast on television each year, which sent the minor leagues into a nosedive. Patton added:

> The major league teams suffered too. Some hurried to sign deals with stations and networks, only to find they had opened a huge knothole in the stadium through which millions saw the game for free. Major league attendance fell from a high of some 21 million in 1948 to just 14 million five years later. Some individual teams suffered attendance losses of more than half. The Boston Braves won the 1948 National League pennant, drawing 1.455 million people. They immediately signed a $40,000 television deal for coverage of all their home games for two years and most of their home games for two more. By the time the contract had run its course, attendance had fallen 81 per cent. In 1953 the Braves moved to Milwaukee and forbade all television coverage.

Some thought that baseball's losses were temporary and that baseball fans would return to the ball park after television's novelty wore off. Branch Rickey, the Pittsburgh Pirates' general manager (and former chief of the Brooklyn Dodgers in both baseball and football), said in an interview with *Newsweek* that he doubted that would happen. Commenting on the effect of both television and radio on baseball's box office, Rickey said,

> Radio created a desire to see something. Television is giving it to them. Once a television set has broken them of the ball-park habit, a great many fans will never reacquire it. And if television makes new baseball customers, as some are claiming, why don't Broadway productions televise their shows? The only way you can see a Broadway production is to buy a ticket—and I cannot concede that baseball has, under the oft-used heading of the "public interest," any obligation to give away continuously at only a fraction of its real worth the only thing it has to sell.

The 1950s saw the birth of the civil rights movement, as well as growing prosperity for professional football. The movement began in December 1955 in Montgomery, Alabama, when a black woman named Rosa Parks refused to give her seat on a city bus to a white man, as required by a city ordinance. Immediately blacks began boycotting the buses, and the cry for equal treatment quickly spread throughout the South.

While the civil rights movement was blossoming, more black players were coming into the NFL. By the end of the decade, more than fifty black players were on NFL teams—about 12 percent of the total. (Today more than 60 percent of NFL players are black.)

Among the black players who arrived during the 1950s are seven who earned induction into the Pro Football Hall of Fame for sterling careers. In order of their rookie years, they are Richard (Night Train) Lane, a defensive back who joined the Los Angeles Rams in 1952 and set the NFL record for most interceptions in a season (fourteen) in his first year; Roosevelt Brown, a 255-pound offensive tackle who came to the New York Giants in 1953; John Henry Johnson, a fullback for the San Francisco 49ers in 1954; Lenny Moore, a running back and split end who joined the Baltimore Colts in 1956; Jim Parker, guard and linebacker for the Colts in 1957; and Bobby Mitchell, a halfback and wide receiver for the Cleveland Browns in 1958.

That's six. The seventh is first in the class. He is James N. (Jimmy) Brown, a 6-foot, 2-inch, 228-pound fullback with speed and power who is sometimes called the greatest running back in football history. Brown was an extraordinary athlete, an All-American in lacrosse as well as football at Syracuse University and a basketball star in high school.

Brown joined the Cleveland Browns in 1957 and quickly established his credentials by leading the team in rushing and earning Rookie of the Year honors. In his thirteen seasons with the Browns, he rushed for more than 1,000 yards seven times, was the NFL's Most Valuable Player in 1958 and 1965, and established a record lifetime rushing average of 5.2 yards a carry.

Brown's predecessor as Cleveland Browns fullback, Marion Motley, was by far the better blocker. Coach Paul Brown called Motley a better fullback than Brown "because not only was he a great runner, but also no one ever blocked better—and no one ever cared more about his team." But as a pure runner, Jimmy Brown was unsurpassed by Motley or anyone else. After his football career ended in 1965, Brown became a movie actor and activist for black economic and youth improvement causes.

In 1956 the New York Giants won their first NFL championship in the age of television (and their first since 1938). They had left the Polo Grounds for the more glamorous precincts of Yankee Stadium. Suddenly they were the toast of New York, including the advertising citadel of Madison Avenue. The players were asked to endorse products and make television commercials. Star halfback Frank Gifford (later a long-time fixture on *Monday Night Football*) had his own show on radio and television, plus a newspaper column. He made a movie in the title role as *The All-American*, continuing a tradition started by Red Grange and furthered by Sammy Baugh.

Phil Patton described the 1956 Giants as the first media team: "A strong New York franchise is the Holy Grail of every professional sports league, but the Giants, by impressing the advertising world at a time when it was booming, began to draw a new type of spectator to the game." He quoted Kyle Rote, an outstanding offensive end:

> When we won it in 1956, we were winning it in Madison Avenue's backyard. These admen were young guys—bright and sharp—but they'd never had an NFL champion in their own backyard. Suddenly, they happened to tie into professional football just when TV advertising was hitting its peak. This propelled football far beyond what it would have been had a Green Bay won the title or a Cleveland.

Three-quarters of all American families had television sets by the mid-1950s, and football on television was rapidly becoming a Sunday afternoon ritual. Interest in pro football grew steadily as games became accessible to almost every fan, but the game still trailed big-league baseball in fans' affections.

That situation would begin to change two years later. The NFL's exciting championship game in 1958 gave the league the jump-start it needed to begin the surge of fan interest that would propel it past baseball in the 1960s.

The New York Giants had dropped back to second place in the

Eastern Conference behind the Cleveland Browns, the dominant team of the 1950s, in 1957. But in 1958 the Giants enjoyed a storybook year. They beat the Browns three times, including the Eastern Conference playoff game, when Pat Summerall, later a well-known sports announcer, kicked a 49-yard field goal with less than a minute left for a 13 to 10 victory.

The NFL title game matched the Giants against the Baltimore Colts, whose NFL franchise had been resurrected in 1953 when Dallas's first NFL team moved to Maryland. The scene was Yankee Stadium, and 64,185 fans were on hand. An estimated 30 million were in the television audience.

It was a classic matchup, with the lately glamorous Giants facing the gritty Colts, led by Johnny Unitas, a ninth-round draft choice quarterback who had been cut by the Pittsburgh Steelers in 1955 without ever getting into an official game. The Colts signed him in 1956 while he was working in construction in Pittsburgh and earning $6 a game for playing with the semipro Bloomfield Rams.

At halftime, the Colts had built a 14 to 3 lead on a plunge by fullback Alan Ameche and a pass from Unitas to Raymond Berry. The Colts started the second half with a long drive that stalled at the Giants' 3-yard line, but then the tide began turning against them. The Giants went ahead by 17 to 14 in the fourth quarter on a 15-yard touchdown pass from Charlie Conerly to Frank Gifford. Then, with less than two minutes to go, Unitas coolly drove the Colts 62 yards down the field on passes to Berry and Lenny Moore. With seven seconds remaining and the Colts on the Giants' 13-yard line, Steve Myhra kicked a field goal to tie the game.

For the first time, the NFL championship would be decided by a sudden-death overtime. The Giants won the coin toss and elected to receive the kickoff. They were unable to move the ball and punted to the Colts' 20-yard line. Unitas masterfully picked apart the Giants' vaunted defense by alternating rushes by L. G. Dupre and Alan Ameche with his own passes to Berry and Moore. Ameche scored the winning touchdown without being touched on a 1-yard plunge.

Ameche had hardly fallen into the end zone when fanatical Colts fans hoisted him to their shoulders and began parading down the field. The goal posts came down instantly, so there could be no extra point kick even if it were needed. Arthur Daley, a columnist for the *New York Times,* wrote the next day, "The enthusiasm shows how completely pro football has arrived. Giants fans were as vociferous as their leather-lunged Baltimore counterparts." Some 30,000 unruly Baltimore rooters welcomed their heroes at the airport when they flew back the night of the game.

The championship game had been blacked out on New York television stations in line with NFL policy, but some homebound Giants fans saw it anyway. Television reporter Jack Gould of the *Times* wrote,

> Thanks to the vagaries of television waves, which sometimes shoot beyond the horizon, station WRCA-TV in Philadelphia—Channel 3—penetrated the New York area for most of the game. The exciting play was clearly visible except for a few minutes at the close of the contest. The picture was badly speckled and streaked but even with the visual handicaps the game was the sports spectacle of the TV year.

Besides the 64,000-plus spectators in Yankee Stadium, fans were grouped around television sets in an estimated 10.8 million homes across America, in addition to the handful of television viewers in New York—all thrilled by the championship game. For a week or more afterward, many of them still tingled with the thrill and made it the topic of lunchtime conversations. Within weeks, the Colts' victory in overtime was being called "the best game ever played."

Writing about that game more than three decades later, Jerry Gorman and Kirk Calhoun, the authors of *The Name of the Game: The Business of Sports*, exclaimed: "What better way to promote a sport and a medium! It was the first glorious moment in a partnership that now, 35 years later, appears to have been conceived in Fort Knox."

What better way to end this narrative than with the climatic game of pro football's early years!

12

EXTRA POINTS

Professional football has climbed swiftly and quite steadily in the affections of sports fans since the 1958 NFL championship game. There have been a few bumps along the way, but by and large the NFL's saga has been one of spectacular success.

Roughly 40 percent of American adults described themselves as NFL fans in a 1991 survey for the Sports Marketing Group. Only 31 percent said they were baseball fans and, ominously for major league baseball's future, twice as many in the eighteen- to twenty-four-year age group preferred pro football to baseball. A CBS News poll conducted in the summer of 1994 found interest in big-league baseball falling even further. However, that survey was done while major league players were on strike, so the fans may have been expressing displeasure over the stoppage rather than a souring attitude toward the game.

An annual indicator of pro football's popularity is the Super Bowl game. Ever since the mid-1970s, the Super Bowl has been far and away the biggest sports spectacular of each year, even though very few of the games have matched the drama of the 1958 title game. Super Bowl telecasts hold 75 percent of the spots on the list of the twenty-four most watched programs of all time. The 1996 Super Bowl ranks number 1, with an audience estimated at 138,488,000. Nearly half of all television sets in the country are tuned in for at least a few minutes of every Super Bowl.

The public thirst for NFL football games has brought television riches beyond the wildest imaginings of George Halas, George Preston Marshall, Tim Mara, and Art Rooney. The NFL's current contracts with the Fox network, NBC, ABC, TNT, and ESPN will bring the league $1.097 *billion* a year through 1997. That's a jump of about 20 percent over the last four-year network-television contracts.

In contrast with the practice in major league baseball, the network-television bonanza is shared equally by all NFL teams. The formula was worked out by former commissioner Pete Rozelle, who succeeded Bert Bell after the latter's fatal heart attack while watching a football game in 1959. The Rozelle plan means that the Green Bay Packers get the same amount from network television as the New York Giants, despite the huge difference in the size of their television market areas.

Buoyed by the television money, players' salaries have escalated exponentially in the past decade. The National Football Players Association estimated that in 1993 the average salary was $600,000, and that figure was expected to rise steeply as the effects of restricted free agency began to take hold. Football players' salaries are far behind those in basketball ($1.6 million average) and baseball ($1.2 million), but even so, they are stratospheric in the eyes of old-timers.

In its annual estimates of the incomes of the "Super 40" in professional sports, *Forbes* reported that Deion Sanders of the Dallas Cowboys was the highest-paid football player in 1995. His total earnings of $22.5 million (number 3 on the list) included the signing bonus of $13 million he got from the Cowboys and $6 million for endorsing Nike, Pepsi, and Sega products. His salaries from the Cowboys and the San Francisco Giants totaled $3.5 million. Drew Bledsoe, the New England Patriots quarterback, was next among the football players (number 12 on the list), with total income of $13.9 million, of which $11.5 million was a signing bonus. Six other football players made the "Super 40." (Number 1 on the list was Michael Jordan, the adman's delight. Jordan, an erstwhile minor league baseball player, went back to basketball in 1995 for wages totaling $3.9 million. His endorsement income from Nike, McDonald's, Gatorade, Rayovac, and Oakley sunglasses added up to a staggering $40 million.)

Such high finance boggles the minds of football players from a half century ago, very few of whom earned as much as $15,000 a year from football, and rarely received money for endorsing products. Bulldog Turner, for example, the center-linebacker for the Chicago Bears from 1940 to 1952, remembered:

> Once I endorsed Vicks cough drops, and I think I got $35 out of that. It was for a short subject for movie houses. It showed me coming out of a game, sitting down all sweaty and dirty, and having trouble breathing. I pick up a box of Vicks cough drops and hold it so you can read the label and put one in my mouth. As I recall, I got $35 for that.
>
> I had one other little deal with Phillips 66 gasoline. I can't remember how much I got out of it. My football number was 66; that's how I got that one. I think the Gillette razor company used a Bears squad picture, and I believe we got a dollar apiece for it. That's how big the endorsements were then.

Players who got their names in the paper for scoring a lot of touchdowns did better than Turner on endorsement income. Bears end Ken

Kavanaugh, who scored thirteen touchdowns on pass receptions in twelve games during the 1947 season, recalled having once earned $500 for making a television commercial for Gillette. (Bulldog Turner intercepted a pass and ran it back 96 yards for a touchdown in the same season, a feat that today would no doubt bring several lucrative endorsement opportunities. But it must be remembered that in 1947 pro football was not yet a national phenomenon and television was in its infancy. Said Bulldog Turner: "I had some first cousins down here in Texas who knew I was up in Chicago playing ball, but they didn't know whether it was baseball or football or what. I don't think anybody was impressed down here in Texas.")

To hold the fans' interest, and especially to keep viewers glued to the tube, the NFL has tinkered with the rules frequently over the years to make the game more exciting. Usually the changes have aimed to handicap defenses and promote higher scores.

Probably the most important rules changes of the past three decades came in 1978 and 1979. From time immemorial, defensive backs had been permitted to bump, or "chuck," a pass receiver at any point, thus affecting both his concentration and his equilibrium. In 1978 the rules were changed to permit only one chuck, leaving receivers with better opportunities to break free. An even more significant rule change came in 1979. Until then, pass blockers had to keep their hands against their chests on pain of being penalized for holding. Henceforth, pass blockers could extend their arms and open their hands in an effort to keep defensive linemen away from the quarterback. The result of these changes was to revolutionize the game. Benjamin G. Rader has pointed out that average total yards gained by passing went from 283.3 a game in 1977 to 408.7 in 1979:

> The swaggering cornerbacks, who sometimes jostled top receivers out of an entire game, suddenly became virtually obsolete. Since they could no longer repeatedly bump receivers, the defensive backs had to retreat into cautious zones. . . .
> The holding now permitted by offensive linemen negated much of the quickness that had earlier been essential to great defensive linemen. When 300-pound blockers were free to plant themselves and embrace onrushing defensive players, even the best of the pass rushers no longer looked quite so fearsome. Linemen in the trenches now locked in "arm ball," or "wrestling matches." . . . To be effective, linemen had to develop immense upper body strength rather than quickness.

Some former players, among them Bulldog Turner, deplore the rules change that permits what used to be a holding foul:

> I don't like the rule at all on blocking. They just stand up and push each other. Of course, that just makes me old-fashioned, I guess. Pass protection now is just standing there and rooster fighting. It's one of the big

gripes I have about the game now because you really don't have to block the guy.

There's another thing that's not even taught in the pros now. I've never seen anybody teach it. Today a center gets ahold of the ball and stands it up on end. Unless they've changed the rules, that's against the rule. You can't move the ball. You put your hands on it, but you can't move it. Today they'll spin it around until they get the laces where they want them.

I used to have to tell the referee where I wanted the laces. He would put the ball down that way, and then all I'd have to do is put my hands on it. I couldn't tilt it on end.

It seems to me that there are too many people in football that don't know football—including coaches and owners and players.

Not all old pro football players disapprove of the changes that have come to the game since their day in the sun. Most agree that today's players are much bigger, stronger, and faster than those of fifty years ago.

Hal Lahar, a guard for the Chicago Bears and Buffalo Bisons between 1941 and 1948 and later a coach at several major universities, had this to say about the modern professional game:

The game is so much more sophisticated today. I think it's a more difficult game for the players. They play more games than we did, and they're working at football a lot longer than we worked at it. In our day, you'd show up at training camp and take off when the season was over; that was it. Now they work year round.

The only real major difference in offensive techniques between today's game and the 1940s is in the blocking rules, which permit the use of the hands now.

Defense is where most of the changes have taken place—pass defense, for example. Because of the great emphasis now on throwing the ball, you have to develop a strong defense or you're going to get run out of the stadium. The defenses in the secondary, with the number of coverages they have now—combination zones and man-to-man, two–three zones and three–two zones, and all kinds of nickel and dime defenses—that's been the major transformation.

And, of course, the coming of the black players—that's been a major difference.

Without exception, the old players who were interviewed for this book were successful in business or a profession after they left the game. Several became high-school teachers and coaches of football and other sports. A few coached in college and the pros.

Steve Romanik, a Bears and Cardinals quarterback, went back to his hometown, Millville, New Jersey, worked in insurance and real estate, and then got into politics and local government. All told, he spent twenty-seven years working for the county in the sheriff's and welfare departments.

Another former pro who entered politics and government was Lon

Evans, a Packers guard during the 1930s, whose widow, Marion, reminisced for this book about their great days as young marrieds in Green Bay. Evans left the Packers in 1937 after his third All-Pro season in five years and went home to Fort Worth. For some years, he worked in business and industry and then became a near-legend as high sheriff of Tarrant County. Evans turned out to be not only an outstanding lawman but an invincible candidate. He was sheriff for twenty-four years, finally retiring undefeated in 1985 at the age of seventy-three.

Some players did not give much thought to the future during their early years in pro football. Vince Banonis was one. He was an outstanding center for the Chicago Cardinals and Detroit Lions, whose salary went from $240 a game in 1942 to $600 a game with the 1953 Lions, plus about $2,300 for winning the NFL championship that year. Banonis recalled:

> At first I didn't work in the off-season. I figured the money would last me forever. Then I woke up. I said to myself, "I've got to do something." So, about 1951, I went to work for one of the local auto-supply houses in Detroit. I got into labor relations and got my feet wet in that field. It was a good introduction because it got me into the plant, where I learned how a stamping was made and how anodizing, plating, painting, and so forth are done. Then I went into sales for the same company. I became vice-president of marketing for a company based in Cincinnati that had an office in Detroit, and I retired from that in 1984.
>
> When I got out of football, I just walked away from it. I didn't retain any connection with it. When I went to a game, I never even went into the dressing rooms—oh, maybe once or twice I did. I didn't want to be a hanger-on. There were a lot of front-runners and well-wishers when I played, and I didn't want to become one of those. I figured that twenty years of football as a boy and as a man was enough.

Like Banonis, Hall of Fame end Bill Hewitt took some time to come to the realization that pro football careers are fleeting. Hewitt, one of the last of the bareheaded players, came out of the University of Michigan in 1932 and starred for the Chicago Bears and Philadelphia Eagles until 1939. (He returned to pro football in the wartime year of 1943 as a member of the Philadelphia–Pittsburgh Steagles and was forced by a new rule to don a helmet.)

In an article titled "Don't Send My Boy to Halas" in the *Saturday Evening Post* in 1944, Bill Hewitt told Red Smith, the era's most accomplished sports columnist, that if he had a son, he would encourage him to play football in high school and college. "But," Hewitt said, "if our muscular young freak ever cracked one word about playing professional football, papa's response would be firm and to the point. Papa would up with his bung starter and rap his loving offspring over the brow until his ears rang like the Chimes of Normandy."

Hewitt staunchly defended pro football from critics who were still belittling professionalism. "Let me say this of pro ball as I know it," he said. "It is rough, it is real, it is smart, and it is for keeps. It is played more skillfully than in college, but with the same earnestness." His quarrel with the sport was that "the average professional football player is the peon of big-league sports. Perhaps a half-dozen players in the National Football League receive salaries commensurate with those paid in other big box-office games."

Hewitt had been signed out of college for $100 a game. As an Eagle beginning in 1937 he went to $200, and as a wartime Steagle he got $400 a game. Those figures added up to a good salary for the period, but, Hewitt explained:

> A youngster coming out of school and going into pro football accustoms himself to a $100-a-week standard of living. I don't claim that proves him smart. But he does it. He tells himself, *Shucks, I'm no longshoreman: I'm a college man, presumably trained for a big job.* He's more than a little spoiled by his publicity. He wants off-season work that will support him in the manner to which he has swiftly become accustomed.
>
> But there aren't any such jobs. At least, there weren't in the Depression, and there probably won't be after the war. Employers don't hand out good jobs in January, jobs with a future, to men who will quit next August and spend four months playing at games. So the player, unable to land anything worth clinging to, either becomes a chronic off-season loafer or accepts whatever ill-paid work he can get to tide him over.

Bert Bell, who was operating the Philadelphia Eagles when Hewitt joined his team in 1937, helped him to begin to focus on his future by arranging a $24-a-week job for him as a grease monkey in a service station for the off-season. "It wasn't a terrific position for a man six years out of college," Hewitt said. "Yet I believe that going to work for $24 a week in 1937 kept me from becoming a thorough-going athletic bum." By the time he left the Eagles in 1939, Hewitt had begun a promising business career. He died in an automobile accident while on a business trip in 1947.

Some pro football players of the period used their football earnings to attend graduate school to prepare for careers in medicine, dentistry, and the law. Others spent the off-season laying the foundation for post-football employment. One was quarterback Ray Mallouf, whose years with the Chicago Cardinals and New York Giants spanned 1941 through 1949. Mallouf remembered:

> So many of the boys came back at the beginning of the season and didn't have any money. They had to borrow money to survive until the season started because they didn't work. I said, "I'm not going to do that." A friend of mine worked at Sears here in Dallas, and I applied for a job there. They hired me immediately as a salesman.
>
> I told the boss, "I may not stay with you because I planned to go

back to football." He said, "That would be fine. I'll hold a job for you when you come back." I made good money all summer long, and when I retired from football after the 1949 season, I had a permanent job waiting for me with Sears. I stayed with them thirty-five years.

Oh, yes, people were interested in talking with me because I had played pro football. Definitely so. It made it a lot easier to talk to people when you were trying to sell something.

At least one old pro got started on his career goal—sales and marketing for IBM—by working for the company during the football season. He is George Buksar, a fullback and linebacker for the Chicago Hornets, Baltimore Colts, and Washington Redskins from 1949 to 1952:

> I started working for IBM while I was with Chicago. They practiced in the mornings. In the afternoons, I was running IBM machines in their office in Chicago so I could learn how to sell them when the season was over. After I got good at it, I sold them during the afternoons when we weren't practicing.

Few people in the company, which at that time had a rigid code of conduct for its employees, knew that Buksar was playing professional football. Thomas Watson, Jr., the chairman of IBM, and the manager of the Chicago office were aware of it, but no one else was.

Some former players who went into sales and marketing believe that their pro football background opened doors for them. Buksar said that he doubted that it had enhanced his career in sales for IBM and later for Reliance Electric, a manufacturer of electric motors. He explained:

> I wasn't selling equipment because I had been a player. One thing you have to remember: During that period of time, people thought that most football players had brains made out of Jello. In fact, I lost an account in Chicago because the guy found out I was a football player. He said, "You're a football player and you're going to check my inventory?" I never forgave and never forgot that guy.
>
> Football was considered a roughneck's sport. I enjoyed playing it, but it was just a means to an end for me.

This random sampling of former players indicating that they made a successful transition to "real life" after football is supported by a more systematic study. Historian Steven A. Riess checked on the occupational status of 48 NFL players from the 1930s and 114 from the 1950s. He concluded:

> Professional football players active in the 1930s and 1950s were extremely successful after their playing days were over. They virtually all wound up in white-collar jobs, mostly in high-level positions. Slightly more than half (52.1 percent) of the 1930s group ended up as professionals, major executives, or owners of large companies—impressive accom-

plishments for men who entered the work force during the Depression. Players active in the 1950s were slightly less likely to secure high white-collar jobs (45.6 percent).

Other surveys of NFL alumni yielded similar results, Riess wrote: "For example, all but one member of the 1948 champion Philadelphia Eagles secured white-collar employment, and he became a farmer. Nearly one-third of the Eagles held high-level white-collar positions, including a judge, an oral surgeon, and a professor."

Brains made of Jello indeed! Riess noted that NFL players from the 1930s and 1950s were far better educated than the general population. That fact, rather than their fleeting fame in football, accounted for their success in other occupations, he wrote.

The players who were interviewed for this book were almost unanimous in saying that their experiences in pro football were highlights in their lives. For some, football was a vehicle for getting a college education. Nearly all looked back with great pleasure, despite the creaky knees and bum hips that are a common affliction among old football players. Steve Romanik, who left the game after playing the 1954 season with the Chicago Cardinals, has the typical outlook of an old player:

> I would have been thirty-two years old if I had gone back the next season. The Cardinals sent me a contract, but I just didn't sign it. I had trouble with one of my knees at Villanova; then in the pros I had trouble with *both* of them. I *still* have bad knees.
>
> When you get up to thirty-one, thirty-two years old, you can feel it. In training camp my last year with the Cardinals, we had two workouts a day—strenuous workouts—and my whole body would be aching. We'd work out in the morning, and the first thing I did when we got back to the dorm was hit the sack until lunch. Same thing after the afternoon workout.
>
> But I enjoyed it. It was fun. You know, you were a hero in whatever town you went to. In every city, people would greet you and want your autograph. It was a different life. On the road we always stayed in the best hotels. It was just a higher class of living. Both my wife and I enjoyed it, living out there in Chicago.

NOTES ON SOURCES

Football players had been paid to play for more than four decades, and the NFL had been in business for almost fifteen years, before anyone thought to record the early years of the professional game. The first chronicler turned out to be an unfortunate choice for the task. He was Dr. Harry A. March, who had been associated with pro football as personnel director of the New York Giants and as an NFL executive for some years when he published his book in 1934.

It was titled *Pro Football: Its "Ups" and "Downs."* The book has much useful information, but it is shot through with errors, due mostly, I think, to March's reliance on faulty memory rather than solid research. Many of his errors were picked up by later authors, including his attribution of the beginnings of professionalism to a team in Latrobe, Pennsylvania, in 1895.

It was not until the 1960s that serious historians began examining the infancy and early adolescence of professional football. The precipitating event was the discovery of a manuscript with a fairly comprehensive account of the earliest professional games that was presented to Dan Rooney of the Pittsburgh Steelers by a man whose name he remembered as Nelson Ross. Ross, if that was in fact his name, had not put a name or an address on the manuscript and never returned to reclaim it. The manuscript told of the birth of professionalism in Pittsburgh in 1892, three years before a player was paid in Latrobe. (The manuscript is now at the research center of the Pro Football Hall of Fame in Canton, Ohio.) Dick McCann, first director of the Hall of Fame, was able to corroborate Nelson Ross's story. Subsequently, J. Thomas Jable nailed it down further in a monograph for the *Western Pennsylvania Historical Magazine.*

During the 1970s, Richard M. Cohen and David S. Neft began publishing authoritative books on early pro football, some with team rosters and records, which are invaluable sources of accurate data. Meanwhile, Bob Curran and Myron Cope, later joined by Richard Whittingham, were looking up the surviving pioneer players for interviews to produce oral histories of the game.

Pro football historiography came of age in 1979, when the Professional Football Researchers Association (PFRA) was organized by six serious students of the game. Many of the books on which I relied are PFRA products. A few of the other books in the list below, such as those by Allison Danzig, are about college football rather than the pros, but they tell us a good deal about the game that was played by the pros too.

Following are the books and monographs I found most useful:

Ashe, Arthur R., Jr. *A Hard Road to Glory: A History of the African-American Athlete.* 2 vols. New York: Warner, 1988.

Barnett, C. Robert. *The Spartans and the Tanks.* North Huntingdon, Pa.: PFRA.

Blair, Sam. *Dallas Cowboys, Pro or Con?* New York: Doubleday, 1970.

Braunwart, Bob, and Bob Carroll. *The Unofficial Chronicle: Part I—Origins, the Journey to Camp.* North Huntingdon, Pa.: PFRA, 1986.

———. *The Unofficial PF Chronicle: Part II—Growth in Western Pennsylvania, the Weekly Wage.* North Huntingdon, Pa.: PFRA, 1986.

———. *The Unofficial PF Chronicle: The First Pros, the Alphabet Wars.* North Huntingdon, Pa.: PFRA, 1986.

Brondfield, Jerry. *Rockne: The Coach, the Man, the Legend.* New York: Random House, 1976.

Brown, Paul, with Jack Clary. *PB: The Paul Brown Story.* New York: Atheneum, 1980.

Campbell, Jim. *Golden Years of Pro Football.* New York: Crescent Books, 1993.

Carroll, Bob. *100 Greatest Running Backs.* New York: Crescent Books, 1989.

Carroll, Bob, and Bob Braunwart. *Pro Football: From AAA to '03.* North Huntingdon, Pa.: PFRA, 1991.

Carroll, Bob, and PFRA Research. *The Tigers Roar: Professional Football in Ohio, 1903–09.* North Huntingdon, Pa.: PFRA, 1990.

Carroll, John M. *Fritz Pollard: Pioneer in Racial Advancement.* Urbana: University of Illinois Press, 1992.

Chalk, Ocania. *Pioneers of Black Sport.* New York: Dodd, Mead, 1975.

Claassen, Harold (Spike). *The History of Professional Football.* Englewood Cliffs, N.J.: Prentice-Hall, 1963.

Cohen, Richard M. *The Sports Encyclopedia: Pro Football.* New York: Grossett & Dunlap, 1974.

———, et al. *The Scrapbook History of Football.* Indianapolis: Bobbs-Merrill, 1976.

Cope, Myron. *The Game That Was.* Cleveland: World, 1970.

Curran, Bob. *Pro Football's Rag Days.* Englewood Cliffs, N.J.: Prentice-Hall, 1969.

Cusack, Jack. "Pioneer in Pro Football." Undated monograph.

Danzig, Allison. *The History of American Football.* Englewood Cliffs, N.J.: Prentice-Hall, 1956.

————. *Oh, How They Played the Game.* New York: Macmillan, 1971.

Davis, Parke H., *Football: The American Intercollegiate Game.* New York: Scribner, 1911.

Duberman, Martin Bauml. *Paul Robeson.* New York: Knopf, 1988.

Eskenazi, Gerald. *There Were Giants in Those Days.* New York: Grosset & Dunlap, 1976.

Gill, Bob. *Best in the West: The Rise and Fall of the Pacific Coast Football League, 1940–48.* North Huntingdon, Pa.: PFRA, 1988.

————. *A Minor Masterpiece.* Volume 1, *The American Association, 1936–41.* North Huntingdon, Pa.: PFRA, 1990.

————. *A Minor Masterpiece.* Volume 2, *The American Football League, 1946–50.* North Huntingdon, Pa.: PFRA, 1990.

————. *Southern Exposure: The Saga of Football's Dixie League.* North Huntingdon, Pa.: PFRA, 1991.

Gill, Bob, and Tod Maher. *The Outsiders: The Three American Football Leagues of 1936–41.* North Huntingdon, Pa.: PFRA, 1989.

Gipe, George. *The Great American Sports Book.* New York: Doubleday, 1978.

Gorman, Jerry, and Kirk Calhoun, with Skip Rozin. *The Name of the Game: The Business of Sports.* New York: Wiley, 1994.

Gottehrer, Barry. *The Giants of New York.* New York: Putnam, 1963.

Green, Jerry. *Detroit Lions.* New York: Macmillan, 1973.

Halas, George, with Gwen Morgan and Arthur Veysey. *Halas by Halas.* New York: McGraw-Hill, 1979.

Hill, Dean. *Football Thru the Years.* New York: Gridiron, 1940.

Jable, J. Thomas. "The Birth of Professional Football: Pittsburgh Athletic Clubs Ring in Professionals in 1892." *Western Pennsylvania Historical Magazine,* April 1979, 131–147.

Johnson, Chuck. *The Green Bay Packers: Pro Football's Pioneer Team.* New York: Nelson, 1961.

Johnson, Pearce B., comp. *Professional Football's National Growth: From Cradle to Maturity.* [A collection of articles, statistics, and art from various sources and years]

Klosinski, Emil. *Pro Football in the Days of Rockne.* New York: Carlton Press, 1970.

Lazenby, Roland. *The Pictorial History of Football.* New York: Gallery Books, 1987.

Maltby, Marc S. "The Origins and Early Development of Professional Football, 1890–1920." Ph.D. diss., Ohio University, 1987.

March, Harry A. *Pro Football: Its "Ups" and "Downs."* 1934. 2nd ed. Albany, N.Y.: Lyon, 1939.

National Football League Properties, Creative Services Division, *NFL's Official Encyclopedic History of Professional Football.* New York: Macmillan, 1977.

————. *75 Seasons: The Complete Story of the National Football League, 1920–1995.* Atlanta: Turner, 1994.

Neft, David S., and Richard M. Cohen. *The Football Encyclopedia: The Complete History of Professional Football from 1892 to the Present.* New York: St. Martin's Press, 1991.

Patton, Phil. *Razzle-Dazzle, The Curious Marriage of Television and Professional Football.* Garden City, N.Y.: Doubleday, 1978.

Porter, David L., ed. *Biographical Dictionary of American Sports*. Westport, Conn.: Greenwood Press.

Professional Football Researchers Association. *Bulldogs on Sunday*. 3 vols. North Huntingdon, Pa.: PFRA, 1920, 1921, 1922.

Rader, Benjamin G. *In Its Own Image: How Television Has Transformed Sports*. New York: Free Press, 1984.

Rathet, Mike, and Don R. Smith. *Their Deeds and Dogged Faith*. New York: Bantam, 1984.

Riess, Steven A. "A Social Profile of the Professional Football Player, 1920–82." In *The Business of Professional Sports*, edited by Paul D. Staudohar and James A. Mangan. Urbana: University of Illinois Press, 1991.

Riffenburgh, Beau. *The Official NFL Encyclopedia*. New York: New American Library, 1986.

Riger, Bob. *The Pros: A Documentary of Professional Football in America*. New York: Simon and Schuster, 1960.

[Ross, Nelson.] "The Birth and Early Development of Professional Football." Pro Football Hall of Fame, Canton, Ohio. Monograph.

Rothaus, James R. *The Philadelphia Eagles*. Mankato, Minn.: Creative Education, 1981.

Smith, Robert. *Illustrated History of Pro Football*. New York: Grossett & Dunlap, 1971.

———. *Pro Football: The History of the Game and the Great Players*. New York: Doubleday, 1963.

Smith, Ronald A. *Sports and Freedom: The Rise of Big-Time College Athletics*. New York: Oxford University Press, 1988.

Smith, Thomas G. "Outside the Pale: The Exclusion of Blacks from the National Football League, 1934–46." *Journal of Sport History* 15, no. 3, (Winter 1988): 255–281.

Spalding's Official Football Guides. New York: Spalding, Bros., various years.

Strode, Woody, and Sam Young. *Goal Dust*. Lanham, Md.: Madison Books, 1990.

Underwood, John. *The Death of An American Game*. Boston: Little, Brown, 1979.

Van Atta, Robert B. "The Early Years of Pro Football in Southwest Pennsylvania." *PFRA Annual*, 1981.

Whittingham, Richard. *What a Game They Played*. New York: Simon and Schuster, 1984.

———. *The Chicago Bears: From George Halas to Super Bowl XX*. New York: Simon and Schuster, 1986.

———. *The Fireside Book of Pro Football*. New York: Simon and Schuster, 1989.

———. *The Giants: An Illustrated History*. New York: Harper & Row, 1987.

INDEX

217